THE
Pious Ones

ALSO BY JOSEPH BERGER

The World in a City: Traveling the Globe
Through the Neighborhoods of the New New York

Displaced Persons: Growing Up American After the Holocaust

The Young Scientists: America's Future
and the Winning of the Westinghouse

THE
Pious Ones

*The World of Hasidim and
Their Battles with America*

JOSEPH BERGER

HARPER ● PERENNIAL

NEW YORK ● LONDON ● TORONTO ● SYDNEY ● NEW DELHI ● AUCKLAND

HarperCollins books may be purchased for educational, business, or sales promotional use. For information please e-mail the Special Markets Department at SPsales@harpercollins.com.

FIRST EDITION

Library of Congress Cataloging-in-Publication Data has been applied for.

ISBN 978-0-06-212334-3

14 15 16 17 18   OV/RRD   10 9 8 7 6 5 4 3 2 1

To my parents, Marcus and Rachel Berger,
who bequeathed to their children the flavor of the
lost *shtetls* and ghettoes of Europe

There are two levels in the study of Torah, Torah of the mind and Torah of the heart. The mind cogitates, comprehends and understands; the heart feels. I have come to reveal Torah as it extends to the heart as well.

If the Bible didn't show us the weaknesses, the vulnerabilities, the sins of our heroes, we might have deep questions about their true virtue.

—Baal Shem Tov

CONTENTS

THE
Pious Ones

PROLOGUE: A PEOPLE APART

We throw around the term "crisis of faith" so casually, applying it to artists, politicians and bankers, not only tormented religious souls, that it has become a cliché of our times. Yet imagine what a crisis of faith must have been like for a man named Shulem Deen.

Deen had grown up a Hasid, a member of a rigorously Orthodox subculture of Judaism. Most strangers recognize Hasidim by the black suits, black hats and broad beards of the men and the wigs and the enveloping outfits of the women but know little else about these people. What many outsiders do not appreciate is how all-encompassing a life Hasidism is, not just a faith for a Saturday or Sunday morning, but one that governs almost every waking hour and virtually every activity of daily life—what one reads and studies, who one marries, how many children one has, how one spends much of a day, even how one goes about having sex.

So when doubts about the literal truths of the Bible and other tenets he had been taught virtually round-the-clock since childhood led to his disenchantment with the restrictive Hasidic life, he had to wrestle with what leaving the fold would mean for his marriage, his intimacy with his children, his friendships, his work, his social life, what he ate, what schooling he would give himself and his family. Yet he could no longer be a Hasid, live what he felt was a consuming lie.

"It started becoming more and more ludicrous," he told me. "I began to realize I didn't want to live in a world I so fundamentally disagreed with. It was something I couldn't do."*

Deen did leave and for the most part won the liberty to think and act for himself that he sought, but his doing so had many of the consequences he feared. His marriage has dissolved and four of his five children refuse to see him.

In studying the Hasidim, which I have often done in more than 40 years as a journalist, I could not help but be struck by the bittersweet, paradoxical outcome of Deen's journey. Yet I also had to balance his tale against many other stories I'd learned, many of them far more ennobling of the Hasidic lifestyle than that of Deen's. And the basic mysteries endured: How do people in an age that venerates personal freedom take on a life of so many commands and restrictions? What is it about that life that draws them and holds them in its grip as firmly as iron filings to a magnet? Why does it come into conflict so often with the wider society? Why do I hear so many intelligent people, especially Jews, revile Hasidim, accusing

---

* Author's interview with Shulem Deen.

them of holding themselves above American laws while exploiting those same laws for their own sustenance?

I felt in undertaking a book on the Hasidim that many Americans are curious about this tribe of people that increasingly presses itself on society's consciousness not just by its offbeat, colorful presence but by its rapidly growing numbers and influence. In a place like New York City, where Hasidim are a forceful, expanding minority, almost every week seems to bring another encounter with the ways of Hasidim—some profoundly troubling like Shulem Deen's story, some enchanting and ennobling. The story of Leiby Kletzky, chilling as it was, gave people a deeper acquaintance and respect for Hasidim.

In the summer of 2011, Leiby Kletzky, an eight-year-old boy, asked his parents if he could walk home from day camp alone for the first time. They assented and he set out on his own through his Hasidic neighborhood of Borough Park in Brooklyn. But he soon got lost and stopped a stranger to ask for help. The stranger, Levi Aron, a bearded thirty-five-year-old hardware stock clerk with an oddly out-of-joint facial expression beneath a newsboy's cap, lured the boy into his beat-up Honda, bizarrely drove him 50 miles north of the city to a cousin's teeming and tumultuous wedding in the Hasidic hamlet of New Square, then drove him back to his apartment in Brooklyn. The next day, he drugged and suffocated Leiby, killing him, then sliced up his body and stored his feet in his refrigerator while depositing the rest in a suitcase and throwing that into in a Dumpster. The security camera film of little Leiby, a yarmulke crowning a face with too-large horn-rimmed glasses and long, dark sidelocks, as he nervously wad-dled along on a sidewalk moments before he was abducted, haunted many who saw it, none more so than parents strug-gling with the amount of independence to give to their young children.

In the days after the crime, New Yorkers—and indeed much of the nation, since the murder of the missing boy was on all the networks—learned much about the Hasidic com-munity. It was astonishingly zealous, cohesive and well orga-nized, with hundreds of rumpled, bearded men streaming in from around the neighborhood and even from their summer bungalows in the Catskills to search single-mindedly for a boy they did not know. And when a funeral became sadly nec-essary after the boy's body was discovered, 10,000 people showed up at nightfall of the same day, spilling out of a syna-gogue to listen to an intense, heartbreaking eulogy, the men in a jostling, swaying swarm surrounding the coffin, the women clustered on the margins in long-sleeved dresses despite the near 90 degree heat. The Hasidic community, those unfa-miliar with them were able to deduce, was impressively pro-lific, with families bulging with six and seven children and some with more than a dozen, in an era when most American couples married late into their 20s and had a child or two.

While most Americans had a monolithic view of the Ha-sidim as insular in their approach to outsiders, and spartan and anachronistic in their lifestyles, many viewers and readers who followed the Leiby Kletzky story closely were surprised at the variety within the Hasidic world. There were dozens of sects with different attitudes toward mainstream society, even distinctive styles of clothing. Some Hasidic men wore the equivalent of black sombreros and others homburgs; some women preferred wigs while others covered their hair with a kerchief. It turned out that neither Leiby nor his killer was Hasidic. Leiby's family was ultra-Orthodox but not Hasidic because it did not venerate a single grand rabbi the way most of the searchers did. Levi Aron did not even merit an "ultra." He came from a plain-vanilla Orthodox family though his father worked in the nationally famous camera and gadget emporium of B&H, which, to the surprise of those bearing views of Hasidim as antediluvian, is owned, managed and staffed largely by Hasidim.

And Americans learned that despite the close-knit nature of the community, which was genuine, Borough Park was increasingly reaching out to the mainstream, most relevantly for help with troubled individuals. True, it had historically sought to deal with problems within the community—through its rabbis and rabbinical courts—but that was slowly changing, too, most prominently as it, like the rest of society, coped with the problem of sexual abuse of minors (though it was never proven that Levi molested Leiby before he killed him). Dozens of cases of abusive teachers, camp counselors, merchants, even rabbis that had been secretly dealt with or hushed up within the community have been turned over to officials like the district attorney in Brooklyn.

Those who chose to delve deeper or simply to google words like "Hasidim" soon learned that the community was also dealing with renegades like Shulem Deen and dis-

senters in its midst, who blogged under noms-de-Web like
FailedMessiah.com and Unpious. And in the year or two that
followed, those googlers would also have learned that, perhaps
in response to the wave of worrisome ferment, the community
had long been unleashing "modesty squads" to make sure its
young Hasidic men and women did not play DVDs or use the
wrong smartphone or wear tank tops or display sexy mannequins in their clothing shops.* They would eventually learn
that Hasidic groups, perhaps flush with the political power
stemming from their growing numbers, were asking the city to
post female lifeguards at a women-only swim session at a municipal pool in Brooklyn, were asking for an exception to a city
ban on the use of well water in food production so they could
bake matzos according to ancient tradition, were asking that
men and women be allowed to sit apart—the men up front, the
women in the back—on a public bus plying a route between
two Hasidic neighborhoods.† Many New Yorkers were out-
raged by what they felt were demands for special treatment
and by the defiance of civic norms and, aware that I had covered such stories for many years, making the Hasidic world
something of a beat, wrote to tell me so. Many of those who
wrote were Jewish and embarrassed by the behavior of people
of their own religious sentiments.

The community, in short, was both more complicated than
the stereotypes and more enigmatic and protean. Still, admire

---

* Joseph Berger, "Modesty in Ultra-Orthodox Brooklyn Is Enforced by
Secret Squads," *New York Times*, January 30, 2013, p. A1.

† Joseph Berger, "Out of Enclaves a Pressure to Accommodate Traditions,"
New York Times, August 22, 2013, p. A19.

Hasidim or detest them, it must be said that the existence of such a rich, colorful, abundant community in Borough Park and others in the Brooklyn neighborhoods of Williamsburg and Crown Heights and still others in Los Angeles, Baltimore, Milwaukee, Minneapolis, Montreal, Toronto and other pockets of North America and, of course, all over Israel, is testimony to the astonishing rebirth of a way of life whose origins stretch back to 18th century Eastern Europe. That was when the rabbis who forged Hasidic philosophy began spurning the austere intellectualism of that era's Judaism and instead emphasized fervor in prayer, an immersion in mysticism and exuberant observance through dancing and singing. A plain-spoken peasant with a zest for God could be as worthy a Jew as the most consumed Talmud scholar. The culture that has evolved since then seems archaic by 21st century standards, but it arguably represents perhaps America's fastest-growing ethnic tribe and one that has much to teach a society that it often tangles with.

Hasidim are reviving a vibrant culture that was nearly extinguished by the Holocaust. They are sustaining the flames of Jewish tradition, otherwise battered by assimilation and geographical dispersal, and the resulting lessons to be learned could have meaning for declining mainstream Protestant and other Christian groups. With their population in the United States doubling every twenty years and now put at more than 330,000 in New York City alone—30 percent of the city's 1.1. million Jews—the Hasidim and other ultra-Orthodox Jews will, according to some population studies, form a majority of America's six million Jews before this century is over.

That fact is breathtaking enough, but it also has profound political implications. Jews are a disproportionately influential ethnic group overrepresented in the halls of Congress, Wall Street, the Ivy League and popular culture. They have always been regarded as America's most liberal and progressive people. But if Hasidim become a more dominant share of the tribe, Jews as a whole may assume a more conservative profile, and politicians appealing to them and seeking their donations will tailor their message accordingly. In New York, Hasidim have been more prone to support Republican and Conservative Party candidates. The views of some Hasidic sects questioning Israel's legitimacy as a state—since they believe the Bible requires the advent of the Messiah before such a state may exist—may one day complicate American foreign policy.

It is also no small matter that Hasidim are preserving a language that is all but dead everywhere else. Yiddish, the homespun tongue of Sholem Aleichem and Isaac Bashevis Singer, is approaching extinction among Jews of a cosmopolitan bent, barely kept alive by the dwindling ranks of Holocaust survivors, a smattering of their children and a few thousand or so young enthusiasts willing to study the language in college. But it is flourishing in America's 30 Hasidic communities, where it is the lingua franca, the language of schooling and the typeface of three weekly newspapers—each thick with ads for their abundant kosher restaurants and clothing, silver, wig and hat shops—and several news websites. (So dominant is Yiddish that many Hasidic youngsters born in this country end up speaking an immigrant's broken, accented English, and otherwise intelligent Hasidim express embarrassment at how badly they write English.)

Yet, to most Americans who encounter Hasidim—literally "the pious ones"—on city streets and increasingly in leafy suburban enclaves, they remain an enigma, a curiosity certainly but nevertheless a puzzle. They are seen by some—Jews and non-Jews—as beguiling and by others as irksome or even off-putting. Why, the curious ask, do they wear those formal black hats on hot summer days (not to mention the round fur *shtreimels* on Saturdays)? Why do their children dress as mini-me versions of their parents, with coiling sidelocks and threadbare tassels dangling out of their shirts? Why do the men scarcely look at passing women, and why do the women refuse to shake a man's hand or the men to shake a woman's hand? Indeed, why do the women spend their days pushing strollers with babies while hanging on to three or four toddlers at the same time? Why do they turn away from the nation's abundant colleges for repetitive immersion in yellowed, dog-eared volumes of the Talmud? Why, in short, do they maintain a lifestyle that is so out of step with the 21st century, or even the 20th and 19th?

The pages that follow will try to answers these questions by delving below the surface of an esoteric world that few from the outside have penetrated and introducing readers to some striking individuals who epitomize the Hasidic experience but also embody its contradictions. By depicting the fabric of daily Hasidic life, I hope to explore how their way of life has allowed Hasidic groups, after the ravages of Hitler, to reestablish themselves in burgeoning communities around the world. But it will also examine the conflicts between the Hasidim and the wider society—over housing, transportation, schooling and more—and the strains that Hasidim have experienced within their own circles over sexual abuse by teachers and rabbis, the role of women and defections.

Americans have much to learn from the Hasidim, eccentric as they are. They are a familiar and intriguing presence in the nation's large cities and their beliefs—on matters of abortion, gay marriage, birth control—somehow insinuate themselves into the national dialogue. As with the Amish, with whom they are sometimes confused, there is something charming about their steadfastness in conducting what seems like an outmoded way of life. But mostly those who delve deeper will realize that their communal bond offers a sharp challenge to the American pursuit of individualistic pleasure and attainment. In a culture that venerates personal fulfillment and reinvention, where everyone is encouraged to venture on a journey of egoistic discovery and transformation, Hasidim put their emphasis on the vibrancy of the group, of its unchangeable, ages-old traditions. For them, those values trump whatever a person can gain from freewheeling exploration of the liberties available in an open society. You may not agree or feel repelled, but that contrast is worth contemplating in a society where consumption has grown ever more conspicuous, where the rich grow ever more remote from the working and middle classes and where too many people spend their days in frivolous worship of Real Housewives and American Idols.

The Hasidim offer a model for how a faith that touches practically every aspect of human life, from work, schooling, eating and sex to clothing and social relations, can strengthen community in an age of anomie and alienation. For families whose kin are scattered far and wide, the Hasidim tell us how community can become the family or enhance it. And whatever others may think of it, Hasidic culture keeps youngsters within the fold, immune for the most part from the distractions of the outside world; studies show that there is actually a negligible proportion of defections. The Hasidic emphasis on the robustness of the tribe has allowed them to tenaciously abide in neighborhoods when more secular Jews have fled at the first sign of conflict with other ethnic groups. Like them or not, the Hasidim offer lessons in survival.

As monolithic as the Hasidic world appears on first impression, it is actually remarkably diverse. Each of America's 30 or so Hasidic communities reveres a different *rebbe*, a spiritual guru of sorts believed to have remarkable, even miraculous insights into such intimate matters as the compatibility of husbands and wives, their fertility, the proper treatment of an illness. Each community, or dynastic court, has subtly distinctive philosophies and traditions and displays singular nuances of worship, custom, even fashion; the width of a hat brim is a telltale clue to whether a Hasid belongs to the Bobov, Belz, Ger, Satmar or Vizhnitz sect. Sketching those differences offers a fascinating course in anthropology.

But underlying all the groups are some unifying principles, few more powerful than the need to wall the faithful in. In the playgrounds of the Williamsburg section of Brooklyn, bright-eyed Hasidic boys with spiraling earlocks race their Easy Rider tricycles against other Hasidic boys. Hasidic girls, in long pinafore dresses, jump to a rope swung by other Hasidic girls. Children of other ethnic groups also frolic in the playgrounds, but the Hasidic children seldom play with them. This is by design.

"If they start to play together when they are children, then later it is too late," Rabbi Joseph Weber, a yeshiva administrator, told me years ago. "The children should know that they have a different background, a different religion, a different tradition and they are supposed to be conducting a different way of life."*

That stance—holding themselves apart from secular forces even as they live amid that world—often explains the tensions that have flared up between Hasidim and the surrounding communities, with their more democratic values. Disputes have arisen over the separation of Hasidic boys and girls receiving remedial instruction in a public school or over a ban on assigning females to drive publicly financed buses ferrying Hasidic boys to school from a village in upstate New York. In these conflicts, Hasidim have often been depicted as contemptuous of the world around them. Many Hasidim no doubt are contemptuous. But Hasidic leaders say that this view is a stereotype and that the truth about them is far more complicated. The barriers, symbolic and otherwise, are not hostile in intent, Hasidim say, though many outsiders are scarcely convinced. They are walls designed to keep people in, not keep outsiders out, to safeguard the community's identity and ensure that observance of the Torah's commandments is protected against erosion. Hasidim are almost universally discouraged from at-

---

* Joseph Berger, "Hasidim Confront the Secular While Living a Life Apart," *New York Times*, July 4, 1987, p. 31.

tending college, to avoid mingling of the sexes and exposure to ideas that could steer them away from what they see as true Judaism. Yet they are far from uneducated, sharpening their minds in the coiling ethical and legal arguments of the Torah commentaries and the Talmud. That women may not have the same access to the Talmud, they would argue, ensures an unswerving focus on their life's mission as keepers of the family hearth.

Most Americans may find demeaning the idea of having a ritual bath—the *mikveh*—where Orthodox women, Hasidic or modern, bathe after menstruation and Hasidic men before they study Torah or before the Sabbath and holidays. But a Hasidic woman like Yitta Schwartz told her daughters how much she looked forward to the ritual. She did not see bathing in the *mikveh* as washing away impurity and uncleanliness, as those terms are understood, but as a mystical transformation that prepares the body for the holiness of sex, or, in the case of men, for study or the Sabbath.

Housing, too, has its own Hasidic twist. Houses have to be large, with room to hold all those children, and most Hasidim are willing to sacrifice backyard space to maximize their living space. Their kitchens, if they can afford to do so, should have two dishwashers and two sinks to ensure that dishes used for meat are kept separate from dishes used for milk products. There must also be room—a backyard or balcony— for the *succah*—the flimsy, shacklike structure that Orthodox Jews build for the autumnal, eight-day festival of Succoth, and in which they eat and sometimes sleep. As a result, the need for roomy housing has become the chief cause of conflict between the Hasidim and the secular towns and villages around them.

To keep themselves apart, Hasidim have created their own fleets of buses, not just to ferry schoolchildren, but to whisk working adults from Brooklyn or a suburb like Monsey, New York, to, say, Manhattan's midtown Diamond District. Among other purposes, the buses make sure that Hasidic men minimize the physically close encounters they might have with the wider public, and they give busy Hasidim a chance to pray. But many of the buses are publicly financed or franchised. So if those buses arrange for separate seating areas to keep the sexes apart in casual social situations—Hasidic men want to avoid temptation and Hasidic men and women will not shake the hands of the opposite sex, as an artifact of menstruation laws—they pose challenges to the First Amendment's religion clause. Some buses even put up a *mechitza*, a curtain, to keep the sexes separate during prayer, yet in places a handful of non-Hasidic women, in a flinty stubbornness reminiscent of Rosa Parks, have refused to change seats.

Within the strict bounds of Hasidic doctrine, what Hasidim can do is often surprising. Unlike the pacifist Amish, Hasidim might serve in law enforcement, as Shlomo Koenig does, as a Rockland County, New York, sheriff's deputy, carrying a gun and badge while retaining his beard and corkscrew sidelocks. Another of the Hasidim you will meet in these pages, Mendel Werdyger, did not go to college nor the professional schools where he might have learned sound engineering. But on his own and with help from mentors whom he sought out, Jewish and gentile, he figured out how to splice and digitally clean the music on old 78 recordings of the greatest cantor of the 20th century, and convert them into CDs that have sold in the tens of thousands. Professional engineers apparently did not have the zeal for such painstaking work for so limited an audience.

Mendel Werdyger, Yitta Schwarz and Shlomo Koenig exemplify the engaging vitality of so many Hasidim that is evident to those who trouble to make their acquaintance. But the darker, flip side of Hasidic life is also part of the Hasidic picture, as are rebels like Shulem Deen, who see the world they grew up in as suffocating and too often unprincipled. The pages ahead will weave those strands together. Through stories like theirs, this mysterious, if controversial, community should come to life and be far better understood.

A WOMAN OF VALOR,
A HASIDIC LIFE

With her kerchiefed hair, long-sleeved frocks and Yiddish tongue, Yitta Schwartz was certainly not a polished chief executive or a stately member of a presidential cabinet. She never wrote a prize-winning book or set a record for speed or distance. Yet when she died on January 4, 2010, at the age of 93, many Americans were astonished by her life story, so many that a less than prominently placed article about her death that I wrote in the *New York Times* ended up at the top of that day's list of most emailed stories and stayed on the list for many more days.

She had certainly lived what almost anyone would consider an epic life—an upbringing in a Hungarian village, survival in the Bergen-Belsen concentration camp (though with the loss of two young children), transplantation to Belgium and then New York City, life in a burgeoning, if sometimes blinkered Brooklyn community of like-minded souls and finally old age in a rural village in upstate New York. But what was most remarkable about her was that at her death she had left behind 2,000 living descendants, an entire tribe, including 15 surviving children, more than 200 grandchildren and hundreds of great- and great-great-grandchildren. They live in the same handful of communities, Hasidic neighborhoods like Brooklyn's Williamsburg and Borough Park and villages like Kiryas Joel in New York's Orange County, and include rabbis, teachers, merchants, truck drivers and plumbers. They ranged in age from a 75-year-old daughter named Shaindel to a great-great-granddaughter born a few weeks after Mrs. Schwartz's death and named Yitta in her honor.

"And she remembered everyone's name," her daughter, Nechuma Mayer, told me in what seemed at first like an antic Mel Brooks line. It was not intended to be. It was meant to distill something essentially Hasidic about her mother—her deliberate attentiveness to the people important to her. That attentiveness was, as she saw it, her payback to God for blessing her with such abundant progeny even after the losses she endured.

In assembling this tribe, Yitta was not trying to gain any special honor or distinction for herself. She was simply living life in the zealous Hasidic way, the way she had been raised, the way she tried to lead her days and nights, the way she taught her children and their offspring to lead their lives. For Yitta as for other Hasidim, the birth of a child is a tribute to God, not just because God commanded Adam in his first directive to be fruitful and multiply but because every child offers an opportunity to inform another soul of the sacred scripture that God passed on to Moses and the Israelites at Mount Sinai. That transmission of Torah enlarges the circle of the innately faithful, producing more believers who can fulfill the commandment of passing on the Torah. And every mitzvah in that Torah, or added on by sages, must, in the Hasidic way of thinking, be executed with the same intensity and intention. That philosophy explains why the Hasidim spend their days the way they do, dress the way they do and live apart the way they do not only from gentiles but from other Jews.

The idea of having 2,000 living descendants may amaze a typical American, who if he or she lives long enough may leave behind a dozen or two dozen living descendants. But in the Hasidic world in which Yitta lived almost her entire life, such numbers are impressive but not surprising. Depending on the sect's claim, the average Hasidic couple has between six and nine children, so, in theory, the ranks of descendants for any family can multiply exponentially into the thousands by the fifth generation. Yet, if the news of Yitta's progeny did not surprise many Hasidim, it did bring a bit of mystical schadenfreude. Before World War II, Hasidim lived mostly in Poland, Hungary, Russia and Ukraine, the lands that were the major target of Hitler's master plan for eradicating the Jews; so Hasidim made up a significant share of the six million killed in the war. Most of the scores of sects were so shattered that they were never able to reconstitute. But more than three dozen did in the United States and Israel, and roughly a dozen of them have flourished in phenomenal fashion. One can jest that Yitta virtually reconstituted a whole group all by herself—though the members of the clan she led are virtually all allied with the Hungarian-rooted Satmar, now the prevailing sect in Williamsburg and in the upstate New York village of Kiryas Joel.

As a result of bountiful procreation, Hasidim of various sects dominate three entire neighborhoods in Brooklyn that were fraying because of white and middle-class flight and the deepening poverty of the remaining inhabitants, and they are major ethnic blocs in cities like Los Angeles and Montreal. They can be seen scurrying—ambling or sauntering on a workday is not the Hasidic style—through the streets of Manhattan's diamond and jewelry district and its Garment Center, two of their largest work locales. Besides a flourishing insular economy, they run the country's largest independent camera store, B&H, with 1,500 employees and an international customer list that includes a fair chunk of the nation's professional photographers. They are so important a slice of the Jewish vote in New York, Baltimore, Los Angeles and a dozen more rural hamlets that Democratic and Republican politicians, to entice their support, pay them unusual obeisance—and engineer a goodly amount of kosher pork for their benefit, as well as sometimes turning a blind eye to violations of zoning, fire and educational laws. In these and other ways, the Hasidim unwittingly compel us to know who they are.

Yitta Schwartz was in many ways the model of a Hasidic woman and her life parallels the same 20th century arc as that of the Hasidic dynasties themselves. She had a boundless zest for life that was expressed, as her children and grandchildren remember it, by a devotion to Hasidic rituals, particularly as they revolved around family, as so many do. She faithfully attended the circumcisions, bar mitzvahs, engagements and weddings of each of her descendants. With 2,000 people in the family, such events occupied much of the year. Whatever the occasion, she would pack a small suitcase and ask a relative or neighbor for a ride from her apartment in Kiryas Joel in Orange County to Williamsburg—about 55 miles away—and sometimes farther afield.

"She would appear like the Prophet Elijah," Nechuma Mayer said of her mother, a few weeks after the funeral. "Everybody was fighting over her!" Nechuma was Yitta's sixth-oldest living child, and at 64 has 16 children of her own and more than 100 grandchildren and great-grandchildren.

I was drawn to finding out more about Yitta because she reminded me so vividly of the men and women my mother would talk about in her hometown of Otwock, Poland, a summer vacation spot about a half hour's train ride from Warsaw that was popular with Hasidic dynasties like Ger, Lubavitch and Modzitz. My mother worked as a teenage helper for the Gerer Rebbe's wife, and my grandfather taught the Modzitzer Rebbe's son the basics of Hebrew. My uncle Yasha, at eight years old, peeked into the Modzitzer Rebbe's window to hear him humming "bim, bum, bim, bum" to a melody he had composed. After all, the Modzitzer Rebbe was so charismatic that when he led High Holiday prayers Jews would line up for blocks to hear him. There was something about Yitta's concession to the whims of life as determined by what she inalterably believed was a higher power, to her unbending loyalty to a tribe, to her steadfast faith in God in the face of the most tragic of losses and a universe gone haywire that reminded me of the clear-sighted common folk, people of simple pleasures, unquestioning beliefs and ironic reflections that my mother, perhaps romanticizing, would reminisce about when she talked to her children about the community she lost to World War II. Her father, a cantor and *melamed*, a poorly paid teacher of little boys, her stepmother, the neighbors, the townspeople and the Hasidim who flocked to hilly Otwock's crisp air hoping for cures of their tuberculosis or simply for a cool retreat would have found Yitta a congenial personality. I realized as Yitta's relatives spoke so worshipfully of her that they were giving me a very one-sided and possibly sanitized version of Yitta's life. After all, Hasidim believe in lionizing the dead and certainly not denigrating them. But I thought her story was worth telling nevertheless because it spanned much of the modern experience of today's Hasidim, from the rural communities of Eastern Europe, to the unimaginable destruction of World War II, to their astonishing regeneration in American and Israel.

Yitta was an oval-faced woman with gray eyes and a soft smile edged by the slightest hint of cunning. She was born in 1916 into a middle-class family of seven children—she was the oldest—in the town of Kalev in northeastern Hungary, a two-hour train ride from Budapest. It is a market town that is esteemed beyond its borders as the hometown of the founder of Hungarian Hasidism, Rabbi Isaac Taub (1744–1828), a man known as the Kaliver Rebbe, who was famous for transposing commonplace Hungarian folk songs into Jewish liturgy. Every year, on the seventh day of the Jewish month of Adar, a week before Purim, rabbis from all over Europe would make a pilgrimage to the grave site. The small town, already teeming with students flocking to its famous yeshiva, would become a frenetic hive of excited black-garbed men. Some of them were Yitta's relatives.

Yitta was not without her own distinguished pedigree, an important attribute in the Hasidic realm, where genetic links to learned rabbis are regarded as innate evidence of virtue (Yitta's daughter, Nechuma, alerted me to her legacy). Yitta's great-grandfather had been the Stropkover Rov, Rabbi Chaim Yosef Gottlieb (1790–1867), head of the rabbinical court in a Slovakian town and a member of a distinguished line of rabbis famed for their piety, scholarship and charisma. Nechuma offered a sense of the mystical atmosphere in which her mother grew up by telling me a family legend of how Rabbi Gottlieb exorcised a dybbuk—the soul of a dead sinner that has migrated into a living person. It was known that Rabbi Gottlieb had a gift for such exorcisms and thus he was called on by a grand rabbi to perform the rite on a possessed young woman. He questioned the woman and her relatives and concluded that the dybbuk had been able to infiltrate the woman's soul because on the day before the Sabbath she had been reading romantic love stories instead of preparing herself for the week's most sacred day. He urged her to repent for that sin; miraculously, she was cured.

Yitta grew up in a world still untouched by 20th century conveniences. Even as a young girl, Yitta had to rise before dawn and draw water from a well and chop wood for a fire while her mother spent much of the day shopping in the market and cooking meals for her large family. That was the lot of most Hasidic women in Kalev. Although Yitta's own father, Nachum Schwartz, owned a "prospering" grocery, the family barely scraped by, for example eating meat once a week—a chicken was slaughtered on Friday afternoon and roasted in time for the Sabbath eve meal. Nachum Schwartz distrusted wealth. "He used to say," Nechuma told me, "that 'I pray my children should not be wealthy because if you're wealthy you turn away from God.'"

In a society where Jews and Christians attended separate public schools, Yitta received a secular Hungarian education just through sixth grade. But her religious education never stopped. It was fostered by her parents in the privacy of their home—in admonitions about what to eat and not eat, what to do and not do on the Sabbath, what to wear and not wear to safeguard her modesty—and Yitta absorbed similar messages of observance from the communal ether. Yitta was a very responsible child. The story is told of how as a girl, she arrived late to school one day and her parents were summoned. They defended Yitta by explaining that just as she was arriving at school she had remembered that the chickens had not been fed that morning and so she rushed back home to do so.

"She was so selfless, even if she put herself in danger," Nechuma Mayer told me, suggesting that Yitta might have been penalized for her lateness.

On Sabbath afternoons, her father would test his sons in the *Chumash*—the Five Books of the Bible—and the *Gemara*—the rabbinic commentary on Jewish law that forms the bulk of the Talmud—that they had learned the previous week. If the boys got the right answers there were candies and chocolates, but if they didn't know their stuff, they got a smack. The Hasidic philosophy then—among mothers as well as fathers—was, as Nechuma put it: "If I do you good you will never remember, but if I give you a slap you will never forget." Yitta would wait outside until she made sure her brothers were not smacked—as if her presence nearby could prevent such discipline. If they were smacked, she was heartsick.*

Yitta was tall and attractive and her parents felt an extra smidgeon of concern that her appeal must not cause her to stray from the Hasidic path. This is clear from another family tale—a story that illustrates the lengths that Hasidim go to protect their children and their way of life. Some of the Kalever Yeshiva students boarded at her parents' house and when Yitta was about 12 her heart went out to one boy who was suffering from tuberculosis. Her feelings were not romantic, the family emphasized, but simply the welling up of a good heart pained by suffering. She thought more food would comfort and help heal him so she put a glass of milk in front of his door. Still, her mother told her that what she did was not the right thing. It might spawn misconceptions by the boy or the neighbors and possibly lead Yitta astray.†

When she turned 17, her parents arranged a *shiduch*—a match—with Joseph Schwartz, a young man from a Hasidic family in the city of Debrecen, about 150 miles east of Budapest and near the Romanian border. Schwartz, distantly re-

---

* Author's interview with Nechuma Mayer.
† Ibid.

lated to Yitta, was a young merchant whose family belonged to the Kossony tribe of Hasidim. He was not a yeshiva scholar, but he was so fervent a Hasid that starting when he was nine years old, he, like other acolytes, walked 40 miles every year to spend the Jewish holidays with his rabbi, the Kossony Rebbe. Yitta moved to Joseph's city of Debrecen, which had a community of 12,000 Jews. As with other fervently Hasidic women, the morning after the *chupah*, the name drawn from the Yiddish word for "canopy" that Hasidim give the wedding ceremony, she took a pair of scissors and cropped her hair down to her scalp. What remained, she covered with a kerchief.

Not long afterward, Joseph was drafted into the Hungarian army. He returned home as often as he could so that he could spend time with his bride, and sometimes Yitta would travel to the army camp where was stationed. Most of the time, though, Yitta lived with her poor in-laws and found life in a bustling city congenial, preferring it to the quiet and isolation of a country village. To be sure, she was not a woman of cosmopolitan tastes; as Nechuma told me, she saw a sojourn in Debrecen as part of God's plan for her—"this was destined for her so this was what she wanted." In short order, the couple had six children—Shaindel, Chana, Dinah, Yitschok, Shimshon and Abraham—and raising those children occupied almost all of Yitta's time and thoughts.

In March 1944, the Nazis marched into Hungary and seized the territory of its ally, declaring that the Horthy government had not done enough to confine and cull the country's 400,000 Jews. (The Horthy government had already barred Jews from holding government jobs and applying for new trade or professional licenses, had severely limited their admission to university and had begun confiscating Jewish-owned land—but that was not enough.) Within weeks, SS commandos, led by Adolf Eichmann, began rounding up Jews, most of whom still believed this late in the war that after the mild experience with Germans in World War I they would be spared any cruel treatment.

Yitta's in-laws were in the middle of a *Shabbos* meal when storm troopers banged on the door and ordered them to put their belongings in a suitcase. Yitta, pregnant with a seventh child, and her husband and their children were taken as well. The family was dispatched by cattle cars to Auschwitz—briefly, it turned out—and eventually transferred from there to the Bergen-Belsen concentration camp in Germany. Whatever she witnessed—the inhumanly crowded trains, the brutal guards, the tearing away of children from their mothers—she comforted herself with her father's words that "every stick has two ends—now we're being hit but one day they will get it all back."

At Bergen-Belsen, her one-year-old, Abraham, died of hunger and the newborn, who was never named, died at birth in ways Yitta never spoke about to Nechuma. Those children were two of the 200,000 Hungarian Jews slaughtered by the Nazis. Yitta never talked much to her children about the war years. But glimpses of what some regarded as her heroic stoicism leaked out from people who had been in the camp with her. At the *shiva* after Yitta's death, Nechuma learned from a visitor—a woman whose mother had been in Bergen-Belsen, too—what kindness Yitta had quietly performed when an old woman died in the camp hospital with no relatives to bury her. Yitta, then 26 years old, took it upon herself to prepare the body according to Jewish ritual, burrow out a grave and bury the woman inside the camp.

"For her it was a matter of necessity," Nechuma said.

Yitta's fierce visceral tenacity in clinging to her faith amid the camps' horrors, in resourcefully finding ways to perform the mitzvahs in the face of anarchy and brutality, was true of many Hasidim, including a woman she would get to know in important ways many years later. The woman, Leah Mayer, lost a young daughter in the labor camp of Wiener Neustadt, an industrial town 40 minutes south of Vienna that was part of the notorious Mauthausen complex, where slave laborers quarried stone, manufactured munitions, excavated mines and assembled fighter planes. She buried the girl with her own hands, but she was, at 23, also eight months pregnant, and so she was brought to Wiener Neustadt's hospital to have a baby who would likely be killed the moment it was delivered in order to have her continue working. At the hospital, she told a Dr. Tuchman, a Jewish doctor assigned by the Nazis to treat the working prisoners, that if the baby was a boy she wanted him circumcised.

"Are you out of your mind?" the doctor replied, with a sneering laugh. "Do you know where you are?"

But he eventually shrugged her off by promising that if Leah could get the commandant's permission, he would agree to perform the circumcision. Leah wrote to a camp official

saying she wanted the baby circumcised "for hygienic reasons."
Amazingly, the official permitted Tuchman to circumcise
the baby. The reasons for the official's decision will never be
known, but perhaps he was aware the war was lost and was
trying to rescue himself with a mercy or was simply tired of
dealing with pesky, troublesome Jews. Leah did give birth to a
boy and, with astonishing chutzpah, she did not let Dr. Tuchman himself circumcise the baby. She found a *moel* working in
the camp, a Hungarian rabbi named Katz, and he did the *bris*.
When the religious ritual was over, Leah pulled out a piece of
bread she had squirreled away from her rations so she could
have the *seudah*—the celebratory meal that tradition dictates
accompanies a *bris*. She even produced some "wine" from a few
grapes she had purloined.*

And who was this baby that was circumcised in a concentration camp? The baby grew up to become the husband of
Yitta's Schwartz's daughter Nechuma, who was her first baby
after the war and the very person who was telling me the remarkable story. Whatever triumph there was for Yitta in that
redemptive trick of providence was to be overwhelmed by the
anguish of her wartime memories.

"She talked very little but sometimes I would get something
out of her," Nechuma told me from the comfort of her Borough
Park home. "When she thinks of it, she told me, she realizes
one of the most painful things that Hitler did was he robbed
away the humanity. People were treading over one another and
hurting each other. They were so hungry they weren't human.

---

* Author's interview with Nechuma Mayer.

This was what hurt her most. My mother always did whatever was within her power, but there are lots of things that were not within her power."

After the war ended, Yitta was slowly to learn that both her parents and three of her six siblings had died in Auschwitz and other camps. Only one sister, Dina, and two brothers, Motchek and Sruel Mendel, survived. All of them chose not to return to Hungary. It was pointless to return to villages whose Jewish population had been all but extinguished and were already under Soviet domination, so Yitta, her husband, their children and her husband's parents were transformed from inmates into refugees. They made their way to Antwerp, Belgium, where other surviving relatives had found sanctuary. Yitta and Joseph's first shelter was in the wreckage of an apartment in a bomb-cratered building.

In Antwerp, Yitta was to give birth to six more children. Before the first baby was born, Yitta and Joseph were penniless and they had trouble finding a hospital that did not require cash up front. When a hospital was found, Yitta could not even afford a diaper to wrap the baby in. But, Nechuma told me, she trusted in God.

"I didn't make plans as to what I'm going to feed this baby and with what I'm going to dress this baby, but God said I should have this baby," she told her daughter when she was grown. Yitta, whether intentionally or not, was articulating the Hasidic view of divine engagement in even the most ordinary events.

She gave the baby, born in January 1946, nine months after the German surrender, the name Nechuma because she was a "comfort" after all the misery and heartbreak of the war. She gave the next two babies—both boys—similar names alluding to comfort—Nachum and Nechemia.

Almost every day, her husband, Joseph, would head to the train station to scan the faces of arriving refugees, looking for other relatives. Often they would take in refugees who weren't related to them. Yitta had the willpower to put up those refugees in makeshift beds in the kitchen of her own ruin of an apartment. She was, her daughter said, driven by a conviction that she needed to live her life morally and kind-heartedly.

"She once said that when the *Moshiach* [the Messiah] comes I'll be ready for him," Nechuma recalled. "I won't have to change my dress and I won't have to change my attitudes, I'm ready to meet my ancestors."

Her husband too carried out the principles that had been imprinted since his infancy. Soon after their arrival, an American soldier came on a Saturday to their apartment to distribute funds earmarked for the refugees. He wanted to give the Schwartzes $100, but Joseph refused to take the money, even after his oldest daughter pleaded with him.

"We don't have anything to eat," she told him.

"*Mir tor nisht nemen keyn gelt Shabbos,*" he told her. "We're not allowed to handle money on the Sabbath."*

And so it went. The war, with its massacre of so many innocents that had disillusioned tens of thousands of Jews, had not disabused Yitta and Joseph of their Hasidic beliefs.

---

* Author's interview with Nechuma Mayer.

While some of the survivors forsook the practices they had grown up with before the war, Joseph and Yitta did not. Joseph, who soon found work as a diamond cutter, learning the craft from another Hasid, grew back the beard that the Nazis had cut off and did not trim it. They became close to other Hasidim who were gathering in Antwerp, including some from the Belz and Pupa clans. They sent their children to Orthodox Jewish schools. When she was six Nechuma started attending a Bais Yaacov school in Antwerp. It was part of a network of ultra-Orthodox girls schools in Europe and the United States founded after World War I by Sarah Schenirer, a seamstress and daughter of Polish Hasidim who, dismayed by the Hasidic girls leaving the fold for secular enticements, thought girls should have a formal religious education as well, if not in the same subjects taught to boys. The concept was controversial among Hasidim, who believed formal schooling was reserved for boys, but Schenirer's schools received the blessing of several notable rebbes and sages. Nechuma learned not only Torah and Hebrew but became fluent in French.

As the family settled in and began to achieve some economic security, Yitta, pragmatic as well as spiritual, was delighted with the fruits of modernism that Antwerp provided in ways she had never experienced in Hungary. Instead of drawing water from a well, she could simply turn a tap. There were sinks, toilets and bathtubs. They even had a primitive washing machine for the clothes. It still required a hand-operated agitator to twist the wet garments so that the water could be drained out. Nechuma remembers helping her mother twist that laundry.

"And my mother thought this was heaven," Nechuma told me.

After nine years in Belgium, they took up a visa they had applied for years before and left for the United States. They wanted to escape Europe, where the Soviet Union was imposing its spartan and despotic communist vision on Poland, Hungary and much of the east and seemed to pose dangers for Western democracies like France and Italy as well. America was a logical refuge because Yitta had an uncle living in Brooklyn's Williamsburg who might help them get started. They arrived in April 1953. The *New York Times* the next day carried a short article about the arrival of 86 European refugees. It bore the subhead "Hungarian Family of 13 Among Newcomers from Europe," and described how the Schwartzes—Yitta, 36, was identified as Julia—and their by-now eleven children—Shaindel, Chana, Dinah, Yitschok, Shimshon, Nechuma, Nachum, Nechemia, Hadassah, Mindel and Bella—arrived aboard a Pan American World Airways chartered flight from Brussels. The children, the article said, ranged in age from 18 years old to nine months. Another newspaper account was accompanied by a photograph of the Schwartzes, dressed in their European finery and smiling, standing on the plane's mobile staircase. Poignantly, the *Times* article quotes Chana, called Eva in the article, as saying the family had endured several concentration camps, including Bergen-Belsen. The Schwartzes, the article said, would be resettled by United Service for New Americans, though

Nechuma remembers that the family lived for a time in a partitioned shelter on Lafayette Street run by the Hebrew Immigrant Aid Society, or HIAS. (Joseph Papp later turned the building into what is now the Public Theatre.) But, even though two children had not survived the Holocaust, the rest of the family was safe. And they had transplanted their Hasidic way of life to America.

2

YITTA'S GOLDEN LAND

The Kaliver and Kossony communities that Yitta and
Joseph Schwartz had belonged to in Hungary were ir-
retrievably decimated, so they looked around New York's
Hasidic neighborhoods to see which transplanted sect was
most congenial. They decided on another besieged Hungarian
tribe, Satmar. Its rebbe, Joel Teitelbaum, had been one of a
contingent of 1,685 Jews saved from a train headed for Bergen-
Belsen by a deal worked out between a Hungarian Zionist ref-
ugee official and Adolf Eichmann—a deal for about $1,000 a
head paid in money, gold and diamonds. Teitelbaum spent the
last year of the war in Switzerland, then after a short sojourn
in Jerusalem, he made it to America in 1947 and began gathering his sect's remnants among the row houses and housing
projects of Brooklyn's Williamsburg.

His was a particularly austere version of Hasidism, one
whose most controversial tenet was its inalterable opposition to the creation of Israel as a state, which had occurred
in 1948. Such an event, the Rebbe in his understanding of

Torah felt, must await the arrival of the Messiah. Still, followers of several Hungarian dynasties who had lost their
spiritual leaders affiliated with the Satmar. And Yitta and
Joseph liked the neighborhood as well. Although more secularized Jews were in the majority—Williamsburg was Mel
Brooks' old neighborhood—they found the sprinkling of stu-
dious, dark-suited, lush-bearded men, the modestly garbed
women frenetic with the chores of home and family, the
ragtag shops increasingly filled with silver plates, candelabras,
and volumes of Talmud reminiscent of the streets of their
Hungarian villages.

The first encounters with the more Americanized Jews
were not always pleasant. The Schwartzes' first Brooklyn
home was in an old brownstone on Penn Street, and Yitta
would dispatch Nechuma—seven years old when she arrived
in America—to the grocery at nearby Marcy Avenue to buy
some food. Like most Hasidic girls, Nechuma usually wore
a long-sleeved blouse and long skirt and stockings, and on
summer days the women on the block, who were less than Orthodox, would say to her: "Little girl. Isn't it hot for you? Why
don't you take off the blouse or roll up your sleeves." Nechuma
would silently walk off, without answering. She was hot, of
course, she acknowledged in our conversation years later, but,
she insisted, she was delighted to be doing the bidding of God,
as her tribe saw it, a God who insisted on modesty. She decided there was envy behind such dismissive remarks.

"I was so strong in my belief," Nechuma told me. "How
come they don't know how much pride a Jewish girl has that for
the sake of God she wouldn't move up her sleeve one inch. But

I understand. Somehow this was the way they relieved their pain by ridiculing instead of saying I wish I could be like you."*

Yitta proceeded to have five more children in America: Israel, Joel, Aron, Sarah and Chaim Shloime. Sarah came along after Yitta had already married off two daughters. Nechuma allows that perhaps her mother wanted to put as many children as she could on Earth because she came from a large family that had been truncated by the war. But her husband, Rabbi Menashe Mayer, now a snowy-bearded yeshiva scholar and administrator, objects gently that "it had nothing to do with that," that Yitta's thinking was another product of her ardently held beliefs.

"The Torah tells us, 'You should not forget what you saw and heard at Mount Sinai and you should tell that to your grandchildren,' and she wanted to do that," he said, suggesting that it was her belief that the more grandchildren she had, the more the commandment would be fulfilled. This white-bearded scholar paused pensively for a moment and with characteristic Hasidic mysticism added: "I can picture her like she was standing at Mount Sinai and that's the way she gave to the children and grandchildren."

The family's apartment at 167 Penn Street occupied the bottom two floors of a brownstone; today it might be given the fancy name duplex. The basement housed the kitchen and dining room. Squeezed into the first "parlor" floor were Yitta and Joseph's bedroom and two children's bedrooms, one for the boys and one for the girls. At one point in the late 1950s,

---

* Author's interview with Nechuma Mayer.

there were ten children still living at home—three daughters and a son were married by then and the oldest son was away studying in the Yeshiva of Nitra in Westchester County's Mount Kisco—so beds occupied the entire floor space of each of those rooms. The closet in the girls' bedroom managed to hold a *Shabbos* dress and two weekday dresses for each daughter. With Yitta's frugal practicality, there were no toys, and the austere outlook was absorbed by the children—at least when they were children.

"Today we raise the kids and don't stop thinking what they're missing," Nechuma told me about the absence of toys. "But as a girl, I went to sleep thinking what can I do to help my mother and father. They worked so hard."

Yitta decorated the space so tidily that Rabbi Joel Teitelbaum's wife, the *rebbitzin*, asked her to host the first school party. The Satmar community was that small in the 1950s; the school's families could fit in her apartment.

Once the family was settled, Joseph, Yitta's husband, opened a furniture shop on Lee Avenue, Williamsburg's commercial spine, right near their home, and Yitta tended to the needs of the family. She was not very educated and was never to learn English well. But tooling around her home with a kerchief over her close-cropped hair, she cooked the meals, cleaned the apartment and washed and mended the clothes, always, according to her daughter, without complaint. Typical of the demands of housework on a woman with so many children were the Sabbath challahs. She had to knead twelve pounds of dough for six loaves; if nothing else, the task gave her strong fingers. In later years, her toil was eased by appliances from KitchenAid or Hobart. Indeed, Yitta, her daughter suggested, had a weakness for modern conveniences, boasting that her mother was among the first in Hasidic Williamsburg in the 1950s and 1960s "to buy silver foil and plastic bags."

Yitta sometimes went into Manhattan to splurge for cream-white blouses—buying 20 for 99 cents each—at that often-lamented discount emporium on Union Square, S. Klein on the Square. Because she believed in living simply and economically, she might buy standard, inexpensive jumpers for her daughters but adorn them by sewing on her own mother-of-pearl buttons. Yitta used to say "the problem today is that people are not happy with their lot." And she would remind them of her life in Hungary, where she chopped wood and drew water for the well and where meat and eggs were eaten once a week. "You don't know what you have—water running in the sink, a fire in the house, meat whenever we want it," she would tell them. But, according to her relatives, lectures like that were relatively few; she passed along this Mishnaic message of contentment with one's lot through her everyday demeanor.

"My mother-in-law had a joy of life," Menasha Mayer, Nechuma's husband, told me. "She enjoyed living every minute and serving *HaShem* [one of God's names], and everybody around her was affected by her natural happiness."

Meanwhile, the children were also affected by their father's burning fervor for matters Jewish, his adding, in the Hasidic way, an extra morsel of zeal to the performance of every commandment. When he lit the Chanukah candles, he wore a *shtreimel*, the round fur hat usually reserved for Sab-

bath, holidays or weddings. Not all Hasidim, not even all
Satmar Hasidim, honored Chanukah with the wearing of a
shtreimel, but to his children it was a sign of his spiritual zest.
The depth of ardor he brought to the blessings he made upon
entering the *succah* or simply the daily *bentshing*—the tuneful
grace after meals—was no less than that for a prayer he might
say when a daughter was married. His *kiddush*, the blessing
over the wine to welcome the Sabbath, and his *havdalah*, the
blessings over a twisted candle and fragrant spices to bid Sabbath farewell, were particularly vigorous and loud, Nechuma
recalled. Schwartz, who was not a rabbi or yeshiva scholar, was
equally scrupulous about not violating any of the prohibitions;
he would not eat a tomato unless it was peeled; he wanted to
avoid the risk, minimal as it was, of biting into a worm and
thus breaching the law against eating a forbidden animal. In
this way, he taught his children upright behavior, according
to Torah, and humility before higher powers and principles.

"What a fiery Hasid he was," Nechuma told me, using a
descriptive that captured the quality that made him more
than just a pious Jew.

How did the Schwartzes take care of so many children?
Older daughters who were still living at home would help Yitta
take care of the younger children, making sure they got off to
school clean and well fed or stayed out of trouble when playing
on the sidewalk. She sent the children to the Satmar day schools,
which where relatively small then but today have 25,000 students, an enrollment larger than that of some cities and one that
comprises 15 percent of the entire Jewish day school system in
the United States. It was not easy paying tuition—which today

is roughly $3,000 per child—for so many children, but she and Joseph made sure there was enough money for education. Even if there hadn't been, the Satmar schools would have accepted the children. Hasidic schools, with heavy donations from more prosperous members of the community, make sure no one is ever turned away; the commandment of teaching the Torah to the young is ironclad and Jewish education is essential to the community's cohesiveness.

Once Rabbi Teitelbaum had set up the Satmar's United Talmudical Academy, the boys all studied there and eventually followed up high school with a *kollel*—an adult yeshiva where young men, usually married already, spend a year or two studying in large groups in the *beis medrash*, or study hall, poring over the large pages of Aramaic Gemara with a study partner in an ageless routine accented by singsong melodies and a raised thumb to clinch a point. Only after finishing *kollel* would a young man take on an occupation. The Schwartz sons all went to *kollel*, either Nitra or, once it was established, the Satmar Yeshiva in Williamsburg.

Rabbi Teitelbaum felt girls should be taught as well— but differently, befitting what he saw as their role as future mothers and homemakers. He liked the Beis Yacov model. He wanted girls to be instructed in the ancient Hebrew of the prayers and the Torah, though he forbade them exposure to the sinuous arguments of Talmud, reserved for men. Still, he insisted that they know how to read English well and be familiar with world and American history, geography and mathematics so they could navigate the demands of the wider society. It is clearly not an educational philosophy that most egalitarian Americans would approve of, but ironically, it meant that the community's women were often more prepared to talk with and understand the outside world than Hasidic men. Nechuma remembers making a scrapbook of American presidents, something it is doubtful her brothers were asked to do. Teitelbaum, however, asked that the girls' schools spurn science, feeling it might breed atheism.

"My mother felt extremely grateful to Rabbi Teitelbaum," Nechuma told me. "He helped her raise her children Hasidic. She did not know if she would have been able to raise them Hasidic in the United States of America without his work. There was nothing before he came. It's really priceless."

There were times when the burdens of so large a family required a little indulgence. Rabbi Hertz Frankel, head of English and secular studies at Williamsburg's large Satmar girls' school, recalled how one year Yitta came to him two weeks before Passover and haggled with him over letting her daughter stay home. She did not seem as intimidated arguing with him as some Hasidic women might have been.

"My name is Mrs. Schwartz," she said. "I respectfully request that you let my daughter take two weeks off to help me prepare for Passover."

"But she has important tests to take at this time of the year and she'll miss them," a skeptical Rabbi Frankel replied. "If I make an exception for you I'd have to let every child go home for Passover."

"Yes, but my situation is a little different," she said. "I have fifteen children."

The rabbi resorted to some other arguments, but when it fully dawned on him what it must be like to prepare Passover for a family of 15 children—cleaning a home so that it bears no trace of *chametz* (the grain products forbidden during Passover), airing out a library full of yellowed volumes of Talmud, preparing the dishes for two seders, not just for her family but for relatives and friends who might be invited—he succumbed. He has gone on to teach four generations of Yitta Schwartz's family.

Yitta supervised her children's spiritual education outside of school as well—often in ways that might repel more secular Americans. Nechuma, who loved to read as a child, tells the story of her delight in finding a nonreligious Yiddish book in a neighbor's garbage. It was on a topic she no longer remembers. But her mother told her, "My dear daughter, you cannot read this book. This is atheistic."

According to her daughter, no matter how many chores were demanded of her, Yitta was never too busy to tend to an unexpected need. Family legend tells of a Friday morning in fall or winter when the sun sets early and the time needed to prepare for the Sabbath is shorter than usual. One of Yitta's brothers knocked on her door to announce that his wife had just had a baby. Yitta dropped her Sabbath duties, scrambled two eggs, wrapped them in foil to keep them warm and snatched up a freshly baked roll. She dashed out of her apartment to catch a bus that would take her over the bridge to Beth Israel Hospital in Manhattan's upper East Village. Her sister-in-law, still feeble from a night of giving birth, was surprised

with a warm, fresh breakfast. Yitta kissed her and congratu-
lated her and sped off to catch another bus back to Williamsburg so she could finish her preparations for Sabbath.

Day after day, Yitta, like almost all other Hasidic women,
clung to a rigorous conception of what modesty should mean.
She wrapped her skull in a kerchief and spurned a wig, though
most women of other Hasidic sects feel wigs fulfill the obligation of remaining modest before male strangers because they
still hide their actual hair, yet are far more attractive. Yitta
never felt that wigs were a transgression, but that wearing a
kerchief was a higher form of observance. Her dresses were
always high-necked and long-sleeved, of dark or plain colors.
When she could afford it, her daughter confessed with a guilty
giggle, she sometimes treated herself to a fashionable scarf by
a designer like Hermès that could be used as a kerchief, but
always in low-key colors.

"I look at the pictures from my mother and I can see she
was dressed at the age of ninety just as she was at thirty-five,"
Nechuma told me. "She never changed her wardrobe because
of this style or that style. She dressed like a dignified Hasidic
woman."

And she made sure her daughters followed her vogue, discouraging them, for example, from wearing oranges or pinks.
She was very particular as well as to where she bought her
food; a label with a kosher certification from the Union of
Orthodox Jewish Congregations of America—satisfactory
for most Orthodox Jews—was not sufficient for her. She insisted on the extra assurance of a certification by a Satmar
or other respected Hasidic *mashgiach*—a rabbinical supervisor

specializing in the attributes that make food kosher or not. She performed all the mitzvahs with that extra dollop of Hasidic fastidiousness. During the nine days leading up to Tisha B'Av, when observant Jews mourn the destruction of the two Jewish temples, she refused to do laundry or clean her house. The holiday occurs in the heat of summer, but Yitta refused to cool herself in a pool and kept her changes of wardrobe to a minimum.

For reasons of privacy and modesty her family would not say much about Yitta's *mikveh* customs. But it can be safely assumed that like other Hasidic women, Yitta was scrupulous about observing the laws surrounding *niddah*—menstruation—and the *mikveh*. For twelve days after the start of menstruation— five days until blood stopped flowing and seven days for the purity interlude known as "the white days"—her husband had to avoid touching her and abstain from sexual relations. After sundown of the twelfth day, she would wash herself thoroughly, remove the minimal makeup and jewelry she wore and immerse her body from head to toe two or three times in the *mikveh*—a cubical tiled pool where some water must be gathered from rain or other natural sources. She would then say the blessing: "Blessed are you, HaShem, ruler of the universe, who has made us holy through His commandments, and has commanded us about immersion." Afterward she would tell her husband that she was *tahorah*—ritually pure—and he was then allowed to have physical contact with her. More than that, he was required to resume sexual relations that night. Hasidim believe *mikveh* night is the most propitious time for conception. For Yitta, it obviously worked.

Just as for other Hasidim, Yitta's week revolved around the Sabbath, its holiest day. The world, it seemed, was created for the exaltation of the Sabbath, the day God rested from creation, and the day that Jews were commanded to especially honor. Yitta would start preparing for *Shabbos* on Thursday when she'd buy carp for gefilte fish, grind it, shape it into oval balls then store it in the refrigerator so it would be cold for the Friday evening meal. On Friday, she rose early. With her older daughters bustling about to help, she packed her children off for a half day of school and started the lion's share of the cooking and baking—challahs, chicken soup, a potato *kugel*, the sweetened carrots known as *tsimmes* and some of her dessert cakes: yeast rolls made with cocoa and sugar, apple pie, napoleons. All the while she and her daughters polished the stove and kitchen counters and mopped the floor. Just before the sun set she covered the dining table with a freshly ironed tablecloth, had the children change into their finest clothes and transfigured herself with a more elegant dress and low-heeled pumps.

"My mother believed the person was the house," Nechuma told me. "So if a visitor came or if she had to leave on the spur of the moment she looked like a *mensch*."

While this whirlwind was swirling, Joseph, on Friday around noon, would shutter his shop—Schwartz Furniture—and head to his home a few blocks away for a nap, a reward for his week's hard work but also a way to arm himself for what was often a long night. He pared his fingernails and burned the clippings—Hasidim believe that evil can reside in our fingernails—and mulled over a page of Talmud, an almost daily exercise for many Hasidim but a particularly blessed session when done to honor the Sabbath. Then he joined other Hasidim at the men's pool of the Satmar *mikveh*—now on East Williamsburg Street—to dip in waters Hasidim believe purify one for the obligations ahead—be they study or Sabbath. Afterward, he returned home to don his finest *kapote*—a shiny black silk frock coat—and his *shtreimel* and head off to synagogue for an hour of prayer. Upon his return, he and his family would savor Yitta's Friday night meal, starting off with Joseph chanting a resonant *kiddush* and blessing over the challah. In between courses, Joseph would lead his clan in several rounds of *Shabbos zmiros*—special songs for the Sabbath. Then he and his older sons would leave to go to the synagogue a few blocks away and sit with the Rebbe at his *tish*—his table—and watch him make another *kiddush* over wine, eat dinner, sing another round of *zmiros* and offer words of wisdom that the Hasidim would digest intensely. As they do at any meal with the Rebbe, the followers grouped around the table would jostle for the Rebbe's *shrayim*—his leftovers, sliced up, placed on little plates and passed around to the agitated acolytes. These evenings were raucous, often rapturous, and could last until two or three in the morning.

That meant that Joseph might only have a few hours of sleep before rising and heading off with his sons to synagogue for morning prayers. Yitta, of course, would help by getting the younger boys ready for *shul*, as a synagogue is called in Yiddish. But synagogue, it seemed, was reserved for men and boys, and widows or elderly women who might watch from behind a screen. The younger girls stayed home and played quietly while Yitta prayed by herself and set the table for the Sabbath *seudah*—the lunch, or second meal. The main course was always *cholent*—a stew of beans lubricated with *schmaltz*, or melted fat—that had baked all night in an oven lit before sundown because lighting a flame to cook is not permitted on the Sabbath itself.

Lunch would be followed by a nap for Joseph and Yitta, seen as a well-earned blessing for the week's hard work. If the weather cooperated, there would be a *shpatzir*—a stroll—partly to greet and chat with familiar faces from the neighborhood but also to visit the homes of each of the grown children and inspect their blossoming families. The day would be capped with another session with the Rebbe—for his *shalosh seudos*—the third of the three festive meals that Hasidim believe Jews are commanded to eat on the Sabbath day. (The other two are the Friday night meal and the lunch.) That third meal is eaten between the afternoon and evening prayer services.

When three stars were sighted, the Schwartz family gathered for *havdalah*—the farewell to Sabbath that honors the division between the holy day and the mundane week with the lighting of a braided candle and the inhalation of an often elegant silver container of aromatic spices. Yitta reluctantly surrendered to the changeover—*motza'ei Shabbos*, the departure of Shabbos—with a Yiddish prayer that she composed herself: "God of Abraham, Isaac and Jacob, watch over your loving Jewish nation, and protect it from evil things. The week ahead should bring blessings, health, splendor, luck and compassion. We should only hear good things. God takes his silver cup and gives his blessings throughout the world and make his blessings so loud and clear that all Jewish children will answer amen and amen."

Only then would she turn on the lights to mark the start of the prosaic workweek.

In the 1960s, Yitta was struck by tragedy again. Like many Hasidim, she had put her younger children in summer camp. She was at home in Brooklyn when she received a call from the boys' camp that her eight-year-old Shloime had drowned in the lake. Heartsick, she mourned again. Nechuma, who was 16 at the time, and the other children felt that the joy that had marked her days drained out of her and that she was never quite the same again. Joseph urged her to take herself out of the house and work and she did, assisting him in the furniture store, with her daughters picking up some of the slack at home. But Yitta persevered—as if she understood in her marrow that losses were woven into the narrative of a life that God had assigned to each one of us.

Watching her family flourish eased the grief or at least distracted her from it. She wasn't passive about that lifelong project; she made sure all of her children were married off well—in the Hasidic manner. Sometimes she used the services of a matchmaker, a *shadkhin*. A *shadkhin* knew that Nechuma needed a clever, charismatic man who also came from an ardently pious home and so paired him off with Menashe Mayer, who had been a good student and whose father was a leading scholar at Yeshiva of Nitra in Mount Kisco. It turned out that the two fathers knew each other, and so it was a sensible match, perhaps *bashert*—predestined. The parents met for one brief session and then Nechuma and her intended met for another brief one in Yitta's dining room, with the parents hovering nearby. With Hasidic matches, if the girl or boy has some misgivings, a second or sometimes third meeting will be held, but after the third meeting a match is either a go or it is not.

"It's really from heaven these things," Nechuma explained to me. "The ultra-Orthodox believe matches are made in heaven, and it's good. Somehow we know God is with us."

Still matchmaking, Hasidim believe, is the preferred way to make sure God's choice is discerned because, as Nechuma explained, "the truth is these boys are so protected they never meet girls, so there's no other way to do it."

Yet, Yitta was not exclusively immersed in her family of 15 children and had some Satmar communal interests to keep her busy. For example, when the Satmar Rebbe's wife, Faige Teitelbaum, decided to make a trip to Israel to visit the sect's girls' institutions, Yitta went along. In all her activities, Yitta always honored Hasidic principles. When two men visited from Israel to raise money in the Satmar community, she put them up. They arrived near midnight, when Yitta was already in bed, but she rose, dressed and prepared a freshly cooked meal. One of her older daughters was visiting at the time, and gently protested that the men should be eating at 7 or 8 p.m. "like everyone else." Yitta took the daughter aside and told her: "Listen. You don't come to my house and tell me how I should serve supper. I love when people wake me up to give them food. This is my hobby."[*]

---

[*] Author's interview with Nechuma Mayer.

At some point, Joseph's aged father, who had survived the war and settled in an apartment nearby, became too frail to live alone, so she moved him into her Williamsburg apartment and converted the dining room into his bedroom. According to Nechuma, Yitta fed him, changed his linen every day and washed his body, tenderly caring for him as if he were her own father. She told her daughters many times that it is a privilege to care for a father or mother.

"He was like the king of the house," Nechuma told me. "And she taught us all to be involved."

By 1976, Joseph too took sick and he died that year. But Yitta never burdened others with her sudden solitude.

"We didn't feel even one minute that she was a widow," Nechuma told me. "She used to say, 'When there are so many problems in life, I should put myself on the scale?'"

In her sixties, a time when her clan numbered just 170, she moved to an apartment in the Satmar village of Kiryas Joel near Monroe, New York, a kind of pastoral Williamsburg where labyrinthine streets and culs-de-sac are lined with stout, closely packed houses. Most of her children were now living in Kiryas Joel, where they could find larger homes and a more rustic pace, so she wanted to be close to them. But still she busied herself with the obligations, as she saw them, of family and community. "A lot of people waste time," Nechuma told me. "My mother had this blessing: she knew what was important and what was unimportant."

As more of her children grew up and married and had their own children and even grandchildren, she spent much of her time shuttling between Kiryas Joel and Williamsburg to wed-

dings, bar mitzvahs and circumcisions, often providing food
she cooked herself. For the *Shabbos* before a wedding, she would
starch tablecloths and bake her standard repertoire of napoleons, cream cakes and chocolate babkas, sometimes enough to
feed hundreds of guests. For a *bris*, she dragged along a pillow
she had embroidered on which to lay the infant boy during
the circumcision. The parents of every grandchild, great-
grandchild and great-great grandchild made sure to have Yitta's pillow for their sons' circumcisions. By one estimate it was
used in more than three hundred circumcisions, with Yitta
washing out any blood that may have splattered on the pillow-
case and ironing it freshly for the next ceremony to come.

She even took the trouble of traveling to a rite that is more
custom than obligation and is celebrated almost exclusively in
the Hasidic and other ultra-Orthodox communities—the *upsherinish*. In that ritual, a boy usually at three years, receives his
first haircut, the "shearing off." The custom dates back to the
16th century and its purpose is to train a child to observe the
commandment of *peyes*—leaving the sidelocks uncut in line
with the instructions in Leviticus that one must not round the
corners of a beard. The child's locks are shorn, sometimes to
his crown, but the sideburns remain there to coil and dangle.
(Some sects confine the length of *peyes* to the cheekbone and
others let them grow beyond the shoulders.) There is a special
honor in being among the first to snip the child's hair, and
sometimes the Rebbe himself will assume the role. And of
course, as with a *bris*, there is usually a bountiful feast, which
meant that Yitta spent the day before cooking, baking and
buying gifts.

Visiting all these children and grandchildren, she spent a good deal of time on buses from Kiryas Joel or in friends' cars when she could cadge a ride. While she traveled to, say, a wedding, she would sing or hum old Hasidic wedding songs she remembered from her childhood in Hungary. There were so many occasions that, to avoid scheduling conflicts, one of her sons was assigned to keep a family calendar.

"From her two-thousand-plus descendants," Nechuma told me, exaggerating only slightly, "she never missed a bar mitzvah, a wedding or a *bris*. Everybody was fighting over her."

Although her family insists that their matriarch had no trouble remembering everyone's face and name, it was among her grandchildren that she was particularly engaged with the young mothers.

"Did you bathe him? Did you burp him? Do you have enough money to live?" she would ask each granddaughter.

Yitta would express her worries about each grandchild, often observing that young people today had more social pressures than when she was girl, and, for those still in school, far more demanding teachers. For the grandchildren approaching adulthood, she would sometimes take on the role of a *shadkhin*, a matchmaker. She was the one who suggested that Nechuma's daughter, Tirtza, marry her first cousin, the son of Nechuma's brother, the kind of inbred match that Isaac and Rebecca made in the Bible and that Hasidim do not shun the way other Americans might. Tirtza is now a mother of twelve.

"We never made a match without letting my mother know what family we were marrying into, and if we didn't tell her we would regret it," Nechuma told me.

The children and grandchildren paid her back, throughout the year but especially around the High Holidays. There is a custom before Rosh Hashanah of visiting parents and grandparents and wishing them a sweet and healthy year. Dinah Wagshal, Nechuma's eldest daughter and herself the mother of 16 and grandmother of ten (she had five children after her oldest grandchild was born), said Yitta's children and grandchildren would show up at her house for a talk or tie her up on the phone all day.

"I used to wish every single minute of my life that I should be like my grandmother," Dinah told me. "She was the heartbeat of every child and grandchild."

Given the pain she suffered during her lifetime—the loss of her parents, of siblings, of three children, of her husband—her resolve to live a robust, vital life was remarkable, and she advised her friends to have the same willpower, to remain upbeat. Nechuma told me the story of how a sixtyish friend of Yitta's came to her once and claimed to be "depressed, down in the dumps." Yitta advised her: "Go to the grocery and buy a sack of flour and bake it up. Make a challah, make rugelach, and give them to your grandchildren. Then let me know how you feel."

Tirtza said that when she was downhearted Yitta applied the same buoyant philosophy. "I had a nine-month-old baby, I was marrying off a daughter and I was pregnant and not feeling well. She gave me a perspective on life—that every child is worth a million dollars."

Though Yitta was not poor, it was not money or possessions she cared about. She told her children: 'If you find money in my house, give it to *tzedakah* [to charity]." It may sound corny, but to her life's rewards were the *simchas*—the joyous ceremonies that mark life's passage—and she kept on attending them almost until the end, the last one being the wedding of a great-granddaughter, Leah, in December 2009.

"She felt if she can't attend an occasion of family, it's not worth living," her granddaughter Briendy Feuerwerger told me.

Her offspring paid her back manyfold. As she lay dying in Mount Sinai Hospital in Manhattan, her children and grandchildren and great-grandchildren and great-great-grandchildren all visited. "In the hospital they couldn't get rid of us," Nechuma told me. The nurses and security guards were overwhelmed at times, given hospital rules. Then when she expired, her offspring streamed into Kiryas Joel from Brooklyn and elsewhere for the funeral.

Satmar men, in black homburgs, many of them her sons and grandsons, jostled to carry her pine casket, draped in a black shroud, through the thick crowd to the village's graveyard. Behind them gathered a teeming cluster of women, their hair wrapped in turbans, many of them her daughters and grand-daughters but many of them women in the community who felt she had been an exceptional specimen of a human being. More than one person used the words *eshes chayil*, a woman of valor, to describe Yitta. The term is taken from a Friday night prayer that lays out the model of a Jewish woman. Yitta was lowered into the ground and the men shoveled the dirt into the grave themselves, the dirt at first landing on the wood with an ominous thud, but later more softly. They continued shoveling dirt into the grave until it was fully covered, fulfilling a Jewish custom of personally burying the dead with Hasidic intensity even as it relieved the unionized grave diggers.

A few weeks later I sat at Nechuma's dining table as she reminisced about her mother, and she pulled out a manila folder of photographs she wanted to show me. She was reluctant to provide them for publication for a *Times* article. Her mother, she said, was too modest to have her photograph broadcast. Yitta did not even want her children to collect photographs of her. "Just keep me in your heart," she used to say. Nechuma finally relented with one that shows her mother at a gathering of women around Faige Teitelbaum, the Satmar Rebbe's widow, during that trip to Israel.*

It was not by photographs Yitta wanted to be remembered but by the sentiments she left behind and the offspring she put on Earth. She had more than fulfilled God's commandment to "be fruitful and multiply" and at her death she was reaping the rewards.

"A baby is worth a million dollars," she used to say. "When you leave a son or daughter after you pass away, it means that you still keep living. If you leave a child or grandchild, you live forever."

---

* Author's interview with Nechuma Mayer.

3

AND WHEN THE REBBE SINGS

The atmosphere in the hall is electric with anticipation, as it might be for Bruce Springsteen at a sold-out concert or at a public appearance at Buckingham Palace by the queen of England. Indeed, this hall is also packed with breathless and enthusiastic devotees. But the star the audience is waiting for is not a musician or a queen, but a simple-living, elderly rabbi—the Rebbe or grand rabbi of the exclusively Hasidic village of New Square, New York. And what he will do is not entertain but simply light a Chanukah menorah.

Inside the castle-like synagogue in New Square, more than 1,000 Hasidic men are standing and jammed together like dominoes along sets of sloped bleachers arrayed like a three-sided amphitheater and rising up almost to the 30-foot ceiling. In front of the bleachers, dense clusters of pale-faced boys with sidecurls squat on the floor, curiosity glinting in their eyes. The boys are squeezed behind steel barricades that separate the crowd from the Holy Ark with a large empty space, as if this area were being readied for a mosh pit. All eyes are turned to a closed door at the bottom right side of the ornately carved Holy Ark.

Suddenly, the door opens and the hubbub flickers into silence. The Rebbe, David Twersky, appears, slight and bespectacled but aristocratic in bearing, sheathed in a black satin caftan tied at the waist with a sash and crowned by the tall, round, golden-brown Ukrainian fur hat called a *kolpik*, a version of a *shtreimel*. Yet he never enters the synagogue interior itself, effectively spurning what could have been his moment onstage, his mosh pit. Instead he is surrounded in that narrow anteroom by relatives—younger men and boys—in a kind of affected familial seclusion. He can be observed by hundreds but the anteroom allows him to maintain a cocoon of privacy, as if he were about to bless the Chanukah candles in the intimacy of his home.

He rocks back and forth murmuring some introductory prayers, his voice laden with emotion, an audible cry sounding as deeply felt as a sob. The Hasidim seem mesmerized, but all they can do is glimpse the Rebbe and keep their ears peeled to those prayers, a warm-up for the two blessings over the menorah on this second night of Chanukah. When he finally recites the first blessing over the candles in a whisper of a voice, a sharp thunderous audience "Amen!" resounds throughout the synagogue. He chants the second prayer and there is the roar of another deafening amen.

Then, as suddenly as it opened, the door closes, the brief ceremony is over and the men disperse into the rainy night, most of them heading for a fast supper at home before they return for the rest of the evening's rituals. This peek at the Rebbe is clearly not enough.

Why is this ritual by the Skverer Hasidim with their Rebbe conducted in this teasing fashion, I ask my three Hasidic escorts, Alexander Rapaport, Levi Meisner, and Yeedle Melber.

"It's the paradox of humility and of stature," Rapaport tells me. "We only get a two-minute peek. The Rebbe celebrates Chanukah traditionally, and blessing the candles in public is not traditional. So he does so in a kind of private fashion. But the Hasidim also want to see the Rebbe. That's why the door is open."

There is one more thing, according to a disciple, Rabbi Mayer Schiller, who teaches advanced Talmud at the boys' high school of Yeshiva University and often acts as a spokesperson for the Skverer sect.

"The belief is strong that watching a Rebbe perform a mitzvah can have a transformative effect on the person watching," says Rabbi Schiller. "And the passion he brings, if we're there, we can capture that passion."

That is why this odd minuet is repeated for different groups of Hasidim every one of the eight nights of Chanukah. So many thousands crave to take part that the nightly attendance is roughly determined in the order of the first names in the Hebrew alphabet. On the first night there were probably many Abrahams and Benjamins, on the second more Chaims and Dovids.

For most of my life I had heard about the awelike reverence lavished on the rebbes—the dynastic rabbis-in-chief who lead Hasidic sects—particularly from my Otwock-raised mother. She often sang playful songs about rebbes and the odd, almost comical devotion that their acolytes felt. "Der Rebbe Elimelech" is a mischievous children's song about how a rebbe's followers gaze with fascination and joy as he takes off his ritual fringes and phylacteries and puts on his hat and his glasses and sends first for his fiddlers, then his drummers, then his cymbalists. Another cheerful song tells of how all the Hasidim sing when the rebbe sings and dance when the rebbe dances. Seeing that devotion in the flesh in a dense swarm of people jammed into a claustrophobic hall can take one's breath away.

New Square, 50 years old, is not Otwock. It is a deliberately planned, rural *shtetl* of coiling streets chockablock with squat, boxy homes made up of 10,000 Hasidim, most of them children (the village's median age is roughly 14). The synagogue along with the yeshiva are its bedrock institutions, the hub for the radiating spokes of the wheel. Though New Square raises millions of private dollars for its own upkeep, it is a village that has been built with considerable outlays of government assistance for institutions like the Refuah (meaning cure) Health Center. The Skverer Hasidim have paid generous politicians back with their votes. And in a gesture of gratitude to America, they have named most of the streets after the presidents of the United States. The synagogue is on Roosevelt Avenue, the bus company on Washington Avenue and my escort Yeedle Melber, a thirtyish Hasid, grew up on Taft Lane. Critics have labeled the village a theocracy and criticized it for having some sidewalks reserved for men and others for women, a waiting room at the health center where men and women are separated by gender and an unwritten rule that the village's women cannot drive.* But it retains many characteristics of an American village nonetheless—closely packed houses on winding streets lead to a town center, in this case a synagogue rather than a city hall.

The intense Hasidic zeal I observed at the candle lighting becomes even more palpable later in the evening when I return to the synagogue. The bleachers have been rearranged for a crowd of roughly the same size but now have been squeezed into a tighter raked amphitheater on the right half of the synagogue. The place has more the intimacy of Fenway Park than the grandeur of Yankee Stadium; the fans, all standing again, are right on top of the action. The rearrangement is needed because the Hasidim want to hear the Rebbe give a sermon without the aid of a microphone. A dais has also been set up where the Rebbe's inner circle and other distinguished rabbis are seated.

Shortly after 9 p.m., the Rebbe ambles to the center of the dais and starts the event off by turning his back to the crowd and murmuring the Kaddish—the memorial prayer for a dead parent, spouse, child or other close relative. It is the *yahrzeit*— the anniversary—of his mother's death and the followers respond vociferously in the appropriate passages. He takes his seat in a gilded, tall-backed beige leather chair, a throne of sorts, which composes the evening's only regal touch, and

---

* Alex Webster, "In New York Shtetl, Where Arson Attack Occurred, the Rebbe's Word Is Law," *Jewish Telegraphic Agency*, June 6, 2011.

the Hasidim break into a deeply felt and vigorous series of *niggunim*, songs without words that are punctuated by characteristic Hasidic nonsense syllables like *ya-ba-bam*. The Rebbe, his penetrating eyes glittering with what seem like merry observations and thoughts, keeps up the tempo by pounding a clenched fist on the table, another gesture typical of Hasidic chieftains.

"When a song has words it limits its meaning," Rapaport whispers to me. "When it has no words the meaning is unlimited."

The melodies are at times plaintive, at times ecstatic, and the overall theatrical effect is spellbinding. In the middle of the floor, an orderly choir of young men and much younger boys rises and breaks into traditional Chanukah songs set to distinctly Hasidic melodies, tunes most Jews have never heard. While they sing, large platters of honey cake sliced in squares are brought in front of the Rebbe, and he passes them out. Hasidim elbow and jostle forward in a surprisingly calm and friendly stampede. The Rebbe hands each Hasid a piece of honey cake and some whisper a "l'Chaim" to him. It is a version of the Sabbath ritual of *sherayim*, the remnants of food the Rebbe has touched, which Hasidim rush to consume during that day's third meal because the food is believed to carry spiritual qualities.

"When a righteous man touches the food it has a transformative effect on the food," Schiller explains.

The handoff to the entire hall takes an efficient 10 or 15 minutes and then the Rebbe launches into his talk. But in the oblique and orchestrated Hasidic style, he begins only after a disciple has asked him a question. The reasons for this nuance is that rebbes are not supposed to sermonize to aggrandize themselves but only to satisfy their followers' curiosity. Reticence and restraint are what are prized in rebbes, something the grandfather of the current Skverer Rebbe, Reb Dovidl Twersky, who died in 1919, once eloquently suggested.

"We keep silent and we keep silent, then we rest a bit and go on keeping silent," he once said.

Dovidl Twersky's silence, his acolytes say, was piercing. "He would sit in silence and everybody around him would hear what he had to say," Mayer Schiller said paradoxically of the grandfather. "Now the Rebbe speaks publicly."

More than speaking, the current Rebbe is clearly holding court. He speaks forcefully for a half hour, with a half dozen long pauses to summon his thoughts before launching into a new idea. His voice is too low for my late-sixtyish ears and my Yiddish is too flimsy to comprehend all that he says. But the Hasidim in the bleachers are visibly enraptured, many of them swaying, twisting and rocking to his words.

My escorts tell me afterward that the Rebbe spoke about three points, all offering a mystical interpretation of the rituals of Chanukah. First he spoke of Chanukah's central miracle: when the Maccabees defeated the Hellenistic Greeks in the 2nd century BCE and wanted to relight the menorah in the holy Second Temple, a tub of oil that was supposed to last for one day lasted for eight. On the scale of spiritual wonders, that miracle was rather small. "It was a wink from heaven," the Rebbe said. Still, it taught an essential lesson. The miracle centered on oil and oil has a distinctive quality: when you pour it out of a container some of its clings to the inside of its container. So, too, said the Rebbe, does the love for Judaism cling to its believers even if you take them away from their Jewish surroundings.

In another segment, the Rebbe also offered a beguiling kabalistic analysis. The Talmudic sages, Hillel and Shamai, argued over whether to start lighting one candle on the first night and move up to eight on the last night—Hillel's position—or start with eight candles and move down to one—Shamai's. All Jews today follow Hillel because, the Rebbe said, rather than emphasizing the steady suppression of the bad impulses we prefer to emphasize the mounting emergence of the good. The point was a quintessentially Hasidic way of looking at life.

Finally, the Rebbe noted that three things are compared to candles in Scripture—the human soul, Torah and God—and all three are sides of the same concept, because when Jews do mitzvahs, they light up the sphere and connect to God and Torah.*

When he finishes, individual Hasidim funnel up to the dais again to ask for his blessing or say a few words. When my turn comes, Levi Meisner, who in daily life is a shofar instructor and kashrut inspector, informs the Rebbe that my mother came from Otwock.

---

* Author's interviews with Levi Meisner, Alexander Rapaport and Yeedle Melber

"Oh, Otwock was a very Hasidic town," the Rebbe says with pleasure in English, flashing me a gentle smile.

Although I did not ask for his blessing, it is my moment with him—and who knows what to make of it. Was this the wisdom I have come 50 miles on a cold, rainy night to seek? But ordinary as the observation is, I have to admit as I head out into the dark that the encounter has left an ineffable imprint, yes heady, even spiritual in its power.

I have many friends who see the adulation I witnessed in the Skverer synagogue as distastefully cultlike, or at a minimum a manifestation of the need of sheep for a shepherd. And it is hard to deny some of the manifestations: the clinging to an almost superhuman figure, the belief in supernatural miracles. But this Rebbe and the others that I know of have never been accused of the typical defects that trip up cults—a leader's sexual abuse of his followers or the financial exploitation of the followers to amass a wealthy lifestyle for the leader. The rebbes live well but hardly in opulent style and none has ever been accused of possessing a harem of young devotees with whom he vacations in luxury hotels in the Caribbean. But it is also worth wondering why the critics do not get as worked up by other popular examples of the human need for transcendence of this mundane sphere through a savior figure. These impulses are almost universal, after all. How else to explain the worship some fans feel toward Bruce Springsteen or John Lennon, the blind devotion to Stalin that many intellectuals felt in the 1930s and 1940s, even the way many young Americans looked to Barack Obama to turn around the country.

Worshipful, willfully ignorant, blindly lost in fantasy are words that can be applied to all those phenomena, so why should Hasidim be singled out for scorn? And the Hasidic tradition has one more argument on its side: while cults tend to be fly-by-night, Hasidism has been around for three centuries and the Judaism it has adapted goes back at least three millennia.

4

REBBES AND REBELS

The whole concept of a mystical Rebbe—perhaps the movement's defining feature today—harks back to the founding of Hasidism. Considering that most American Jews think of Hasidism as an anachronism, some ancient throwback or relic with archaic customs and dress, it is striking how young the movement actually is in the span of Jewish history. Hasidism emerged less than 300 years ago, around the time that a few American colonists were beginning to think of their land as worthy of a separate nation, an idea sometimes encouraged by the writings of such contemporaries of the first Hasidim as the philosophers Voltaire and Montesquieu. Those comparisons are not accidental since Hasidism generated a revolution of its own, one that, as Elie Wiesel wrote in *Souls on Fire*, "shook the very foundations of Judaism, by revolutionizing its thoughts its perceptions, it way of life."[*]

---

[*] Elie Weisel, *Souls on Fire* (New York: Random House/Vintage, 1972), p. 8.

At a time of turbulence in the Jewish world, the Hasidic upheaval coalesced in one man, the Baal Shem Tov, the Master of the Good Name, or Besht for short. His title alone was a marker of his significance because it originated in ancient times to honor someone who had secret knowledge of the names of God and therefore knew how to exploit those names in working miracles. The details of his life (1700–60) are overwhelmingly speculative, the gleanings of mystical tales filled with prophetic annunciations about his birth and revelations about his saintly mission that were handed down orally by his disciples. These tales created a messianic aura not unlike that surrounding Jesus of Nazareth, about whom similar tales were told. To Hasidim the obscurity and tentativeness of the biography only augment the Besht's mystical magnetism and so intensify their veneration.

His name was actually Israel Ben Eliezer, and he was the son of Eliezer and Sarah, an elderly couple living in what legend says was Okop, a small village in Podolia, a historical region of what is now southwest Ukraine. Some say Eliezer and Sarah were rich, some poor, but legend had it that they were exceedingly pious and generous, and that they died early, leaving Israel an orphan. The sketchy outlines of his life available through oral tradition suggest that he worked as an assistant in a school for young Jewish boys and as a night watchman, then married a woman who died soon after the wedding. He remarried, had two children and variously toiled as a clay digger and innkeeper. But he spent most of his twenties living quietly in the Carpathian Mountains, gearing up his mind and soul for what he, like some ancient Hebrew prophet, saw as his divine destiny. By the age of 36, he revealed himself: he was a healer, blessed with miraculous powers, and he wanted to blaze a new religious trail.

Clutching his signature pipe in his mouth, the Baal Shem Tov traveled around the small villages, marketplaces and taverns of Poland and Ukraine, effecting cures, expelling evil spirits, promising children to the childless and getting the curious to join him in ecstatic prayer. He preferred conversing with peasants and laborers to rabbis or power brokers. He assured listeners that they were not inferior because they spent their days toiling at a workbench or in the fields rather than in the study hall. The fallen were as good as the angelic. No sinner was irredeemable.

"To pull another out of the mud, man must step into the mud himself," he once said. Using another term for spiritual leader, he added: "Small *tzaddikim* like small sinners, a great *tzaddik* likes a great sinner."*

He could be warm, approachable, generous, deeply curious and instantly intimate. His fiery gaze and palpable charisma attracted hundreds, and widespread reports of his miraculous cures gained hundreds more. Yet surprisingly, he rarely displayed any depth of Talmudic scholarship. Instead he taught that every Jew, no matter how undistinguished or ill-educated, is a limb of the Almighty so that a prayer sincerely uttered by an untutored peasant carries as much power as the informed worship of a scholar. Indeed, esteemed saints have the humility to acknowledge that they too are beset by impure thoughts.

---

* Wiesel, *Souls on Fire*, p. 20

For his age, these were remarkably democratic ideas—and enticing ones.

"The Hasidic emphasis was on the value of each individual," Rabbi Schiller told me as we spoke during my visit to the Skverer Rebbe. Schiller is a broad-bearded man who wears a black hat, but he is not formally a Skverer Hasid, and he is comfortable in more secular realms like Yeshiva University, a modern Orthodox institution, which is why he serves as a Skver spokesman. Confounding stereotypes, he acquired some fame in the Orthodox world as a hockey coach for the Ramaz School and for Yeshiva's high school division.

"God is concerned with every Jew, not just the elite," Schiller went on, elucidating the Besht's philosophy. "Every individual is beloved. That yields a sense of joy."

There were groups resembling Hasidim before the Besht's arrival, but he gave a diffuse, inchoate movement an enduring shape and system of beliefs. The time was ripe for the Besht's message. Some historians of the movement talk of how ossified and stratified the Jewish world had become. Rabbis were admired for their ability to recall or analyze passages of Talmud, not for their kindness to their fellow human beings or their soulfulness in prayer. Learning was valued above all else, leaving the untutored to feel they were somehow less worthy no matter how pious they were in their hearts and daily routines. Moreover, the Jews of Europe were mired in gloom; oppression persisted for them even as enlightenment and emancipation were sweeping across Europe. Vicious pogrom-like violence was commonplace—there were at least two large-scale massacres in the second half of the 18th century—and

Jews, particularly in remote villages, were discriminated against in access to jobs and schools. Jews were also recovering from their heartbreaking disillusionment with a 17th century Messiah manqué—Sabbatai Zevi—who had beguiled tens of thousands but ended up converting to Islam under threat of execution. So to the despondent Jewish masses the Baal Shem Tov offered a heady message of hope.

The Baal Shem Tov left behind a few letters, but no substantial essays or books, deliberately refusing to put his teachings into print and discouraging his followers from doing so. "I said one thing, you heard another and you wrote a third," he was supposed to have gently rebuked one of his disciples.* Yet disciples like Rabbi Yaakov Yosef of Polnoye proceeded anyway to set down what they could remember of his sermons and sayings, hundreds of them. As a result, it is possible to cobble together a coherent philosophy that constitutes the bedrock of Hasidism.

Though outsiders sometimes look upon Hasidim as dark and dour—an impression deepened by what seems like an ascetic lifestyle, the rejection of so many secular pleasures and their staid garb—Hasidism actually is an exuberant philosophy. There is profound pleasure imbibed in the performance of the dozens of daily observances and rituals that mark reverence for the deity they casually call *HaShem*—the Name. This should not be mistaken for frivolity. Rather, the Baal Shem Tov emphasized ecstatic worship in prayer to the point of exaltation as the most important avenue to God and to re-

---

* Wiesel, *Souls on Fire*, p. 9.

demption. He spoke of a cleaving to God, a concept called *devekut*, which, combined with a "burning enthusiasm" for God, enriched prayer, observance and even everyday physical pleasures like eating and sexual relations. He emphasized study of the Torah as well, but spiritually absorbing the letters of the Torah, the literal *aleph beis*, losing oneself mystically in them, was as important as comprehending or dissecting the context the words conveyed.

Among the tales Elie Wiesel tells is one in which the Baal Shem Tov and his scribe find themselves lost on an uncharted island and chant the *aleph beis* so they can "transcend the laws of time and geography." They are soon transported back home.

"This tale is characteristic because it contains most of the basic elements of Hasidism," Wiesel writes. "The fervent waiting, the longing for redemption; the erratic wanderings over untraveled roads; the link between Man and his Creator, between the individual act and its repercussions in the celestial spheres; the importance of ordinary words; the accent on fervor and on friendship too; the concept of miracles performed by man for man. It is also characteristic because it may well . . . not be true."[*]

Wiesel's grandfather was a Hasid and filled Elie with tales about the Baal Shem Tov and his disciples in which "facts became subservient to imagination and beauty." What difference did it make if dates and events did not match? "An objective Hasid is not a Hasid," his grandfather told him. Passionate subjectivity should be the ideal.

---

[*] Wiesel, *Souls on Fire*, p. 5.

"What mattered to me was not that two and two are four, but that God is one. Better still that man and God are one."[*]

Far from preaching an austere lifestyle, the Baal Shem Tov eschewed asceticism. Though some pious Jews expressed their intensity by fasting frequently and for long stretches, the Besht felt that fasting should be confined to Yom Kippur and the other less taxing fasts sprinkled throughout the year that all Orthodox Jews observe. His disciples, far from preaching extreme self-denial, encouraged spirited singing and dancing as an expression of faith. One, Rebbe Leib of Shpole, known among Hasidim as the Shpole Zeide (grandfather), turned dancing into a ritual, and another rabbinical worthy said of him: "Your dancing counts for more than my prayers."[†]

Particularly relevant to what distinguishes Hasidism today, the Besht articulated the idea that a *tzaddík*, a man of superior soulfulness and righteousness, could exert spiritual influence on others, elevating sinners and stirring them to repent or generating sinfulness in others by his own base or malicious thoughts. With his magnetic influence, the *tzaddík* would attract a circle of followers, and so the Baal Shem Tov became a model for the Rebbe and his court, the Rebbe as the intermediary between Heaven and a whole Hasidic tribe. Thus 250 years after the Baal Shem Tov's death, Gerer Hasidim or Satmar Hasidim or Skverer Hasidim look upon their leader, chosen dynastically like a monarch, as an intercessor to God—someone who loves them and cares for their well-being

---

[*] Wiesel, *Souls on Fire*, p. 7.

[†] Ibid., p. 46.

and, because of his holiness and pedigree, has remarkable powers to reach the Heavenly Court that determines one's fate. The Hasidim pay the Rebbe back with their ardor and love. That idea explains the devotion to Rabbi David Twersky that was so palpable among his Hasidim on the second night of Chanukah.

Stories about the Baal Shem Tov and the concepts he passed down were spread widely by his associates, chief among them the Maggid of Mezhirech (1704–72), also known as Reb Dov Ber. If the Besht was the Mazzini of the Hasidic movement, its revolutionary thinker, then the Maggid was its Garibaldi and Cavour wrapped up in one, the apostle who turned Hasidism into an earthbound organizational reality. The Maggid was nearsighted, lame and bashful in his way and so led a spare housebound life, eating and sleeping as little as possible and avoiding public speaking. But he was inspirational nevertheless and he gathered around him the handful of disciples who would implant the Hasidic message. He was celebrated for his ability to listen, for his mystical insights and for the simplicity of his message. Unlettered, unassuming people, he preached, could be worthy of redemption simply by reciting the *Shema*, a core prayer that observant Jews recite at least three times a day, and that message was manna to tens of thousands of downtrodden Jews. The Maggid, a name that means "tale teller," also preached that "self-perfection could be attained only through others"* and so his message stressed the importance of brotherhood, of praying with and living

---

* Wiesel, *Souls on Fire*, p. 76.

with like-minded believers, an idea that turned a philosophy into a movement that set up courts in town after Eastern European town.

Hasidim quote the disciples as they might quote the wisdom of the prophets that followed Moses, recalling maxims that celebrated the modesty, humility and sincerity of their rebbes, not just their insight. Rabbi Nahum of Chernobyl was supposed to have said, "I like poverty. It is God's gift to man, a treasure." And Rabbi Mikhal of Zlotchev, when asked why, as a penniless man, he thanked God for taking care of his needs, reportedly replied, "For me, poverty is a need."

As Hasidism flowered into a robust movement that stretched from what is today Hungary into the heart of scholarly Judaism, Lithuania's Vilna, it began to draw critics, even enemies—known by Hasidim as the *misnagdim*, or opponents. The Vilna Gaon, the leading rabbinical scholar of the era, issued an order of excommunication against Hasidim, charging that the ballyhooed miracles were delusions and that the Hasidic veneration of rebbes amounted to idolatry. Under his and other orders, Jews were forbidden to marry Hasidim, have any business dealings with them or even assist at their burials. The Gaon urged Jews to preserve their stress on Torah learning as the path to God and to rely on the worth of rabbis hired by their synagogues and yeshivas for their erudition.

A few rebbes, like Israel Friedman of Rishin (1798–1850), a great-grandson of Reb Dov Ber, were singled out by detractors for the opulent, almost royal courts they had gathered. "Visitors to Rizhin," writes Jerome Mintz, "found the Rebbe seated on a throne, as elegantly dressed as a Russian noble,

His hat was laced with gold embroidery. He had a moustache but only a small beard, and his eyes were said to be hypnotic."* But to his followers the Rebbe's lavish home, carriage and furnishings were expressions of his stature as God's intermediary and they were certain that underneath the luxurious veneer the Rebbe was actually the most humble of men.

Whatever the critics said, they could not halt the spread of the Hasidic fever, and by the middle of the 19th century the map of Eastern Europe was dotted with Hasidic courts headed by rebbes—each court with its own synagogue, study hall, *mikveh* and bureaucracy. Disciples made regular pilgrimages so they could breathe in the aura of their rebbe, sit at his *tish* (table), share his leftovers and beseech him for advice or a wonder-working blessing. The decentralization of the movement led to variations, often subtle, in styles of worship, garb and tenets, but the essential contours kept Hasidism an identifiable subculture. Various histories have put their numbers in the millions and asserted that they may have constituted a majority of Eastern European Jews. The Hasidic idea thus became arguably the most significant religious movement in Judaism since the destruction of the Second Temple.

Parallel universes evolved. In the secular realm, the laws of the Russian or Polish state persecuted Jews and barred them from whole territories or occupations, so Hasidim paid lip service to those laws, observed them in fear but, like the Sicilians did with various conquerors, ignored or broke them

---

* Jerome R. Mintz, *Hasidic People: A Place in the New World* (Cambridge, MA: Harvard University Press, 1992), p. 11.

outright when they could because they were the oppressive laws of a powerful invader. What was paramount was the Torah, as enforced by the rabbis and rabbinic courts, where the reckoning for transgressions was divine or in some cases could lead to communal ostracism. That history of a dual system sometimes explains, though it does not excuse, what outsiders today view as a cavalier disregard that Hasidim have for America's tax laws, fire codes, educational standards and other manifestations of the governmental authority.

What did set back the Hasidic groundswell was not *misnagdim* or other critics, but the new gods of socialism and communism and a rising Zionism that lured so many of the young and took them away from a life of pious observance. One response of the Hasidic leaders as they tried to retain pious Jews within their orbit was to set up formal yeshivas where their young people could study and absorb the Torah ways. To many observers the cultures of the Hasidim and *misnagdim*— later known here as the *Yeshivish* or *Litvak* (Lithuanian) Jews— began to overlap, becoming almost indistinguishable under the umbrella of what Americans now call ultra-Orthodox Jews and Israelis call *Haredim*—"those who tremble in fear of God" and reject secular ways. Except for Hasidic veneration accorded the rebbes, both groups wore somber attire, required thick beards for the men and wigs for the women and centered their daily lives on Torah observance.

The emphasis remained distinct, however. As Meisner told me: on Chanukah, the yeshiva crowd—called that partly because the *rosh yeshiva* (head of a yeshiva) rather than a dynastic rabbi is a group's esteemed figure—might probably light candles for his followers to see, but then the yeshiva crowd would spend the hours afterward studying the Gemara passages that concern Chanukah.

"By us we sing together, and eat together and schmooze together," said Meisner. "Why do we have vodka and a piece of cake after praying. The Lublin Rebbe said food brings a certain closeness. Studying doesn't always bring closeness."

World War I and the political turbulence that followed, particularly the Bolshevik Revolution in Russia, shook up Hasidism as well, forcing leaders to move their courts to new towns or even cities. Then there was the irresistible lure of America across the Atlantic. More than two million Jews immigrated after the 1880s, and an uncountable portion had been Hasidim, including a few rebbes. Once in America, the Jews found the liberty to be who they wanted to be and the opportunities to make money and realize grander ambitions, and these enticements were even more inimical to Orthodox mores than the Enlightenment had been in Europe.

But all that—the losses suffered to emigration and political idealism—did not extinguish the movement. What almost did was Hitler. Most of the courts were so decimated by the systematic killings of Jews that they could not reestablish themselves in the United States or in Israel. But a relative handful did, often through the miracles of money and wile, like the Satmar, whose rebbe made it to the United States. The Bobover were not so lucky at first; that sect's rebbe was discovered hiding out in Lvov in 1941 and then, dressed in his satin kaftan and Sabbath finery, was beaten about the head by the rifle butts of a Ukrainian mob and shot in a forest the next day. All but three hundred of his followers also perished. However, his son, Shlomo Halberstam, did make it to America and reestablished the group, which has flowered into what is today the largest sect in Borough Park, with 50,000 strong just in that neighborhood, larger than the Bobov dynasty before the war.

Also successful were the followers of the Lubavitcher Rebbe, Rabbi Menachem Mendel Schneerson, who built an impressive network of yeshivas and synagogues and—in singular departure from other Hasidic groups—proselytized among more secular Jews. The Lubavitch have drawn tens of thousands of *baalei teshuva* (repentant returnees to Orthodox Judaism) on college campuses and Jewish suburbs who have enlarged their ranks beyond their already high natural growth.

Indeed, the Hasidic birthrate and their emotional energy have given all the remnant groups impressive vigor on the Jewish landscape, and their revival out of the cinders of the Holocaust is one of the great Jewish stories of our time.

5

MODERN MIRACLES

The Baal Shem Tov's teachings and the corollaries of his disciples remain very much alive today, quoted and analyzed by the Hasidim in the way that Madison and Jefferson's writings might be by students grappling with what the founding principles of American democracy mean today. The Hasidic philosophy continues to emphasize a oneness with God, the idea that all expressions of creation—a rock, a leaf, an animal, and man—are part of God's ubiquitous garment. Prayer and the performance of *mitzvot*—prescribed good deeds—are aimed at achieving a mystical consciousness of that union with God, absorbing the divine light but also releasing the "holy sparks" that Hasidim believe are contained in all things. (Some say the holy sparks explain the lingering fondness of Hasidic men for smoking, despite its contemporary links to lung cancer.) Serving God therefore is a joy, and passionate immersion in God—which paradoxically produces not just rapture but trembling at God's awesome presence—will bring down blessings from above.

With all his flaws, man cannot do this alone, which is why he needs the elevated soul of a *tzaddík*—the Rebbe—to help him along, to draw him closer to God and intercede so that God showers blessings down upon him. That is why Hasidim exalt their rebbes and seek their advice and blessings on all important matters. Nevertheless, within its own microcosm, Hasidic thinking is surprisingly democratic. Three hundred years later, at least in theory, it does not elevate the learned man above the sincere worshipper and urges the wealthy individual to help care for the poor one.

"Until the Bal Shem Tov, people used to serve *HaShem* out of fear," Levi Meisner tells me. "The main focus was to avoid doing bad things. A good Jew was someone who studied a lot and the plain worker was looked down upon. But the Baal Shem Tov said you actually serve God better if you go out and work and do business in the world in the Torah way than if you just study. Every Jew is counted by the Baal Shem Tov. Even if he's a worker, he's counted."

Even in an age of iPhones and space stations, much of Hasidic thought is rooted in the archaic mysticism of the medieval kabalah and is physically expressed in curious ways. In my visit to New Square, I was surprised to find that the Skverer Hasidim have placed their yeshiva next to the village's cemetery, where the body of the previous Skverer Rebbe is buried. The yeshiva is thus an expression of his mind and soul and studying there is an homage to him, my guides told me.

"The yeshiva should be a merit to his *neshama*," Meisner tells me, using the Hebrew-Yiddish word for "soul."

Hasidim, some of whom can trace their lineage to the disciples of the Baal Shem Tov, believe that their rebbes still perform miracles. They visit at least once a year, usually around Rosh Hashanah, to receive his blessings, often handing him a *kvitl*, a petition for help, as well as a *pidyon*, a donation for the upkeep of his court. They may ask for advice about whom to marry, what doctor to see, what job or business strategy to take. Hasidim believe that the Rebbe has prophetic insights into these matters.

When I went to see the Skverer Rebbe on the second night of Chanukah, his chief fund-raiser, asking only that I not mention his name, told me two so-called miracle stories. I'm sure they were stories he has told before while enticing contributions. But they reflect Skverer faith. He told me of a four-year-old girl who had undergone chemotherapy and whose parents—one non-Hasidic, but Orthodox, the other nonobservant—brought her to the Rebbe for a blessing. "The parents bring the girl to the Rebbe and the Rebbe says: 'Everything will be okay,'" the fund-raiser told me. "The next day, the doctors tell the girl that the tests have come back and she is completely clear of cancer."

I followed up this story with a call to the girl's father, Irving Botwinick, shortly before New Year's 2012. He was a man in his mid-sixties who lives in Rockland County not far from New Square, and at the time ran a lucrative Manhattan firm that served subpoenas and other legal papers on hard-to-reach defendants like Donald Trump and on professional athletes. The name of the firm is Serving by Irving and its motto is

"If they're alive we'll serve them; if they're dead, we'll tell you where they're buried." Folksy and warm in manner, he seemed like a down-to-earth individual who would not be especially susceptible to mystical or New Age notions. I asked him about the so-called miracle and he readily told me the story.

Sometime around 1995, his daughter Samantha, then four and a half, complained of abdominal pain. She was taken to the hospital and diagnosed with a rare childhood cancer on the kidney, called Wilms' tumor. The tumor was surgically removed at Columbia-Presbyterian Medical Center in New York and 15 months of chemotherapy followed. At the end of the treatment, the doctors came to him with bad news. CAT scans showed the cancer had spread and was moving toward the lungs, a development requiring such desperate treatments as a bone marrow transplant. A biopsy was necessary and would need to be performed the following Monday.

Botwinick was not a Hasid, not even Orthodox at the time, but on his wife's urging—a kind of "it can't hurt" notion—he took Samantha and three of his seven children to see the Rebbe. They waited in a line of a hundred Hasidim also seeking the Rebbe's blessings, but finally were let in and met with the Rebbe for eight minutes. The Rebbe shook hands with the children and gave them all blessings in Hebrew, specifically praying that Samantha be healed and experience a full recovery. The following Monday, the biopsy was performed and the doctors came in and told Botwinick: "We have something unusual going on. We have to call a team in." An hour later, the doctors told him: "It's gone."

"I'm thinking my daughter is gone," Botwinick, weeping at times, told me. "But the chief doctor tells me. 'Whatever she had last week is gone. I can't explain it. You had a miracle.' He couldn't believe his eyes."

A few days after the conversation with the doctor, Botwinick spoke to the Rebbe's fund-raiser, who passed on some more mystical details. The Rebbe does not shake hands with females, but because Samantha had such short hair as a result of the chemotherapy, he mistook her for a boy and shook her hand.

"That was the hand of *HaShem* reaching out to your daughter," Botwinick remembers the fund-raiser telling him.[*]

When Botwinick and I spoke, Samantha was already twenty-one, a student at Hunter College in Manhattan, and was planning to move to Israel, where her boyfriend lives. Botwinick had become a yarmulke-wearing modern Orthodox Jew, not Hasidic but Orthodox nonetheless. He visited the Rebbe several times a year for blessings and gave generous donations to the Skverer community. He also believed he had been the beneficiary of at least one other miracle—his survival of a heart attack 10 years before, when his heart stopped on the operating table. And nothing had occurred in the intervening years to change his belief that his daughter's overnight recovery was clearly a miracle.

"I was always against having faith, never into religion," he told me. "But after this thing happened I said to myself, *You know, some miracles happen.* This has to be a miracle because

---

[*] Author's interview with Irving Botwinick.

we were in the best hospital in the world. They wrote in the report 'an unexplainable event.' How can you explain that?"*

Ever the skeptic, I looked up Wilms' tumor on medical websites and learned that depending on the degree of the cancer's spread there can be a 90 percent cure rate. But telling that ambiguous factoid to Mr. Botwinick would probably not change his mind. As Jerome R. Mintz wrote in a sociological study of Hasidim, "X-rays, surgery, and antibiotics do not eliminate faith in the power of the Rebbe. Believers inevitably discover that mystical aid was necessary to locate the right doctor and to select the appropriate medicine."†

The second miracle story the fund-raiser told me is a founding myth of New Square. Rabbi Yaakov Yosef Twersky, the father of the current Rebbe, felt that he and his followers should settle in a rural area—much like their Ukrainian hometown Skvyra—and so in 1954 purchased a 130-acre dairy farm near Spring Valley, New York. On a certain Friday, the Rebbe urged that the deal had to be closed that day. The lawyers said it would be impossible to finish the paperwork before sundown and the start of Sabbath. The Rebbe insisted that it be done and the deal was indeed consummated. The following day, Governor Thomas Dewey announced the path of the final portion of the Palisades Interstate Parkway, whose Exit 11 runs right near New Square. The land instantly became several multiples more valuable, and would have been unaffordable to the Skverer sect had the deal not been signed beforehand.

---

* Author's interview with Irving Botwinick.

† Mintz, *Hasidic People*, p. 3.

Hasidim visit the court of their rebbe as frequently as they can because staying in touch with their rebbe is essential to their faith and lives.

"It's not uncomplicated for me to go to Spring Valley for Rosh Hashanah, " said Meisner, using the name of the larger nearby town that existed before New Square was incorporated in 1961. "I have to pack up. But when I *daven* [pray] over there I feel uplifted. It says in *Shulchan Aruch* [the Code of Jewish Law] when you *daven* with more people your prayer goes up quicker. You have the merit of the people around you."

As Hasidism has evolved, so have the disputes and differences. They can be as small as subtle distinctions of dress, ritual or custom.

"Imagine there's a band with only one kind of instrument, how would it sound?" Meisner tells me. "You need all kinds."

Skverer emphasize humility, Ger the study of Torah. Sartorially, Skver, Bobov, Belz and most other Hasidic dynasties wear the bow on the hatband of their beaver hats on the left side; Vizhnitz prefers the bow on the right. Many Hasidim even wear white socks on the Sabbath, harking back to a fashion among aristocrats of the 18th century. Hasidim will maintain such hoary styles because it is a fundamental belief that they do not change simply to keep up with the whims of society or for personal vanity.

"We did not change our names, we did not change our language, we did not change our dress code," Meisner said. "We wear modest clothes."

But Hasidim like him do make calls on iPhones, drive with a GPS in their cars and exploit other modern devices to pursue their livelihoods and their needs. These would not be considered an expression of vanity, but pragmatic tools. When I was with Meisner, Rapaport and Melber, the GPS on Melber's van guided us to the all-important visit to the Skverer Rebbe. Given the darkness and the labyrinthine warren of New Square, the GPS too seemed something of a miracle.

The one philosophical issue that has deeply split Hasidism, resulting more than a few times in violence, has been the establishment of Israel as a state. The Satmar Rebbe believed that the idea that Jews can have their own government and state before the coming of the Messiah was a misguided, even arrogant presumption that went against Torah as he interpreted it. Most Hasidim felt similarly, opposing the state's creation by secular Jews and the secular bent of subsequent governments, but they chose to accommodate themselves, not to challenge. In time, many accepted government posts and welcomed government funds for education.

"All of them felt it was a danger," Rabbi Schiller told me. "But not all of them felt it was more than sinful, it was heretical. 'The thing is here, ninety-five percent of them said. 'Let's make the best of it.' That's why in the Satmar *shul* you won't see a Star of David."*

Yet despite these differences there is an impressive uniformity—of religious observance, lifestyle and worship—that allows most Americans to see Hasidim simply as Hasidim and to classify their fraternity as a coherent movement,

---

* Author's interview with Rabbi Mayer Schiller.

one that they are coming to realize is consuming a larger political and existential place for itself in Judaism.

The one trait that seems to unite almost all Hasidim is the intensity they bring to every sacred act. Whatever God has commanded, Hasidim will go an extra mile to fulfill. I saw this most palpably around the holiday of Yom Kippur, the most sacred, awe-filled day of the Jewish calendar. The Bible commands Jews to "afflict your soul" on Yom Kippur as a sign of atonement, and while it does not specifically mention fasting, the commandment has come down to mean acts of repentance like fasting, the wearing of leatherless shoes and abstinence from sexual relations. Fasting from sundown of Yom Kippur eve to one hour past sundown the next day has assumed totemic status across much of the Jewish cosmos, with the prohibition against eating becoming a tribal taboo. Even many Jews who do nothing else Jewish the rest of the year will fast; a 2011 study of the New York area's Jewish population sponsored by UJA–Federation of New York found that 61 percent of those surveyed fasted on Yom Kippur.

Since preservation of life trumps almost any other commandment, rabbis have long held that those who are sick, very elderly, pregnant or are taking crucial medications are not only permitted to eat, but obligated to do so. But because violating a fast is stressful for many observant Jews, some rabbis will, depending on their custom, recommend eating no more than the size of a large date at intervals of about nine minutes or drinking less than a cheekful of water. Others urge all necessary consumption of food. But many Hasidim spurn eating altogether, even if they are sick (which may explain why Yom

Kippur is one of the busiest days of the year for Hatzolah, the Jewish volunteer ambulance service).

That Hasidic zealousness explains why Yitzchok Fleischer, a Hasid from the Bobover sect, the largest in Borough Park, has since 2002 organized a program to offer intravenous feeding to those who cannot fast.* The scheme strikes many Jews as excessive, even bizarre, but it seemed to me to epitomize the lengths the most scrupulous Hasidim are willing to go to make sure they do not violate their understanding of *halacha*, Jewish law. All day long on Yom Kippur in the main Bobover synagogue, fasting men and women are praying upstairs, but if you make your way to downstairs to a special room in the basement, you will see what looks like a scene from a hospital ward: twenty people—elderly, ill or pregnant—are lying prone on hospital cots and receiving intravenous nutrient drips to nourish them through the day. Medics stand by to monitor them. There are five similar but smaller programs in the neighborhood also organized by Fleischer, who is a leader in the Bobover *bikur cholim* society, the group that provides aid and comfort to the sick. Medics he drafts will visit the apartments of those who are homebound to provide intravenous nutrition.

"It's not considered eating if it goes through a vein," Fleischer, a slight, bearded father of nine, told me. "You're not supposed to take anything through the mouth or stomach. Anything. Even if you're allowed to, nobody wants to

* Joseph Berger, "A Successful Yom Kippur Fast with a Medical Assist," *New York Times*, September 24, 2012, p. A17.

eat. It's very hard for a person who has always fasted to face the reality of a situation where they have to eat. This way they still feel they fasted and *halachically* they didn't eat. The mouth is still dry."

Some might see the effort as exploiting a loophole, but actually every one of those receiving the IV could simply have been eating without violating any Orthodox law or principle. Indeed, Moshe Feinstein, the rabbi regarded as the greatest Jewish legal scholar of his time, an ultra-Orthodox adjudicator so respected that his views on the execution of a law were often obeyed by Hasidim and non-Hasidim alike, ruled that it is preferable to eat rather than receive an intravenous drip. Feinstein, who died in 1986, explained that one premise he relied on in reaching his conclusion was that the Torah forbids inflicting a wound other than for purposes of healing. But Hasidim take the ban against eating so literally that they find the IV nutrition an elegant solution to the dilemma. In fact on Yom Kippur 2012, more than 200 frail Hasidim fed themselves intravenously. Some might call it fanaticism, but like the outdated Hasidic clothing styles, the stigma against college educations, the prohibition against physical contact between men and women who are not married to one another and so many other features of Hasidic life, the Yom Kippur intravenous program was testimony to the fervor and literalness with which Hasidim take their religious obligations. Hasidim will tell you that it is precisely such fanaticism that has allowed Judaism to endure for thousands of years.

6

A GHETTO GROWS IN BROOKLYN

Borough Park, in the heart of Brooklyn, does not quite look like an American neighborhood. Walk through the low-rise streets of two-story brick houses on a sunny day in late summer as Jews are getting ready for Rosh Hashanah or on a crisp fall day as they are hurrying to get ready for an early Sabbath, and what is striking are the contrasts to the streets of, say, Brooklyn Heights or San Diego or Des Moines. Almost no one is wearing jeans or tank tops. There are no bare shoulders or revealing décolletage among the women, no muscle shirts or sagging pants on the men, few sneakers or sandals. Instead, pale-faced teenage boys scurry by already crowned with various permutations of a black felt homburg hat and below that the Hasidic uniform of a white shirt buttoned at the neck and a baggy black or navy blue suit. They look like miniature clones of their fathers, who are also dashing through the streets, their faces thick with beards, sideburns spiraling down to their shoulders.

These men are not carrying gym bags or electric drills or
the *New York Times* but rather purple-covered tomes of Talmud
or velvet bags tucked into in a clear plastic all-weather sleeve
that contains their ritual tools—a prayer shawl and two sets of
tefillin, the odd contraption that accompanies morning prayers
and is made up of two black leather boxes, containing commands to love God with all one's heart and soul, each with
leather straps to bind the boxes to the forehead and left fore-
arm. Why two sets of *tefillin*? Hasidim—in contrast to most
other Orthodox Jews—are not certain which of two conflicting Talmudic rulings about the sequence of the Torah
passages inscribed on rolls of parchment inside the tefillin is
the right one. So they don a set containing one sequence for
most of the prayer and a second set for a short prayer. That
scrupulousness about observing what they see as the Law—
halacha—is quintessentially Hasidic.

A large Hasidic man with a stately, confident bearing sails
by, his three sons close alongside as if they are escort vessels,
absorbing every one of their father's words. Young women in
glossy, wavy wigs, silk blouses, dresses to mid-calf and dark
stockings inspect fruit at a market. Suddenly, in what looks
like a whimsical scene out of a Truffaut movie, a Hasid wheels
by on a beat-up bicycle, balancing his round black hat on his
head. But he is not taking a leisurely ride or training for a
triathlon. Instead he has the frenzied look of someone on an
urgent errand.

Indeed, no one is strolling, dawdling, loitering. The walks
are clipped, fevered; nothing is frivolous or indolent about
anyone's gait. Everyone is hurrying to do the work of the

Creator—be it study or prayer or shopping for the ingredients of a kosher weekday meal or heading off to one of the countless obligations: giving to charity, or visiting the sick, or bathing in a *mikveh* or picking out a *shofar* at Levi Yitzchok Meisner's shop tucked away in a corner of his home's living room. Everything is done with earnest or zealous intention. There is much to squeeze in. In addition to work or schooling, there needs to be a time and place for prayer, study and the fulfillment of the various rituals that define the week and the season.

"There are hundreds of pressures that Hasidim take on that are unknown to the public," Alexander Rapaport, my de facto tour guide through Borough Park, reminds me.

Borough Park is a ghetto of sorts, a cheerful, open ghetto with an almost suburban feel, but a ghetto nonetheless, a place where Jews by their own choice live and work among like-minded souls. Like other such Hasidic ghettoes in Brooklyn's Williamsburg, or Kiryas Joel and New Square upstate in New York, it is astonishingly self-sufficient—with practically all the businesses, services and institutions to function as a thriving island in the tumultuous sea of the city. This virtual isolation is not an accident. Hasidim believe the implicit walls of their neighborhood will keep their members away from the enticements of the outside world, which could sabotage their meticulously cultivated lifestyle. That view has been impressively prescient. Whatever other Jews think of the insular philosophy, it explains why Hasidim have flourished when other Jewish communities struggle with dilution of daily observance, assimilation, intermarriage or simply a de facto shrugging off of Jewish identity. Civilization, of course, keeps invading, with technologies like the Internet and smartphones that Hasidim cannot forestall forever. Some like Mendel Werdyger and Shlomo Koenig have founds ways to accommodate these modern intruders, remaining devoutly Hasidic yet absorbing what is useful and not profane. A handful like Sholem Deen flirt with blasphemy and leave.

Borough Park is approximately a square mile, squeezed in between 11th and 18th Avenues and 40th and 60th Streets. Yet in that square mile there are 200 synagogues and *shtiblech* (room-sized synagogues). Every block seems to have one and— and every other block a stout institutional yeshiva. Commerce is transacted on the avenues, but most of the shops are not the kind you would find on Main Street. On 13th Avenue, every other block seems to have a wig store, like Sheila's Wigs, that outfit women with stylish—and often expensive—hairpieces that conceal their actual hair, which only their husbands are permitted to view by their more rigorous interpretation of Jewish law. There are hat stores, like Kova Hats, that sell felt hats in a dazzling variety of crowns, brims, bands and bows, and materials that various Hasidic factions wear—but all in basic black. There are stores devoted entirely to the silver utensils like menorahs, ornamental Passover plates and spice boxes that are used in various rituals scattered throughout the Jewish calendar, which Hasidim feel they must adorn as elegantly as they can afford. There is at least one shop that sells only *shtreimels* in several flavors like sable or gray fox, and one can learn that these donut-shaped hats single out the specialness of a Sabbath or festive holiday just as the nobility in Eastern Europe wore crowns for royal ceremonies.

Even the more mundane stores seem geared to Hasidic tastes—a men's suit shop where the fabrics are various tints of black, furniture stores whose ceilings are incongruously crowded with chandeliers, bookstores lined with volumes of Talmud or children books based on biblical tales, electronics stores that sell digital cameras that don't shoot video, a feature that otherwise might encourage watching of television. There is a relatively new store called Treasures Forever, which advertises *tznius* fashion accessories to maintain modesty. Guaranteed you won't find those kind of wares at Macy's. A Hasidic woman may buy a suit at Macy's, but she will go into Treasures Forever to purchase a dickie, or a full slip or separate sleeves or a "neckline kit" to make sure that she can adapt the suit so that it never crosses Hasidic strictures for modest clothing. She can even buy a "maid of honor," a kind of housecoat to make sure her cleaning lady does not work around her house without modest clothing.

Within the clothing stores, the stock reflects the esoteric patterns of which kind of Hasid buys what. Gerer Hasidim tuck their pants into their socks in a knickers-style known as *hoyzn-zokn*, so they need long socks for this custom. The hat stores carry nuanced styles to accommodate the subtle variations in the brims, bands and crowns of the stiff beaver felt, homburg-like hats. A Satmar hat, as has been said, has a shallower crown and wider sombrero-like brim; a Bobov hat has a higher crown; the Lubavitch wear wide-brimmed fedoras turned rakishly down in the front. But all Hasidim have their names engraved inside. How else could you tell yours from everyone else's when you leave it on a hook outside the *mikveh*?

The streetscape is broken everywhere by posters advertising various services and celebrations or by billboards for homegrown shops like the *tefillin* and *mezuzah* center, which sells the sets of hard black leather boxes and straps as well as the small ornamented cases containing a biblical passage inscribed on parchment that is nailed to the doorpost of a Jewish home. Here and there on the horizon towers an industrial loft building like one at 14th Avenue and 37th Street, but those buildings too are different, honeycombed not with laborers, but with accountants, Internet consultants and do-gooders for Jewish community organizations. One thing you don't see as you pan across the landscape are satellite dishes or TV antennas of any kind. Hasidim, to repeat, do not watch television, and the few who do would not want their neighbors to know.

If it is morning or late afternoon, the streets are crowded with buses. There are streamlined Greyhound-like buses to ferry men to work in the garment or diamond centers in Manhattan or to other Hasidic enclaves like Williamsburg or Monsey. And there are yellow school buses, each engraved with the Hebrew name of its yeshiva, names that offer clues to the Hasidic sect to which they belong. "Yeshiva Kehilas Yaakov Bnos Yaakov Pupa," says one bus, referring to the Hungarian-rooted Pupa dynasty and the first name of one of its sages. When it stops in front of the school, out scamper little girls with shy smiles or earnest glances, dressed in similar outfits of long-sleeved dresses, long skirts with dark stockings and schoolbags. On colder days, they are sheathed in quilted down jackets, part of the unofficial uniform in these parts. No dawdling; they move hurriedly to enter the building, waved in by one of their teachers.

"In the two zip codes of Borough Park there are probably two hundred buses every day," Rapaport tells me on a Friday morning as the eve of Sabbath nears. "By twelve thirty today everybody is finished, so it becomes like a railroad of buses. And everybody is doing the last-minute shopping. So it all crashes at once."

Rapaport, when he gave me the neighborhood tour, was the father of six children, ranging in age from three years old to 12. He operates a food pantry called Masbia, which literally means satiation, a reference to the phrase in the *Shema* prayer that promises that Jews will not only be fed but satiated. Bred in the Vizhnitz tribe, he wavers among rebbes and sects, though he firmly regards himself as a Hasid.

"Rapaports are very independent people," he tells me. "They're not Joe Six-Pack kind of people."

He is an odd duck among the Hasidim, a man who speaks in an articulate English flavored with beguiling American phrases and homespun metaphors even though he has trouble reading because of congenital dyslexia. I asked him to explain how he acquired his silver English tongue in a Yiddish-speaking community where many people have trouble speaking English fluently.

"NPR!" was his one-word answer, adding that he turns on the station whenever he is driving and at home.*

---

* Author's interview with Alexander Rapaport.

It is another bolt of his sly sense of humor, one that is almost never telegraphed to call attention to his wit and only strikes the listener a few seconds after the bon mot is issued. His grandmother was a survivor of the Bergen-Belsen concentration camp. She told him stories about getting beaten by SS men for stealing a potato peel and of digging through piles of bodies to see if any of the Jewish victims were still alive. His father was loosely raised in a Satmar colony in Montreal after the war, then studied in a Vizhnitz yeshiva in Bnei Brak, outside Tel Aviv. He stayed with the Ukrainian-rooted Vizhnitz after returning to America until he was perplexed by one of those battles over dynastic succession that strike many Hasidic sects, this one erupting between the two sons of the Vizhnitzer Rebbe, Moshe Hager. The father, now in his sixties, as well as Alex, who also studied in Bnei Brak, have since allied themselves with the Kosover Rebbe, Shraga Feivel Hager, who is distantly related to the Vizhnitz leaders. That rabbi's fervor, sincerity in prayer and commitment to personal Torah study on a high level remind them of Moses Hager in his prime.

"The Kosover Rebbe has the obvious sense of humility," said Rapaport. "He doesn't have the handlers and the whole rebbe apparatus. He answers his own phone calls."*

As we strolled through Borough Park, I was struck by the paucity of white-tablecloth restaurants. Although there are many coffee shops, luncheonettes and kosher pizza shops for a hurried lunch, there are very few places where a family might

---

* Author's interview with Alexander Rapaport.

spend a few hours savoring a meal that is served to them, as there would be in, say, an Italian neighborhood. Part of the reason is that in the Hasidic philosophy the holiest persons eat only what is needed to keep them healthy enough to serve God. Eating solely for pleasure can be seen then as something of a sinful indulgence. Of course, few people—even Hasidim—reach such an ideal; it defies nature. And Hasidism is for the masses, not just for the elite few. So people might take great delight in a piece of well-cooked stuffed cabbage or gefilte fish or the bean stew known as cholent, eaten at home and prepared by a relative. But going so far as to entertain oneself with food in a restaurant crosses a boundary and is customarily avoided. Still, newsstands that refuse to carry fashion magazines that feature slightly undraped women will carry magazines filled with recipes for food.

"Food becomes the only pleasurable thing in Borough Park," Rapaport told me with a chuckle. "So these magazines filled with recipes show there's food porn in Borough Park."*

In fact, Rapaport points out that with so few pleasures available to a Hasid outside the religious realm, "a Hasidic millionaire has nothing to do with his money except give to charity."

The streetscape is evocative of a certain way of life, antiquated in some ways, but congenial nonetheless. Despite a feeling by most Americans that they would choke under such narrow-mindedness and conformity, would find the sameness of daily and weekly customs suffocating, the sense on the streets of Borough Park is one of pleasant ease, of belonging

---

* Author's interview with Alexander Rapaport.

to the right neighborhood and of optimism. People are intent and sometimes anxious but they are not perpetually somber or miserable. From their point of view, the only point of view they have ever known, the rules are clear, the values ingrained, the rhythms prescribed; there is no mulling over endless choices of hobbies, possessions, events, fashion, lifestyles. The communal limits seem to reduce certain tensions; there may be anxiety about getting all the needs of a day completed—the prayers, studies, shopping, cooking, fulfillment of dozens of rituals—that go into making life possible, but there is little fretting about the wisdom of the activities themselves. They are all laid down, understood and often ironclad, just as the life of a farmer dictates getting up long before dawn to feed and milk the cows. For many Hasidim, the seeming monotony seems to carve out a core of tranquility.

The optimism is also driven by a boomtown zest—baby boom, that is. In 2004, the city's Department of Health reported that the neighborhood had recorded 4,523 births, the highest in the city and a rate of 24.4 per 1,000 residents, almost double that of New York State.[*] The corridor that runs from Borough Park, through Kensington, Flatbush and Midwood is probably the largest concentration of ultra-Orthodox Jews in the world, at 60,000 households, which, given the size of Hasidic families, may mean more than 300,000 people. That would make the area twice as populous as Bnei Brak, east of Tel Aviv, which was founded by *Haredi* Jews in

---

[*] Carl Campanile, "Fertile Grounds—Baby Boom in Borough Park," *New York Post*, January 23, 2006, p. 7.

the 1920s. Though an outsider probably might not spot the differences, Midwood is not Hasidic, but has incorporated a variety of Orthodoxy variously known as "Black Hat," Lithuanian or *Yeshivish*. They are descendants of the scholarly Jews from Lithuania and thereabouts like the Vilna Gaon, who believed in rigorous study of Torah but spurned many of the Hasidic customs. They do not venerate a particular rebbe.

Still, Borough Park is the heart of Hasidic Brooklyn. A population study of the Jews of New York City and three suburban counties that was released in January 2013 painted a compelling sketch of the neighborhood. It found that Borough Park had 131,900 Jewish residents, an increase from a decade before of 71 percent. Yet despite that fertility—and perhaps because of it—68 percent of the households had incomes below $50,000, with 44 percent qualifying as poor under federal definitions, allowing many to receive Medicaid and food stamps. Almost half the population were children under 17. Despite the official poverty, 94 percent of those children attended yeshivas or other Jewish day schools where the tuition can average more than $3,000 per child.

But Borough Park should not be seen as homogeneous. Most important, there are lots of different sects—Belz, Bobov, Ger, Klausenberg, Vizhnitz, Pupa, Satmar, probably two dozen in all—as well as a shrinking minority of modern Orthodox and Conservative and Reform Jews. That variety is a distinction of Borough Park because Brooklyn's Williamsburg, New York's next-largest Hasidic neighborhood, is overwhelmingly made up of Satmar Jews—perhaps 80 percent—while Crown Heights is almost entirely Lubavitch.

That diversity of Orthodox sects has meant that Borough Park is much more open to various styles of worship (within the basic ultra-Orthodox canon, of course), nuances of life-style and apparel and custom. Women, for example, will be less self-conscious wearing a wig among peers who feel the preferred expression of modesty is a kerchief covering the skull.

"There's no dos and don'ts, at least from our perspective," Rapaport told me. "When I was a child the more *frumakh* [extremely pious] Hasidim lived in Williamsburg. They used to say of them: 'He doesn't kiss the *tzitzit* [ritual fringes]; he bites it.' So moving to Borough Park gave you more freedom. But today there are lots of *frumakhers* in Borough Park."*

A good illustration is the difference between Borough Park and Williamsburg on the issue of the *eruv*. Observant Jews are forbidden to carry anything on the Sabbath because carrying—or transferring anything from one "domain," like a home, to another "domain," like a synagogue—is one of the 39 proscribed forms of work, as the Torah is interpreted by the Talmudic sages. (Other forms of prohibited work include lighting a fire, writing, building and tearing; even winnowing is forbidden, so Jews eat gefilte fish on *Shabbos* rather than pick out the bones of a filleted fish.) Orthodox Jews are technically forbidden to leave their homes carrying house keys or umbrellas when it rains and cannot even push a baby carriage, making it difficult for younger mothers to attend synagogue. But observant Jews find loopholes to ease their lives and one

---

* Author's interview with Alexander Rapaport.

of these is the *eruv*—a boundary usually delineated by fishing line or wire strung between telephone poles that figuratively extends the domain of the home to the neighborhood outside. The Satmar do not give much credence to such loopholes. In Williamsburg, despite an *eruv* put up by smaller sects like Pupa and Klausenburg, a Satmar Hasid might reprimand a fellow Hasid whom he sees bearing a prayer-shawl bag on *Shabbos.* Not in Borough Park, where there are many Satmar but where the neighborhood attitude is more "live and let live."

Still, Borough Park is hardly a liberal bastion. The forces of more rigorous, fundamentalist Judaism have gained the upper hand in recent decades throughout Judaism, and the residents of Borough Park have been subjected to this trend as well.

"When I was a child, you used to see lots of people on the *Shabbos*—husband and wife—holding hands," Rapaport told me. "Now it's unheard-of. Any romance in public is halachically forbidden, even with one's own wife. Even speaking with a woman on the street is kept to a minimum."

Rapaport is thirty-four years old, and long before he was born, the neighborhood was fairly secular; most of the synagogues were either modern Orthodox, Conservative or Reform. These were, after all, the streets where Sandy Koufax hurled a ball and Alan Dershowitz split his first legal hairs. Koufax attended public school. Now there is only one Reform synagogue, and almost no Jews attend the neighborhood's public schools. Young Israel Beth El is the only prominent modern Orthodox synagogue. (The modern Orthodox observe all the commandments and even separate the sexes for prayer, but many are quite immersed in the secular life of their surrounding cultures, working in such fields as television.) And Young Israel Beth El, itself a merger of two modern Orthodox survivors, is losing members. If it closes, it may be taken over by a Hasidic congregation, as happened to its rivals, and get a remake as well. Hasidic synagogues and yeshivas are not ornate. In response to the churchlike opulence of Reform synagogues and their own rigid adherence to modesty, the Hasidim seem to tone down or shear off a house of worship's architectural decorations, its turrets, arches, domes and columns. When they build new or renovate, they prefer plain façades and spartan sanctuaries, containing a spare Holy Ark and, rather than pews, tables or counters with room for prayer book and *tefillin*.

The community seems to revolve around its synagogues and yeshivas. It is hard to come up with a list of the yeshivas but one indication are figures in the *New York Times* Schoolbook blog of private Jewish schools in three Borough Park zip codes. They show there are 77 yeshivas of various sizes, with 31,177 students, figures that do not include schools for men of college age and older. Even a partial list of the yeshivas paints a picture of Borough Park's Hasidic variety, with references to many of the sects or onetime rebbes or, in the case of girls' schools, rebbes' wives: Bais Ruchel D'Satmar, Bais Yakov D'Gur, Bais Brucha Karlin Stolin, Bais Simcha, Bobover Yeshiva Bnei Zion, Bais Esther, Bnos Belz, Bnos Margulia Vizhnitz, Kehilas Yakov Pupa Borough Park, Torah Vayira D'Satmar, Talmud Torah Sanz Klausenberg, Talmud Torah D'Chasidei Belz, Talmud Torah Karlin Stolin, Talmud

Torah Tiferes Yisroel Vizhnitz, Yeshiva Imrei Chaim Vizhnitz, Talmud Torah Toldos Yitzchok Bnei Mordechia Skver, Tomer Dvorah Skver, Mosdos Spinka, Yeshiva Tzemach Tzedik Vizhnitz, Yeshiva Yagdil Torah D'Gur, Yeshiva Chasan Sofer, Yeshiva Novominsk. Many of these yeshivas have several buildings, one, say, for older boys, another for young girls, a third for older girls.

At the boys' yeshivas students sit on worn benches or classroom desks in front of battered volumes of Talmud, the 63-volume collection of rabbinical debates and interpretations of Jewish laws. For 10 hours a day and beyond, the air is clamorous with explications of ambiguities and paradoxes and quarrels over superfine distinctions. At a particularly passionate thought, a student may break into metronome-like swaying, his eyes twinkling at a particular insight or finessing of logic. While girls do learn secular subjects almost on par with their secular peers, the boys seldom learn science, mathematics or history—despite state laws requiring some basics—except what they may glean from the Talmud itself. After all, they are being prepared not for professions, but for what will be a lifelong commitment to *Torah lishmo*, Torah study for its own sake, even if that pursuit arguably contradicts the Baal Shem Tov's emphasis on the dignity of work.

Just as fevered in their atmosphere are the synagogues. Unlike more conventional synagogues, Hasidic synagogues are full of life every day of the week, not just on the Sabbath and holidays, and at any time there may be several groups praying, not just one. At the Satmar synagogue where I joined the men in prayer, there was a maze of a half dozen rooms on different levels, each with men praying in *tefillin* and prayer shawls known as *talesim*. Each room contains a *minyan*, a quorum of at least 10 men, though sometimes there are hundreds to join them, either rocking in place or pensively absorbed in the words and looking up and murmuring with great energy as if they were talking to God himself. More than a few, it should be said, interrupt the prayers with schmoozing and gossip.

Different *minyans* start at different times to accommodate different work and study schedules throughout the morning. The ritual day is set not by a digital clock, but according to an astronomical one whose springs were wound in antiquity. The prayers that compose *shacharit* (morning prayer) can start at sunrise. *Tefillin* and a *tallis*, a prayer shawl, can be worn "when one can recognize a familiar acquaintance from a distance of approximately six feet." But given a Hasid's busy life of studying and family obligations, the morning prayers can be chanted as late as the midway point between sunrise and sunset.

For morning prayer, each Hasid will put on the *tallis* even though he is already wearing *tzitzit,* or a *tallis katon*—the smaller *tallis* worn throughout the day—to remind him of his religious duties. The Torah says in Numbers 15:38, "Speak to the children of Israel, and say to them, that they shall make themselves fringes on the corners of their garments throughout their generations, and they shall put on the corner fringe a blue thread." So most modern Orthodox men wear these *tzitzit,* twisted ritual fringes attached to a four-cornered woolen or cotton poncho-like garment, under their shirts. But Hasidim do them one better. They usually wear their *tzitzit* on top of their shirt or at least they let the twisted fringes themselves dangle out. And the garment they wear is broader than that worn by Orthodox men—an *amah* in width, a biblical measurement that is the equivalent of approximately two feet—broad enough to cover their entire chest.

"It's nice of you that you have *tzitzit* on but you don't have the full mitzvah unless it's an *amah*," Rapaport told me, speaking of a typical religious Jew.

Why then wear a *tallis*, which Jews who do not wear *tzitzit* will put on for morning or Sabbath prayers to fulfill the ritual-fringes requirement? Whatever the reasons that other Jews add a *tallis* along with *tzitzit*, Hasidim do so for kabalistic reasons—it wards off Satan.

The synagogue is not forbidding to an outsider like me. As Rapaport explains: "In a Satmar *shul*, you're always welcome. If you're a Jew, by default you're one of them." I arrive at noon on a November day, but men are still here strapping on their *tefillin* and wrapping themselves in *talesim*. Some have slept late because they had a wedding in, say, the Hasidic satellite colony about 40 miles north in Monsey, New York, and got home in the wee hours. Others come late in the morning because they were shopping for *Shabbos*—a duty that can take precedence in time.

"It's much more what you do with your heart inside the *shul*," Rapaport told me. "Even the big *shuls* have some *shtibl* flavor."

Among the anomalies that stand out in the Satmar synagogue—and at other Hasidic synagogues for that matter—are the racks of CDs. But these are not recordings of Tony

Bennett or Heavy D. Rather, these CDs all contain lectures on the week's Torah portion or that of a recent week—some designed for adults and some for children. Most synagogues also have a large study hall—a *beis medrash*—which sometimes doubles as a prayer room, though sometimes the main sanctuary is designated as the *beis medrash*. In a continuation of their yeshiva educations, bearded, sidelocked men in white shirts and large skullcaps sit around long tables where copies of the Talmud, the Five Books or prayers books are scattered, seemingly higgledy-piggledy, though there is an orderly system to the tumult. Just like the high school youngsters but with more confidence and élan, they read various texts to each other and interpret them in a characteristic singsong, often rocking as they do, as if their entire body were in the throes of enchantment. Their *chavrusah*—or study friends—shoot back corrections or emendations or their own exegesis. Points are made with a raised thumb or a fist. Take the opening words of the first tractate, Bava Meziah—the laws of found objects.

"Two are holding on to a garment. This one says 'I found it,' and this one says 'I found it.' This one says, 'All of it is mine,' and this one says 'All of it is mine.' This one shall swear that he does not have in it less than half of it, and this one shall swear that he does not have in it less than half of it, and they shall divide it."

For hours, the men analyze this simple passage and the rabbinical commentaries and dissections that follow because so many things are at stake: What is ownership? How do impartial bodies make a determination? And how can a judge rule when there is confusion or seemingly equal claims? How does one acquire something and when does ownership pass to someone else? What is the power of a sworn oath? How is a garment different from an animal or a silver vessel? What role does mercy play?

Each question branches out into other questions and is disputed among different sages who have epiphany-like observations about why an even more respected or ancient scholar would have said something the way he said it. The students in the study hall echo these primeval modes of analysis and often these students make discoveries or have epiphanies of their own. They are absorbed in these questions; those who do not have full-time jobs or are retired spend many hours each day, every day of the week for years until the Talmud is completed. Then they start all over again because now they are more learned, older and wiser, and new ideas they have gleaned from other tractates will inform their renewed encounter with a text.

However austere these lives may seem to outsiders, they appear to provide enormous opportunities for pleasure, and pleasures inside the religious realm are pleasures nonetheless. I met Zev Yankel Neiman, a wiry Hasid of 30 years old with a thin, untidy beard who finds deep gratification in memorizing the Talmud, all 68 tractates, studying it 10 or 11 hours a day. I didn't test him, but Rapaport claimed he did, and Neiman modestly acknowledged that he tries to remember it all.

"First you learn it and then you go deeper and deeper," he told me. "The learning itself, this is what life is about. For *HaShem*, everything, *HaShem* wants people should know the whole Torah and I'm trying to fulfill it."

Though he was born in New York, he spoke in a clotted, accented English more suitable for an immigrant, which suggests that growing up in the Borough Park Yiddish-speaking ghetto can be the equivalent of growing up in a foreign country. Like so many other married men, he gets a stipend from his *kollel*, or adult yeshiva. The money for these stipends—which can be as little as $100 a week for beginners and rise from there—is contributed by Hasidim who work full-time at jobs or businesses. The theory is that that since Jews are required to occupy themselves with the study of Torah, those who work to support the more studious share equally in the worthy deed, or mitzvah, of learning and are equally rewarded in the World-to-Come. (Orthodox Jews sometimes refer to this relationship as an Issachar-Zebulun partnership after the deathbed instructions of the patriarch Jacob that the more practical Zebulun support his more cerebral brother.) *Kollels* have grown to mammoth proportions in the postwar period, with 1,500 scholars studying at the Beth Medrash Govoha in Lakewood, New Jersey, an ultra-Orthodox but not Hasidic yeshiva.

Since no one could survive in New York on just a *kollel* stipend, Neiman and his wife mostly support themselves and their five children by her work as an office secretary. When the wives can no longer work—they need at times to be home for their small children—the men find jobs through the community. Rapaport takes a mild amusement in this archaic system where most Hasidim work for schools, *shuls* and other religious organizations

"God is the biggest industry by Hasidim," he said with a self-mocking chuckle. "The Hasidic economy, ninety percent of it is God."

In a Hasidic neighborhood, the synagogue, if it is large enough, will also likely have a *mikveh*, a communal ritual bath, for, in another practice that distinguishes Hasidism, men go to the *mikveh* every day. Plain-vanilla Orthodox Jewish men will rarely bathe in a *mikveh*, or perhaps, in some communities, do so once a year, before Yom Kippur. But among Hasidic men daily immersion in the *mikveh* is regarded as essential before reciting prayers or studying Talmud. The literal reason: "seed" can be spilled during the night—either in sexual relations with one's wife or through a wet dream. Modern Orthodox men, if they think about it at all, regard taking a shower as sufficient, but the Hasidim believe a man must be ritually purified afterward by immersion in the *mikveh*'s waters. There is also a sense that a dip in holy waters washes away the temporal detritus of the night and previous day, leaving the bather feeling spiritually cleansed. So a Hasidic man will wake, dress, head to the *mikveh*, undress, shower in a room of benches and hooks, then immerse himself in the waters of the *mikveh* for about a minute or two, though some luxuriate slightly longer. It is a quick dip, but the entire body must be underwater, the head as well.

"*Shuls* that don't have a *mikveh* don't attract people," Rapaport, my guide to Borough Park, told me. "They have very low traffic for *shacharit*."

The *mikveh* I saw in the Satmar synagogue on 53d Street between 13th and 14th Avenues has three tiled rectangular pools—one that can hold about 30 men, another 15 and a third about 10. The temperatures of each pool vary: warm, hot and cold. The water feeding the pool is mixed with water from a rooftop cistern that captures rainwater—since all *mikvehs* must have a certain quantity of water from a natural source. The Satmar *mikveh* has a turnstile at its entrance that collects money—two dollars a shot or about one dollar with a monthly card—to pay the Latino man who provides clean towels and soap for the showers taken before immersion. After his dip, the Hasidic man gets dressed and heads upstairs to the synagogue to pray.

Outside the yeshivas and synagogues, there is a strong network of communal organizations—sometimes hidden below the surface of daily life but powerful nonetheless. Five hundred men volunteer to drive a fleet of 25 ambulances for the local branch of the Orthodox rescue corps known as Hatzolah. Residents call Hatzolah before a city ambulance because they sense that the drivers will respond more urgently and pleasantly to a fellow Jew's need. Others volunteer for the Shomrim, a civil security patrol that prowls the neighborhood looking for potential crimes and alerts the police. The Shomrim have been embroiled in a number of controversies, some racially tinged, where volunteers interceded in what they said was a mugging or attack and beat up the accused black or Latino assailant. In 2008, prosecutors called the beating of a black man in the Lubavitch neighborhood of Crown Heights a bias attack, and for years afterward tussled with the Lubavitch in their efforts to extradite the accused volunteer from Israel.

And then there are the Chaverim, which literally means friends. They are there to assist in such daily emergencies as a flat tire, a lockout from home, an elderly person's need for a ride to a subway station or a call from someone who had too much to drink and needs a ride home. The Borough Park group claims to have logged more than 100,000 calls in its 10 years. For people who need medical advice—perhaps a couple that has been unable to have a child and wonders what remedies for infertility would meet halachic standards or a cancer patient wondering whether the ingredients in a certain kind of chemotherapy are kosher—there are rabbis who offer guidance and referrals, rabbis like Binyamin Landau, a white-bearded Hasid who never went to college but acquired his mix of medical and Talmudic knowledge by reading and talking to doctors.

The benevolence of the Hasidic community toward its own members is impressive. That benevolence is largely inward, though sometimes it extends to outsiders. Rapaport's narrow soup kitchen on 14th Avenue—one of three he runs—feeds Hasidic Jews but also Muslim Bangladeshis, Catholic Poles and Pentecostal Latinos, any poor people from the neighborhood. The food is kosher even if the customers are not. Masbia serves 500 meals a weekday as well as weekend take-home packages that include such Sabbath delicacies as gefilte fish, according to Rapaport. Even though Hasidim scarcely celebrate Thanksgiving—it's just another workday—Masbia's 200 volunteers distributed 500 turkey meals and 50 raw turkeys on Thanksgiving 2011. The fixings included *cholent*.

Rapaport contends there are many poor people scattered around Borough Park, hidden in seedy apartments in basements or alleyways. It is hard to pick out—on my visits I did not see any homeless people or derelicts—but Rapaport shows visitors photographs of what he calls *bubbes* (grandmothers) and *zaydes* (grandfathers) picking food out of Dumpsters. On one occasion, he flashed slides for a kindergarten class from a nearby school operated by the Munkacz sect.

"You see that Yiddish grandmother getting food from the garbage," Rapaport told the children. "That's why we set up Masbia so she would have some place to eat."

He told them it was a mitzvah to feed hungry strangers and to illustrate his point he reminded them that in that week's Torah portion, Abraham feeds the three disguised angels by having his servant roast them a calf. It is more than coincidence that the three angels repay Abraham with a mitzvah of their own, promising him that his barren wife, Sarah, will have a baby.

Every spot in Borough Park seems to have a Hasidic twist, so that even those shops that sell commonplace goods never forget that they are catering to Hasidim and their fussy eccentricities. Take Double Play Toys. It appears to be a standard toy store, but it has its own unwritten rules and customs. It will, for example, not carry Batman and Spider-Man action figures or Xboxes or other video games. Barbara Shine, the manager and former owner, told me such characters encourage interest in television and the Hasidic and other ultra-Orthodox Jewish families who make up more than 95 percent of her customers do not watch television. Those toys might also teach lessons that Hasidic parents don't want their kids to learn.

"Thomas the Tank Engine is a kosher character," she said, illustrating her store's philosophy. "He's not hitting and killing people. We don't want kids to learn violence."

She sold the store a few years ago to another merchant to limit her hours and responsibility. Still, as either an owner or manager, she has been able to keep her business thriving for 18 years because she has not alienated or irritated her picky clientele. Over time, she has developed a keen understanding of the neighborhood's unwritten codes, even when they extend Jewish law beyond what most Orthodox Jews observe. Hula hoops are a hot item among Hasidic children, but Shine keeps them out of sight because the packaging has pictures of scantily clad women. She stopped selling a game that featured a girl with a nose ring on its cover; Hasidim associate piercings with idol worship. She successfully lobbied the manufacturer to change the packaging on the popular card game Perpetual Commotion because she considered the clothing immodest. She knows that some Hasidim have qualms about their bar mitzvah–age children playing with Legos on *Shabbos* since that might violate the ban on construction.

Toys are crucial year-round in Hasidic life. Families tend to have flocks of children, and mothers need ways to amuse them when the fathers are studying or at synagogue and when the parents take their customary Sabbath naps. So Shine, an effervescent mother of seven who is ultra-Orthodox but not Hasidic, knows she has a ready market. The store is not the kind of airy, decorous shop that might be found in one of the

city's tonier neighborhoods, with charmingly arrayed cubbies
and lots of floor space for children to try toys out. The aisles
at Double Play are narrow and the shelves run floor to ceiling.
But they are crammed with all manner of toys and games so
the dark-suited men and women in long skirts and wigs can
pick out what they need.

"You have something for an *upsherin*?" a bearded Hasidic
customer asks Shine, inquiring about a gift appropriate for
the celebration that marks an Orthodox boy's first haircut.
Shine steered him toward a tool set. Parents do the shopping,
even when their children are not with them. Little boys in
coiling earlocks and girls in long sleeves do come in and search
out toy figures like the Mitzvah Kinder (mitzvah children),
but their chances to do so are constricted because schools days
stretch to 5 p.m.

Shine, now in her early forties, grew up in Minnesota and
was not raised Orthodox—her mother went to a Zionist camp,
Camp Herzl in Wisconsin, with Bob Dylan when he was still
known as Zimmerman—but she was deeply influenced by her
Minneapolis yeshiva. In 1994, she started Double Play out
of her home to earn some income for her burgeoning family,
rented a shop at another Borough Park location and saw the
business flourish until she bought the larger shop on 14th
Avenue. Rapaport told me that, even though Shine is not Hasidic, the community has confidence in her judgment. "She
is her own *mashgiach*," he said, using the Yiddish word for an
inspector of kosher foods. She knows not to sell stuffed lions
to a Lubavitch family because members of that movement do
not want their children playing with unkosher animals. She is

very careful about stocking books because some themes may not sit well—like the *Chronicles of Narnia* series and its Christian symbolism. On the other hand, she is not afraid to sell an Advent calendar made up of intriguing toy pieces. Though the set literally counts down to Christmas, it does not trade in religious imagery or mention the holiday by name, only Advent.

"And nobody in the neighborhood knows what Advent is," she said.*

A trip to a Borough Park grocery is also instructive. The products at Super 13th Grocery—a market on 13th Avenue—are not just kosher but have extra supervision by rabbis trusted in the neighborhood. So many of the brands in the supermarket— like Ostreicher's, Lieber's, Unger's or Kemach—are local, produced or distributed by Borough Park businessmen. The milk and cheese are not just ordinary milk and cheese, but are certified as *cholov Yisroel*, which means they were produced either by observant Jewish farmers or under the supervision of an observant Jew. Many Orthodox Jews see such scrupulousness as excessive, even fanatic. Towering Non-Hasidic rabbis like Moshe Feinstein have decreed that milk approved by the United States Department of Agriculture as 100 percent cow's milk (and not, say, from a horse or other nonkosher animal) is more than suitable for drinking. But Hasidim demand that extra measure of scrutiny.

Similarly, Hasidim will only buy Romaine lettuce or other leafy vegetables in packages that have been inspected to make

* Author's interview with Barbara Shine.

sure no insects have crept in; the bugs could be accidentally ingested and they are not kosher. Some of the packaged lettuce may have four different stamps of certification because "Hasidim are particular about who washes the lettuce," Rapaport said. But Hasidim like Rapaport, wanting to economize, sometimes buy a cheaper unpackaged head of lettuce and examine the leaves themselves to make sure there are no insects trapped.

It is also instructive to note that many if not most customers at Super 13th do not pay with cash or by credit card, but simply give the cashier a phone number, then the sum of purchases is added to their "tab." It seems like the kind of trade found in intimate villages, not in urban neighborhoods. But here too there is a Hasidic aspect to the transactions. There is an ethos in Borough Park that people will either pay their bills on time or, if they cannot, they must be given time to do so. The arrangement is further testimony that Borough Park is one cohesive, symbiotic community.

"There's no class divide," explains Rapaport. "The fishmonger and the stockbroker sit on the same bench in the synagogue. People help each other a lot. The rich Hasidic person lives here. There's no mansion in the Hamptons."

Still, it should be noted that as Rapaport was explaining the system to me, one of the cashiers overheard and joked: "Borough Park is Schnorrers Park." He was using the sometimes affectionate Yiddish term for a parasite who lives off the generosity of others.

One reason for all that trust is a communal understanding that residents have of one another's lives. Whatever the sect distinctions, every family mirrors the neighboring families in so many ways. On Friday, for example, everyone will be getting ready for the Sabbath in pretty much the same way and on the Sabbath everyone will celebrate it in virtually identical ways.

"There isn't a single house that won't eat gefilte fish tonight—not one," Rapaport tells me. "That's twenty thousand houses eating gefilte fish. If a teacher will hear from a pupil that the family is not having gefilte fish, he will call the Tomchei Sabbos [a kosher food pantry that provides Sabbath meals for poor Jews]. Everybody will have some *kugel*. Everybody eats *cholent*. When you're given all the choices the world has to give, you're more in a pickle."

And what could be more a sign of a clearly defined and identifiable community than 20,000 Jews all at the same time eating gefilte fish.

7

THE WAY YOU WEAR YOUR HAT

Most Americans recognize Hasidim by their clothing, but the façade they present to the world is far more intricate than it seems at first glance, shot through with esoteric lore, customs, and rituals.

Although there are subtle variations, a Hasidic man will generally wear a dark three-piece suit with an elongated frock coat–like jacket that might reach to the knees and is known as a *rekel*. The jacket is worn over a matching vest and a white shirt that can be buttoned or unbuttoned at the neck. Hasidim do not favor ties, a relatively modern addition to men's formal wear. Unlike the clothing worn by most American men, Hasidic men's shirts and jackets are specially manufactured so that the buttons are sewn on the left side and the buttonholes on the right. It is a custom whose origins are obscurely kabalistic, but when a shirt is buttoned it's done, as Hasidim say, "right over left." Women too are asked to observe this custom, but American women's fashion is already made with the buttons sewn on the left side.

In between the vest and the white shirt is added a fringed undergarment known as *tzitzit*, which by biblical commandment reminds a Jewish male of his ritual obligations. The entire outfit is then crowned by a black homburg-like hat made of steamed rabbit fur. Rabbit? An unkosher animal? The Bible only commands Jews not to eat animals like rabbit and pig; it doesn't say that wearing clothing made of that animal is forbidden. So as long as a Jewish man doesn't literally eat his hat, he is obeying the law.

A Hasidic woman's clothes have more color, but her outfit too generally shuns bright hues like red or orange and her blouse covers her arms at least to the elbow and often to the wrist; it is buttoned at the neck while her skirt falls halfway or more between the knees and the ankle. The contours of her figure are often hidden by an additional sweater and the legs are covered by densely woven stockings. With a married woman that outfit is topped by either a wig, known as a *shaytl*, a turban or a kerchief wrapped around the head, the style differing with different Hasidic courts. In most cases the hair underneath is either close-cropped or shaved.

In the Hasidic world, a traditional fashion code and age-old interpretations of Jewish law dictate modesty for a woman—a concept known as *tznius*—so even on sizzling days women conceal any sexually intriguing parts of the body from men other than their husbands. While Hasidic men do not feel the modesty obligation to the same degree, they believe that it is a mark of humility and respect for others to dress formally when encountering the world—even on casual days.

"Does anybody ask a congressman why he walks into Congress with a suit or a Wall Street executive why he goes to work in a suit?" is the question that Isaac Abraham, a leader in the Satmar Hasidic community, poses to critics of the Hasidic wardrobe.

To make this wardrobe possible, a whole industry has arisen in Hasidic enclaves like Borough Park and Williamsburg. Borough Park alone has four stores that sell black beaver hats—almost exclusively, since you won't find a boater, beret or a newsboy's cap there. Walk into G&B Clothing, a men's suit store, on 14th Avenue, and you have entered a singular world. Its second-floor loft has none of the polished elegance of Brooks Brothers, but its cluttered racks—narrow as the stacks of a research library—have many more suits in various lengths and styles. They sell for $149 in polyester and rayon summer versions and up to $250 in heavier winter styles. A neophyte in the Hasidic world may think on first glance that all the suits are black, but Joel Czin, a salesman who belongs to the Satmar sect, will point out the subtle variations in color tones—dark gray, navy blue, charcoal black, ebony—and in fabric design—with petals, triangles, checks or stripes brocaded into the weave. Even the length of the *rekel* has some variations. It used to be 10 inches off the ground, and is now shorter—15 or more inches off the ground, perhaps a slight adjustment to contemporary taste. And there is a Sabbath version of the *rekel*, made of more silken fabrics, that is known as a *bekishe* or *kapote*, as well as a *tish bekishe*, a more solid-colored fabric worn at the Sabbath table accompanied by a *shtreimel*—

the tall, cylindrical Russian sable hat that stays on the head throughout the festive meal.

The vest, I thought, was a particularly curious part of the outfit—more Savile Row than Hungarian *shtetl*—and I asked Czin about it. He said it is only minimally a tradition since it has become a practical necessity. It is equipped with extra pockets, which allows Hasidic businessmen to stuff them with receipts, bills, checks, phone numbers and to-do lists.

"Instead of walking with a briefcase, you have lots of pockets," Czin said.

The clothing and fabric are made in China; Hasidic clothiers travel there to arrange contracts with certain factories and make sure the Chinese manufacture the clothes to the eccentric Hasidic specifications. Still, all clothing must be inspected in a laboratory in Williamsburg's Lee Avenue for *shatnez*, the mixture of linen and wool that is forbidden by edict in Leviticus 19:19 and in passages in Deuteronomy as well.

Czin explains that this formal wear—rumpled as it sometimes seems on some men—is a way of demonstrating deference for God.

"Like the yarmulke, it's a sign of respect," he told me. "Somebody's watching. You're under control."

Yeedle Melber, a 34-year-old Hasid who has an unusual business advising people on improving their social interactions and was shopping in G&B the day I was there, made the same point more colorfully. "You wear a suit and tie when you go to a meeting; you wouldn't dress casual. We don't ever dress casual; respect is part of our culture. We look at every encounter in a respectful way." When he heard Melber, Alex Rapaport, my guide in the store, added wryly. "If you're *haredi* [trembling before God] you're not casual."

But as I investigated further, I realized such explanations barely scratch the surface. For beyond the requirement to wear *tzitzit*, the austerity of Hasidic attire is the result of customs that grew up willy-nilly but have almost no explicit scriptural justification. The identifiable style of Hasidic clothing—even some witty Hasidim call it a uniform—serves many purposes. It honors the way ancestors dressed in Europe starting in the 18th century, when the Hasidic movement was founded. Many dress patterns, like the round fur hats and knee-length frock coats, imitated the attire of the nobility. A style adopted by a movement's grand rabbi filtered down to the ardent acolytes.

"The equation of burden doesn't come into play when that's the tradition you're brought up in," Amram Weinstock, a 65-year-old Satmar Hasid who was shopping at G&B Clothing, told me. "We are happy to live that tradition and feel uplifted by living that sort of life. This is how our parents went; this is how our grandparents went."

Weinstock was born in Budapest after World War II, lived as a child in Antwerp after Hungary's takeover by the communists, then came to the United States with his parents in 1956. He points out that Hasidic clothing is more "a tradition than a rule, which means if somebody does not wear this style of clothing he is not deviating from the rules of Orthodoxy. You can go without a jacket and hat and still be an Orthodox Jew. You don't become a non-Hasid by wearing a short jacket."

Even Hasidim take off their jackets when driving around for work or while running errands, though any extended stroll demands a more formal *rekel*.

Dark, austere clothing also serves to separate Hasidim from the rest of the world by making them identifiable to one another and different from everyone else, which helps keeps members inside the fold. A young Hasid seized by an impulse to sneak out for a night on the town would not only have to think about snipping off or disguising his side-locks and finding casual clothes to wear; he would also have to have the strength to endure scornful glances on the way to the subway station. To maintain that wall between their tribe and society, even eyeglass frames in some sects tend to be distinctive. No streamlined designer styles for Vizhnitz Hasidim, who prefer black, heavy frames. Indeed, not too long ago, one of the two Vizhnitzer Rebbes, Israel Hager, warned his followers not to wear contact lenses or metal-frame glasses.

"We must wear the exact opposite of what is worn in Paris," he said.

Samuel Heilman, a professor of sociology at the City University of New York who has studied Hasidic life in Israel and also written a book about the Lubavitch Rebbe, Menachem Schneerson, told me that Hasidic clothing "is the way to show you're dedicated to your belief."

"Even the vagaries of weather and seasons don't affect you," he said. "You have the ability to suffer for your beliefs."

To Americans who find themselves in summer wilting in 90-degree-plus temperatures, even while dressed in shorts and tank tops, Hasidim can look absurdly, onerously over-dressed. But Hasidim will tell you they have learned to live comfortably in all seasons with their daily attire.

"I think I'm not as hot as other people because the sun is not on me," Chany Friedman told me as she was shopping in Borough Park with two of her five children in tow on an after-noon where the mercury flirted with 100 degrees. "If I'm cov-ered the sun is not on me. I'm happy that I'm not exposed to the world. That's what *HaShem* wants from us. We try to stay in an air-conditioned room. But we're not going to change. God wants us to stay modest."

Some Hasidim even contend that their concealing cloth-ing keeps them cooler.

"Look at the Bedouin," Nuchem Sanders, who owns an eponymous hat shop in Borough Park, told me "They live in the desert and they have layers of clothing. Why? It protects them from the heat. When I was a child we had one air condi-tioner in the dining room and we never thought we were hot. The point is the body gets used to weather."

Hot and cold is all in the mind anyway, argues Shea Hecht, a Lubavitch Hasid who chairs some of the movement's ed-ucational outreach arms. In his dark suit and gray fedora—Lubavitch garb is different from that of other Hasidim, though conservative—he sometimes chuckles at people in Bermuda shorts.

"Why are they spending so much money on only a half a pair of pants?" he told me.

Indeed, Hasidim have found subtle ways to beat the heat. In Borough Park, women snatch up neckline-hugging shells that allow them to wear thin long-sleeved and open-necked blouses from, say, Macy's (not see-through, of course). Meanwhile, Hasidic men search out frock coats made of lighter-weight, drip-dry polyester fabrics without canvas or any other kinds of linings. They also look for lightweight weaves in the fringed, four-cornered woolen poncho. Even the *shtreimel* has in recent years been modified with holes inside the crown that provide a kind of ersatz air-conditioning.

"It's a new invention in the sculpture of the *shtreimel*," Rapaport told me with a chuckle, tenderly mocking his own culture's odd ways.

Those innovations may not seem to offer that much relief, but Hasidic philosophy says it is more important to go the extra mile to please God.

Since the fringed ritual garment adds another layer for men on a torrid day, Jacob Roth, of Malchut Judaica, one of the largest distributors of prayer shawls, is working on finding a way to make both *tzitzit* and the *tallis* lighter.

For those extra-scrupulous Hasidim, he has come up with a summer wool version of the *tallis,* the Sabbath prayer shawl, that is half the weight—"light as an eagle" is how it's name translates from the Yiddish; it is made in Israel. It can be accompanied by an imitation silver collar band to replace the heavy band of real silver that the most traditional Hasidim insist upon.

For daily *tzitzit* wear, polyester won't do because, as Roth explained to me, the *tzitzit* must be a woven *beged*, an article of clothing; the Israelites wandering in the desert were not weaving polyester. So Roth has found cotton alternatives and—what he is very proud of—has secured a sleeveless undershirt with slits and fringes at four corners that is made of cotton and avoids the need for a separate T-shirt. The brand name is PerfTzit. It has taken off in the wider Orthodox community, particularly among children, but the most exacting Hasidim will not wear it because they insist on wearing *tzitzit* over their white shirts and also prefer wool rather than cotton even in *tzitzit*.

"My father wears one hundred percent wool," Roth told me. "Me myself? I go with cotton."

Roth is working on finding a version of *tzitzit* that more parched Hasidim can wear.

Why would they wear such thick clothes on a sultry summer day? Heilman points out that Hasidim do not spend idle time outdoors, at best going "from the shop to the yeshiva to the study hall to the house," and since "they're not Amish or Luddites they have air-conditioning."

"They're not exposed to the weather in the same way. And they don't go to the beach." Indeed, Hasidim believe that casual time outdoors exposes them to the temptations of the streets, not the least of which are skimpily dressed New Yorkers. So given all these reasons for modesty, suffering a little heat is not too great a burden.

"You *shvitz* [sweat]!" said a Hasid named Joseph, who didn't want to give me his full name. His what's-the-big-deal expression seemed to shrug off the problem as a piddling price to pay for a virtuous lifestyle.

Winter too has its own Hasidic garb. Hasidim have an article of clothing some jokingly call hoodies, but theirs is intended only for winter Sabbaths. It is a hooded plastic rain-coat worn on top of an overcoat in snow, sleet or rain. The hood attached to the raincoat's collar is large enough to cover the round *shtreimel*. They can cover the black hats they wear on ordinary days with a transparent plastic sheath or even a torn plastic shopping bag, but on the Sabbath that covering is for-bidden because many Hasidim believe donning an accessory that is not part of standard garb constitutes carrying, a species of work forbidden on the Sabbath. A hood attached to a rain-coat gets around the prohibition and has the added benefit of safeguarding a man's expensive *shtreimel* against the rain.

In winter, or at least for six days a week, a long, dark over-coat is standard for men and the hats are the same black homburgs they wear year-round. Some Hasidim prefer tall fur astrakhan hats called *kuchmas*. Footwear is standard, too, always black, though the men in some Hasidic sects may wear high boots as their ancestors did in Europe. Women, mean-while, garb themselves in long coats and prim, bonnet-like hats that emphasize modesty.

What is particularly distinctive in winter outfits is what Hasidim wear on the Sabbath, the day for which food, cloth-ing, furnishings and customs all have sanctified and some-times elegant variations. To lend the day its distinction, Hasidic men in winter wear a satiny overcoat known as a *resh-vulka*, made of genuine silk for the few who can afford it but glossy polyester for the majority who cannot. The cheaper version is usually made in China and comes with a zip-out lining made of either artificial down or artificial fur, and costs about $200. What makes the *reshvulka* particularly Sabbath-like is that it has no pockets—pockets could imply carrying—and the buttons are hidden by a seam, a custom that some Hasidim say harks back to centuries ago when coats worn in Eastern Europe were robelike.

"It's the Hasidic way," Samuel Dresdner, a salesman, told me as he showed off an elegant *reshvulka*.

The grand rabbis and other Hasidic dignitaries will wear a *reshvulka* all week as a sign of their status, and theirs comes adorned with broad fur collars known as "pelts." In January 2013, Hasidic newspapers and blogs carried photographs of one of the two Vizhnitz grand rabbis, Menachem Mendel Hager, whose seat is in Israel, receiving visits in Williamsburg from the grand rabbi of Spinka, Isaac Horowitz, and from one of the two grand rabbis of the Satmar sect, Zalman Teitelbaum. All three leaders wore pelt collars so wide they looked like stoles, and had they not had long beards one might have mistaken them for flashy dandies.

When it's biting cold, a Hasidic man will also wear earmuffs or a band known as an ear warmer. Both come only in black. The gloves are also black. But a Hasid will not wear gloves on the Sabbath, Jacob Feder, the manager of Crown Dry Goods in Brooklyn, told me, because that constitutes carrying. So coats are styled with extra-long sleeves, which allow a man to draw in his hands against an icy wind.

The rules for women do not seem to have as many Sabbath nuances because they can wear a good coat of any kind as long as it comes in muted colors and covers their arms and much of their legs. However, married women will wear plastic see-through bonnets to guard their wigs—often costly, glamorous concoctions—against snow or rain and so forestall an expensive appointment with a stylist. Doesn't that violate the prohibition against carrying? I asked several customers at Silksation Plus. They explained that the plastic bonnets are not seen as a violation because a wig, unlike a man's hat, is considered virtually part of the body—if it gets wet the skull gets wet—and so a plastic bonnet is entirely permissible. Go figure. Of course, most Satmar women do not have to be so fussy—they prefer to cover their shaved skulls with a kerchief.

Not all women, it must be said, are comfortable with all that goes into wearing a wig, particularly the insistence in some sects that women shave their hair. In an article she wrote for the *Forward* in 2013, Frimet Goldberger, an Orthodox woman who once belonged to Satmar, described her repugnance at having her head shaved by her mother the morning after her marriage. She had just turned 18. "I remember the first time I felt the cold prickly air on my newly shaved head," she wrote. "I remember staring at the pile of auburn hair in the vanity sink of the cozy basement apartment I now shared with my husband."

She was shaving her head because according to the Talmud, a woman's uncovered hair is equivalent to physical nudity. Some Hasidic rabbis take this idea one step further, insisting that women shave their skulls so that not a single hair can be seen. Goldberger recalled how the founding Satmar Rebbe, Joel Teitelbaum, implored women in emotional speeches against growing hair. "Jewish daughters, our mothers and fathers gave up their lives to our Father in Heaven for the sanctity of His name, but you, their daughters, don't want to give up even a few hairs?" he once said.

But after she became pregnant with her second child and stopped going to the *mikveh* in Kiryas Joel, she let her hair grow, telling herself she would shave it off after her daughter's birth. Then she would return to the *mikveh* and the other women would see she was still shaving her head. But when the time came, she could not do it. She and her husband had formed friendships with Orthodox and non-Satmar Hasidic families where the women did not shave their heads And she decided to stop doing so as well.

The decision had consequences. Goldberger described how her three-year-old son was expelled from a Satmar school and how she and her husband were summoned before an intimidating Va'ad Hatznius, a Satmar modesty committee. Wondering how they found out—her neighbors in Kiryas Joel "must have ratted me out"—and frightened, she did shave her hair immediately after meeting with the modesty committee. But it was the last time she did so. Enraged by the community's behavior toward them, Goldberger and her husband decided to leave Satmar for a more tolerant Orthodox crowd. Today, she no longer even covers her hair with a wig and is finishing up a bachelor's degree at Sarah Lawrence College.*

During my exploration of the vagaries of Hasidic clothing, Sanders and G&B Clothing instructed me about another aspect of Hasidic life—that many of the most singular Hasidic practices do not have to be carried out by Jews. The hats in the factory Sanders has in the rear of his store and

---

* Frimet Goldberger, "Ex-Hasidic Woman Marks Five Years Since She Shaved Her Head," *Jewish Daily Forward*, November 7, 2013, p. 1.

in the basement are manufactured by Ecuadorians, almost all related to one another, who have been blocking, steaming and stitching those characteristic rabbit fur hats for twenty years. The suits in G&B Clothing are altered and sometimes custom tailored by a half dozen Muslim men from Senegal and other countries in West Africa and have been for years. Despite the store's Jewish ambience, the Senegalese lay out their prayer mats several times a day in the business's lunchroom to say their Islamic prayers, sometimes while Hasidim are having lunch. Hasidim, after all, appreciate the obligation to pray several times a day. Could there possibly be a shortage of Jewish tailors? Well, apparently, there is. Tailoring appears to be another once-common Jewish trade—see Motel, Tevye's son-in-law in *Fiddler on the Roof*—that is seldom carried out by Jews any longer. In the United States, Jews long ago clambered into the middle class and are no longer an immigrant people willing to work for little more than the minimum wage.

As Ecuadorian music played, Sanders took me around the hat factory. Daniel Zangari, a 40-year old Ecuadorian immigrant, has been blocking hats for 21 years, operating a heavy metal machine that looks like an inverted crab. He placed a wooden mold for a certain head size inside a flattened circle of fur and steam rushed up from the bottom of the blocking machine and shaped the fur to the contours of the mold. Afterward, other workers stitched the headband and hat rim (each operation requiring a distinct sewing machine), curled the brim, brushed off the fur and did some additional tucking and shaping of the crown. Sanders showed me cubbies containing wooden blocks in different sizes and crown shapes to match the preferences of various sects.

Sanders got into the hat business through marriage. His store's forerunner was a small hat shop on Clymer Street in Williamsburg owned by his wife's grandfather. As a young reporter for *Newsday* in the 1980s, I interviewed the grandfather—his name was Kraus and the business was called Kraus Hats. What I remember is that the wizened man showed me his hat blocking and sewing machinery and told me he had carried it with him from Hungary after the war, and he would not be able to replace its parts.

The beaver hats start at $70 and can cost as much as $165. Sanders also sells the Sabbath *shtreimels*, which are typically made of sable, and the taller *spodiks*. *Shtreimels* sell for between $1,000 and $5,000, and usually a bride's father will buy one for the groom at the time of the wedding, part of his dowry in a way. In the United States, many Hasidim have two *shtreimels*. There is a cheaper, sturdier one for a rainy *Shabbos* so any damage caused by water is less upsetting. And then there is a more expensive one; it can be shown off in the balmiest of weather.

8

A WORKING HOLIDAY

To understand how Hasidic philosophy works out in practice, it helps to appreciate the punctilious and painstaking manner in which Hasidim go about observing a crucial holiday like Passover. All Orthodox Jews avoid *chametz*, leavened or fermented products of any of five grains specified in the Talmud: rye, wheat, barley, oats and spelt. Thus, their bakers make sure that any flour used in matzo or other grain products has not been exposed to water for more than 18 minutes before being placed in the oven; otherwise it might violate the Torah's prohibition against leavening as interpreted by the Talmud. But Hasidim go the extra mile, and then some.

Go to Gourmet Glatt, a relatively new supermarket in Borough Park that has the polish and tidiness of a Whole Foods but is aimed entirely at the kosher crowd. It has two sections of vegetables—washed and unwashed. Most Orthodox Jews will trust that the vegetables were properly washed in water. Hasidim worry that some grain alcohol might have been mixed in with the cleaning solution, so they prefer carrots, beets, parsnips, radishes straight from the soil, with granules of earth still clinging to them. That way they can wash the vegetables themselves and know for sure, or at least as humanly possible, that they are free of *chametz*.

Most American Orthodox Jews use matzo meal—essentially finely grounded matzos that have been baked before any leavening could take place—to make matzo balls for the soup they serve at the Passover seder, for flourless chocolate tortes or as a thickener in meatballs and other dishes. But matzo meal is not a big seller at Gourmet Glatt; potato starch is. The reason: Hasidim worry that matzo or matzo meal still contains some microscopic amount of unbaked flour that might leaven when exposed to water. They spurn matzo meal entirely for the holiday and will put cooked or scrambled eggs inside their chicken soup rather than matzo balls. Most will not even smear a liquid substance like jam on a matzo lest any water cause the flour in the matzo to rise. Hasidim take the prohibition against *chametz* as absolute, and even have a name for crumbled matzo that might possibly be exposed to liquid—*gebrochts*, from the Yiddish word for broken.

As Rabbi Menachem Genack, the rabbinic administrator of the Orthodox Union, which certifies kosher foods in more than 80 countries, points out, a Jew can eat a speck of bacon or shrimp as long as it amounts to less than one-sixtieth of the portion consumed. But the prohibition against *chametz* has no such wiggle room and Hasidim—in contrast to more modern Orthodox Jews—stringently see the rule as incontrovertible. Forebears of today's ultra-Orthodox Lithuanian-leaning Jews, like the Vilna Gaon, who assertively opposed many Hasidic practices, would deliberately eat matzo dipped in water or some other liquid on Passover to show that the extra Hasidic rigor was pointless. In modern times, esteemed American Ashkenazi rabbis like Moshe Feinstein (1895–1986), viewed as his era's most reliable authority on questions of Jewish law, and Joseph Soloveitchik (1903–93), the head of Yeshiva University's rabbinical school, felt such unnecessary scrupulousness imposed obligations that sucked the joy out of a holiday where Jews are commanded to be joyous. But Hasidim persist and will search out signs at, say, a hotel where they may want to spend Passover, that promise them no *gebrochts* is used. This way they can be sure the establishment will not serve them matzo balls and other foods that mix matzo with water.

To maintain this fastidiousness, Gourmet Glatt covers its shelves with brown butcher paper to make sure Passover products are not exposed to the year-round boards that could be flecked with *chametz*. At the entrance, the store promotes a tall stack of Easy-Off to help Hasidic homemakers clean the oven two or three times to make sure not even a speck of *chametz* from the past year contaminates dishes they might bake. The store also retains a rabbi on the premises—a *mashgiach*, or kashruth supervisor—to monitor the precision of Passover observance. Indeed, across Borough Park and other Hasidic neighborhoods there is a seasonal uptick in employment of experts in the finer points of keeping kosher, experts who greatly supplement their livelihoods during Passover.

Gourmet Glatt even features a bin of unwaxed apples; wax might be contaminated with *chametz*. It sells jars of natural honey—straight from the hive—for those Hasidim who spurn sugar not because of the calories but because sugar is processed and who knows what might have happened during the processing.

"On *Pesach* people don't want anything chemical, even if it's not *chametz*," said Rabbi Shmuel Teitelbaum, the store's *mashgiach*, told me. "They don't want any stories."

Gourmet Glatt also has a sprawling section of *shmura* matzos—matzos that have been "guarded" by rabbis from the time the grain was milled, through the mixing with water and the kneading of the dough, all to make sure no leavening occurred. (Hasidim even guard the grain while it is growing, and one branch of Satmar is extraordinarily rigorous: it grows its wheat on a Christian farmer's land in the scorching heat of Yuma, Arizona, where there is almost no rainfall.) Again, only 18 minutes can pass between the mixing of the water and flour and the insertion into a very hot oven. The process echoes the haste of the ancient Hebrews as they rushed to bake bread before escaping from Egypt. These matzos, usually round like pizzas and often charred, can cost $25 a pound, which adds a major expense to Passover since a typically large Hasidic family may require more than 10 pounds for the holiday's eight days.

There are a number of *shmura* matzo bakeries scattered through neighborhoods like Williamsburg and Borough Park that come to life for roughly three or four months a year in the season before Passover. I spent time in one of them, Chareidim Shmurah Matzah Bakery, which is planted inside a nondescript brick one-story factory that sits in the cool shadows of the elevated subway in Borough Park. The bakery turns out 80,000 pounds of hand-kneaded, flattened and perforated matzos in an atmosphere of high-wire tension, monitored by timers.

One of the thrilling sights of Jewish life is watching a dozen fretful men and women with kerchiefs wrapped around their hair stand around a long table and roll out balls of dough into pancakes using stainless steel rollers, all while a stop-watch set to an 18-minute alarm ticks away and a rabbinical supervisor and the bakery's owner look on. The discs of dough are slipped over a long rod wielded by a young man who sprints to rush them into the oven. At times, he looks like an Olympic pole-vaulter running down a track before his leap, as if the gold medal were at stake—all to make sure the deadline is met. Any cakes of dough that exceed 18 minutes from mixing are thrown away. The steel rollers are washed after every use to make sure they contain no flour or dough that has exceeded the 18-minute time limit. Many Hasidim will buy their matzos straight from the bakery rather than at a store like Gourmet Glatt, to add an extra scintilla of fastidiousness (and perhaps because the price is slightly less).

Passover, which celebrates the seminal Exodus of the Hebrews from Egypt, transforms the entire Hasidic neighborhood almost like Christmas does to Fifth Avenue or a Currier & Ives village. Passover consumes many Jews who observe it, but in Hasidic neighborhoods the visible degree of fevered rigor is breathtaking.

On any ordinary day, yellow school buses with the Hebrew names of yeshivas dominate the ultra-Orthodox landscape of Borough Park, but in the days before Passover a visitor is

struck by the many large trucks parked along the sidewalks
with signs bearing a word obscure even to most Jews: *sheimos*
(pronounced SHAME-os), a term for religious books containing the Hebrew name of God that need to be ritually
buried in the ground. Because Orthodox Jews strive to rid
their homes of even the slightest trace of *chametz*, almost down
to the molecule, Bibles, prayer books and volumes of Talmud
receive a thorough airing to make sure there are no particles of
bread trapped in the pages. (Indeed, Hasidic wives will often
admonish their husbands not to eat while they study Talmud
so they won't have to deal with stray food or stains on a *Gemara*
page when Passover approaches.) The most dog-eared books
are often discarded, but Jewish religious law considers throwing religious books with the Hebrew name of God in the trash
a desecration. So parked all day on streets in Borough Park are
trucks whose drivers will cart books to an upstate cemetery
for a fee of about eight dollars a box.

In my travels through Borough Park, I spotted a large white
tent in a homeowner's driveway with a sign offering "*Hagalas
Keilim.*" Inside the tent the homeowner had set up are large
vat of boiling water. Many Hasidim come and have the metal
pots and pans they use year-round dipped for a few seconds
in the bubbling water. Immersion in boiling water is believed
to liberate the pots from the taint of *chametz*, thus eliminating
the need for poorer Hasidim to buy a special set of pots and
pans restricted to Passover use. Earthenware, china and glass-
ware dishes cannot be koshered in this way and so Hasidim,
like most Orthodox Jews, have special sets of Passover dishes
and flatware.

The frenzy for perfection is also evident in the stacks of food processors for sale at the Buzz, an appliance store that is a kosher cross between a Williams-Sonoma and a Best Buy that is especially bustling before Passover. Juicers become a particularly hot item. All year long, ultra-Orthodox Jews drink Tropicana and other processed juices that bear rabbinical certification. On Passover, particularly fussy ones buy juicers to squeeze their own and avoid possible *chametz* contamination in the manufacturing. But food processors are the big seller. The Buzz sells thousands. The most popular, one of the owners, Heshy Biegeleisen, told me, is a 14-cup machine made by Gourmet Grade that has the "ultimate *kugel* blade" for making a starchy potato pudding that does not require grain products. The blade prevents the potato batter from having a soupy consistency associated with some food processors. The blade was designed—for convenience, not religious reasons—by engineers in China after Biegeleisen spent three weeks there with them figuring out how to forge a device that could create the granular texture of a hand grater (minus the blood that often comes with a cut finger). The answer was a blade that alternated large holes with small holes.

The fastidiousness goes on. Hasidim from the Belz sect will not touch garlic during the holiday. Not because garlic is *chametz*, but because generations ago in Europe garlic was preserved inside sacks of wheat. Since their ancestors did not eat garlic, Belz Hasidim will not eat garlic, even though almost no one preserves garlic in sacks of wheat anymore. Tradition is tradition. Hungarian Hasidim will not eat gefilte fish because in Hungary fish came from afar and was often preserved in alcohol, which might be processed from grain. Though fish can be bought straight from the ocean in New York, Hungarian Hasidim will still hew to tradition and spurn gefilte fish, or they will eat it made only from carp because it can be bought live and killed and cut up in one's home. Stores feature gallon bottles of Kedem grape juice because little children may not drink the required four cups of wine during the seder but they will be required to drink four cups of grape juice to inculcate them in the observance of the Passover ritual.

When I visited Gourmet Glatt, Mordechai Rosenberg, a 50-year-old Bobov Hasid wearing an astrakhan fur hat, was pushing a cart loaded with boxes of sugared cereal made from potato starch. He felt compelled to explain apologetically to another Hasid that they were for his grandchildren. "I eat what my parents taught me," he told me.

All Jews are commanded to collect their *chametz* on the evening before the first seder, a symbolic gesture since the home has already been scrubbed clean. Still, many families set out pieces of bread and pursue the last elusive crumbs of *chametz* with feather and candle in a kind of treasure hunt as a fun way to teach their children about the tradition. The *chametz* is then burned the following morning in the backyard or kitchen sink. That is not enough for Hasidim. They set up large bonfires on nearby street corners—the police even supply steel barricades so that the fire is contained, and to be extra cautious a city firefighter sometimes looks on—and the men and boys gather round, throw in their bags of the forbidden *chametz* and mutter prayers as they rock back and forth. The fire crackles and sparks, and billows of acrid smoke fill the air above the low-rise houses and sting the nostrils. It is a dazzling sight for many of the young sidelocked boys and it happens to provide a soupçon of fun that draws them further—cynics might say seduces them—into the demanding life of a Hasid.

The punctiliousness extends to the holiday itself, of course, but most residents of New York become aware of it not in the *shmura* matzo the Hasidim eat but in the presence of Hasidim in places they otherwise seldom visit. Suddenly, on the four intermediate days of the eight-day Passover holiday, when Jews are allowed to work, travel, spend money freely and do all the everyday chores, places like Central Park, the Bronx Zoo and Brooklyn Bridge Park are teeming with Hasidim. All Jews are told that the three festivals of the Hebrew calendar—Succoth, Passover and Shavuot—are a time of joy and pleasure, but Hasidim take these words proactively, going out of their way to have a good time. In the new state-of-the-art Brooklyn Bridge Park, dozens of boys and girls, dressed in heavy clothes that conceal their arms and legs, scamper in a jazzed-up version of a sandbox or scoot down the long, twisting sliding ponds, screaming with glee while their parents look on with delight and take photographs. In Central Park, Hasidim can be seen riding bicycles on the paved drives or navigating motorized sailboats in Conservatory Pond. At the Bronx Zoo, Hasidim sometimes dominate the landscape as they gawk at lions, giraffes, polar bears and tigers. The Hasidim must be a curious site to tourists from Kansas or New Mexico who have come from even farther away to see the famous wildlife park, perhaps even more curious than a rhinoceros or a snow leopard since they may have seen pictures of those species in animal books. It would be understandable if more than a few tourists concluded after the visit that most New Yorkers have thick beards and sidelocks and wear heavy dark clothes even on a warm spring day.

A high point of sorts in Passover observance was reached a few years ago. An ultra-Orthodox group in Brooklyn rented Madison Square Garden for a command performance—with restrictions—of the Ringling Bros. and Barnum & Bailey Circus that drew 19,000 men, women and children, many Hasidic, though many were from the Lithuanian-rooted yeshiva crowd that dominates the neighborhood of Midwood. They fulfilled the Torah commandment to be joyful on Passover.

Here's how they made the circus kosher for Passover. They sold hot dogs without rolls and bought two brand-new cotton-candy machines uncontaminated by leavened grain products. They insisted there be no female performers, including the Lycra-clad star aerialist Sylvia Zerbini, known as the Circus Siren, since Orthodox Jews insist upon modest dress for women.

"It's not because we don't like ladies," Rabbi Raphael Wallerstein, a yeshiva principal and organizer, told me. "I'm married with thirteen children and over thirty grandchildren. We love ladies. It's out of respect for them."*

They also asked Crazy Wilson Dominguez, who crosses himself as he begins his gravity-defying walk on the spinning Pendulum of Pandemonium, to do so out of audience view. The circus performers had to stage extra rehearsals to make

---

* Author's interview with Rabbi Raphael Wallerstein.

sure none of the elements violated Orthodox strictures. The circus agreed to a number of other uncommon accommodations. They let the organizers bring in their own potato *kugel*, and they allowed them to reserve whole swaths of seating for those spectators who wanted to sit only among members of their own sex.

Wallerstein, only partly in jest, told me that he and the other organizers also prayed to God that the New York Rangers would not make it to the National Hockey League playoffs—their home games are held in Madison Square Garden—so the circus performance could be held on the only intermediate day that worked in that year's quirky Hebrew calendar. God, or that year's hapless Rangers team, obliged.

Wallerstein has become the impresario of such Orthodox holiday events, and the money raised helps finance two yeshivas he runs in Brooklyn as well as tuition and summer camp for children who are poor or learning disabled. Although in previous years he had arranged for the Passover and Succoth intermediate-days events to be held at the RexPlex amusement park in New Jersey, in 2004 he booked the circus at Madison Square Garden because, to twist a popular Passover saying, he wanted that year to be different from all other years.

I was at the 2004 performance and it was certainly different. The band started the afternoon by playing "Dayenu," a rousing song that often delights children seated around the seder table. And David Larible, the master clown they call the Prince of Laughter, wore a yarmulke to perform a miracle that more than one youngster must have thought was right up there with the parting of the Red Sea and the Ten Plagues: for several heart-stopping seconds, he turned another performer into a goat. But mostly the children shrieked, gasped and gazed in wonder like all children at circuses, maybe more so because most of these children don't have televisions and have never seen a circus extravaganza. I watched the lion tamer, Jason Peters, put his head in a lion's mouth and then asked some of the children what they thought. Lazer Schlesinger of Flatbush, then a side-curled 12-year-old from Flatbush, told me: "It was very scary. I was scared he was going to rip him up and eat him."

Of course, seeing such secular amusements has its dangers within the Orthodox fold; it opens up new worlds, as Elliot Zimet can testify. He grew up in an observant home in the Riverdale section of the Bronx and was enchanted by visits to the circus as a boy. Now he is no longer Orthodox and was at the Garden that afternoon, not in the audience, but as a carrot-haired Ringling Bros. clown, making a dove fly out of the fist of a delighted boy named Shimy.

9

KOSHER SEX

Hasidim do not have sex through a hole in the sheet. How this myth, believed by otherwise erudite people, got started is anybody's guess. Some people posit that it cropped up in the ghettos of Europe and was somehow linked with *tzitzit*, the poncho-like fringed garment an Orthodox man wears, which does have a hole for a man's head (not his penis), and which was sometimes seen flapping in the wind on a wash line. Nevertheless, the myth is a good way to approach the subject of sex in the Hasidic community because there is a widespread belief in the puritanism and prurience of Hasidim. In fact the matter is far more complicated, and by some lights their traditions may pose a sharp contrast to the puritanical.

Take frequency. Once Hasidim are married they are commanded to have sex as often as they can in order to procreate. Except, that is, for the five-day *niddah* period when a woman is menstruating and the seven "white" days afterward—a total sometimes of 12 days, give or take a day depending on a woman's menstrual cycle. Since a wife is not fertile during the 12 days, most Orthodox Jews believe sex should be avoided, in obeisance to interpretations of a commandment in Leviticus, though emotional and spiritual bonding is encouraged. But the 12 days ends with the wife's nighttime immersion in the communal *mikveh*, and then sex with her husband—*tashmish hamitah*, as it is called—is prescribed for right after she comes home. The *tahara* period often carries a woman to the point of ovulation, which may be the motivation behind the whole exercise.

Hasidim, of course, take this paradigm to their own levels (cynics might say extremes) and believe that God wants them to enjoy themselves during sexual intercourse. Procreation is a sacred act that can be infused with as much joy as eating at a Passover seder or dancing with a Torah. Even if a couple, for medical reasons, can no longer have children or their years of fertility have ended, a man is obligated by the Torah to give conjugal pleasure to his wife, and by the Talmud to satisfy his own desires within marriage lest they sidetrack him from the study of Torah. Of course, sex before and outside marriage is forbidden, though therapists tell me that they have been told by female patients about Hasidic husbands who visit gentile prostitutes during the *tahara* period, seeing this as a lesser sin than the willful spilling of the seed explicitly prohibited by the Old Testament.

Still, the sex and love life of Hasidim would strike modern Americans as peculiar. Starting in elementary school and all the way until marriage, boys and girls are kept quite segregated from one another, except for what Saul Bellow's Herzog called the "potato-love" intimacy of siblings and parents; boys play with boys, girls with girls and attend separate schools in discrete buildings. Both boys and girls are taught almost nothing about sex, even into their teenage years. Shulem Deen, a defector from the Skverer Hasidim, told me that it is not uncommon for adolescent boys to explore their sexual urges with other boys through mutual masturbation, because in "an all-male environment" they have no other outlet for their roiling hormones. But all sexual activity before marriage is dismissed by their rabbis and teachers with the Yiddish phrase *shmut-zezeh zachin* (dirty things), and Deen does not think this experimentation breeds later homosexuality or abuse by men of young boys.

"Most adults are not attracted to children," he told me.

A psychotherapist in Rockland County, where Hasidim live in such suburban communities as Monsey, told me of meeting with the mother of a 15-year-old girl who complained that her daughter was "sneaking out of the house to meet a boy." The therapist, who asked me not to reveal her name because she continues to do both counseling and testing in the community, told the mother, "This is not abnormal." But the principal told the mother he "cannot have the girl in school anymore—she's a bad influence on the other girls. We don't want her influence. She's not a *bas Yisroel*—a daughter of Israel." The therapist then met with the principal and cautioned him that if he expelled the girl she would end up in a local public school, where dating is commonplace at her age and things would get even worse. The principal backed off from his expulsion threat.

The schools have difficulty coping with sexual misbehavior. Fifteen years ago the therapist worked with a case of incest where a boy was molesting a sister. The family preferred to deal with it on their own. An Irish cop who was called in because the conduct was a law enforcement matter told the therapist that the society-wide problem of sexual abuse of minors is aggravated in the Hasidic community "because they hide it." Parents are leery about revealing any blemish or family problem that could hobble a child's ability or the ability of a sibling to find a marriage match when they are older.

"I had one child who had a hearing impairment but the parents did not want him to wear a hearing aid and wouldn't put it on him," the therapist told me. "They didn't want people to know he was very hard of hearing."

Segregation continues even after marriage. Men and women are urged to avoid contact with the opposite sex except for spouses, children and immediate kinfolk. A Hasidic man will not shake a woman's hand and a woman will not shake a man's hand. Idle talk between the sexes, except for the necessities of business or other practical purposes, is also discouraged. Whenever I've interviewed a Hasidic woman in person, it has been done with her husband in the room. Once Nechuma Mayer wanted to exchange a photograph she had given me and, rushing out alone, tracked me down at a local eatery in Borough Park. The conversation did not last long. Both of us felt awkward simply chatting by ourselves.

There are also communal pressures that enforce the mores about contact across sexual lines, and sometimes these take forms that strike democratic Americans as sinister if not illegal. In my encounters in the Hasidic world I began to hear about modesty committees—shadowy, sometimes self-appointed squads that use social and economic leverage to enforce conformity. I heard of billboards signed by such squads and plastered on lampposts or store windows that cautioned Hasidic women against wearing certain kinds of wigs, or skirts that were too short or stockings that were too thin— all so they would not make themselves attractive to strange men. One family reported being harassed because the wife had stepped outdoors with a robelike housecoat rather than a dress, even though most women in a neighborhood like Borough Park wear housecoats indoors. Store owners have received rough verbal warnings from committees to stop selling magazines that carry provocative photographs or even articles that dispute the Satmar view that refuses to accept Israel as a state.

Visiting shops along Lee Avenue, the main street of Brooklyn's Williamsburg, I learned that store owners were often threatened with communal shunning if they exhibited mannequins deemed too erotic or almost any mannequin at all. The manager of one women's clothing store related how the store owner received a call at home one evening from a man who said he was from a modesty committee. The committee, the man said, was concerned that the mannequins in the window might arouse passing men and boys.

"Do the neighborhood a favor and take it out of the window," the caller cautioned the shopkeeper. "We're trying to safeguard our community."

For a day or two, the shopkeeper wrestled with the implied threat to her business—a boycott or unfavorable posters—and to her family's status in the community. But she ultimately decided to obey. "We can sell it without mannequins so we might as well do what the public wants," the shopkeeper told the manager.*

The power of these modesty committees was evident in the fact that of the half dozen apparel stores along a stretch of Lee Avenue that I passed, only one had mannequins, and those were relatively shapeless and faceless torsos. The Brooklyn district attorney's office has received allegations of members of a modesty squad forcing their way into a home and seizing an iPad and other computer equipment used by the children. The district attorney was also said to be investigating a modesty committee that threatened to publicly expose a married man who was having an affair unless he paid the committee money for what the committee described as therapy.

"They operate like the mafia," Rabbi Allan Nadler, director of Jewish studies at Drew University in New Jersey, told

---

* Joseph Berger, "Modesty in Ultra-Orthodox Brooklyn Is Enforced by Secret Squads," *New York Times*, January 30, 2013, p. A1.

me. "They walk into a store and say it would be a shame if your window was broken or you lost your clientele. They might tell the father of a girl who wears a skirt that's too short and he's, say, a store owner, 'If you ever want to sell a pair of shoes, speak to your daughter.'"* He and others told me that these committees do not have addresses or business cards and few Hasidim even know where their authority originates, though it is highly unlikely that they would be operating without the tacit blessings of rabbinical leaders.

"There are quite a few men, especially in Williamsburg, who consider themselves '*Gut's polizei* [God's police],'" Yosef Rapaport, a Hasidic freelancer journalist, told me. "It's somebody who is a busybody, and there're quite a few of them—zealots who take it upon themselves and they just enforce. They're considered crazy, but people don't want to confront them."

As a result of the pressures to keep separate from the opposite gender before marriage, Hasidim are often ignorant of the basic details of sex until the moment they get married and even sometimes afterward. The sociologist Samuel Heilman, in his book on the Hasidim of Israel, *Defenders of the Faith: Inside Ultra-Orthodox Jewry*, tells a wonderful joke about the Hasidic bridegroom who meets with a rabbinic counselor just before the wedding and is appalled to learn the physical mechanics of sex.

"Why shocked?" the counselor asks. "After all, your father did this as well." "Yes, of course," the bridegroom replies. "But

---

* Author's interview with Rabbi Allan Nadler.

he did it with my mother. But me, I'm going to have to do it with some woman I don't even know."*

Nevertheless, some Hasidim I have spoken to are open in talking about menstruation, intercourse and other aspects of sexuality because to them it is not much different than the details of food or Sabbath, all part of the austere daily pageant of being a pious person. This first struck me about 25 years ago when, as a new religion writer for the *Times*, I reported on a conference at Mount Sinai Medical Center on sex therapy and Jewish law. The keynote speaker was the late Dr. Helen Singer Kaplan, one of America's best-known sex therapists at the time. Her brassy X-rated talk was sometimes startlingly concrete. For example, she talked about the pornography she had sexually timid clients watch but noted that she did not do this with Orthodox couples, encouraging them instead to fantasize only about their spouses in sexually titillating positions. Her talk was followed by responses from three different rabbis, one Reform, one Conservative and one Orthodox. It sounded like the beginning of an old Jewish joke, and it almost became one. The Reform and Conservative rabbis spoke in trite, hollow generalities about the sanctity of the sexual act and the harmony of marriage but danced around specifics, while the Orthodox rabbi, Moshe D. Tendler, professor of Talmud at Yeshiva University and chairman of its biology department, waded in with prescriptions and proscriptions for masturbation, oral sex and other quite specific

---

* Samuel Heilman, *Defenders of the Faith: Inside Ultra-Orthodox Jewry* (Berkeley: University of California Press, 2000), p. 325.

sex acts. The Bible forbids a man from willfully and fruitlessly "spilling his seed," but Rabbi Tendler pointed out it does not prohibit women from masturbating, although it would be regarded as "an antisocial life style."*

"A marriage without sexuality is a weak marriage," Rabbi Tendler told the audience. Every sex act should give maximum pleasure to both parties, and even eroticism has its place "if it does not violate modesty." Under Jewish law, the rules of modesty forbid a man from engaging in acts that violate the woman's sense of privacy and are associated with prostitution—but Tendler did not specifically rule out all forms of oral sex during a procreative sex act. The audience, most of whom were ultra-Orthodox and modern Orthodox Jews for whom sexual dysfunction is a serious religious matter, not just a matter of emotional gratification, never blushed.

Hasidim will take the Orthodox canon several steps further. First there is the marriage itself. Hasidim believe marriages should be arranged by mature people like one's parents or professional matchmakers. Romance, if it develops, is a nice bonus, but the essential purpose of marriage is to produce children and help a family live a pious life. So parents or wise professionals are shrewdest at determining what two people might best be compatible for such purposes. That means, according to Hasidic wisdom, that there is no need for long dating periods and long engagements. Therefore, the parents of a prospective match will meet first and discuss the

* Joseph Berger, "Sex Therapy and Religion," New York Times, March 12, 1986.

wisdom of proceeding with a marriage. Then the young man
and young woman will be introduced, given two or three private meetings over a dinner table set with drinks and snacks
and with relatives ensconced in an adjoining room. In some
sects, like Skver, the meeting may last only 15 minutes before
an engagement is sealed. Deen, the Skver defector who at the
time we spoke was writing a memoir about his Hasidic life,
said that the 15-minute meeting is a formality and that immediately afterward the couple will head to the Rebbe's house
"and he will give them a piece of *lekech* [sponge cake] and *shnaps*
[whiskey or other spirits] and say 'Mazel Tov,' and then it's official." Satmar, often regarded by outsiders as the most backward of the Hasidic sects, is, according to Deen, actually more
enlightened and worldly when it comes to marriage, allowing
for longer meetings between the prospective groom and bride.

If either the young man or young woman rejects the match,
often for reasons having to do not so much with beauty or
character as with a woman's views on wigs or a man's on the
frequency of Torah study, then there is no deal. Hasidim do
not believe in forcing a young person into marriage. If either of
the prospective spouses discovers that the other has a chronic
illness or handicap or there has been a divorce or other scandal in the family, then the arrangement can be broken off. If
a match is made, the couple usually does not meet again until
the wedding celebration, which is organized by their parents.

Nechuma Mayer told me that marriages have to be arranged because Hasidic boys and girls are so protected from
one another that they have no way of making a wise choice.
Parents, on the other hand, know a prospective mate's family.

"They would decide if the two people have something in common and the thing might go," she told me. "My father was a Hasidic person. My father-in-law was the *rosh yeshiuva* in Nitra [head of the Yeshiva of Nitra, a rabbinical college in Mount Kisco, New York]. They happened to be friends, but he made a good guess. He came to me and said they have this boy, that he was a good student, that he not only has charisma, but good character attributes. With all matches, the parents meet first and then the boy and girl meet and they have a chat in the dining room of the girl's house. Sometimes they want to speak again. One or the other may be uncomfortable about a certain thing. They meet one or two times or even three times. If everything seemed fine you made an engagement and that's the way it is to this day. It's really from heaven these things. The ultra-Orthodox believe matches are made in heaven."*

In her own case, Nechuma told me, "it turned out to be perfect."

These marriage customs may strike most Americans, for whom freedom of choice is a bedrock principle, as primitive and antediluvian and guaranteed to produce scores of mismatched couples and loveless unions. But Hasidim will argue that men and women who are judged by wiser people to be congenial are more likely to share the same aspirations and wishes. They even come to know one another more deeply so that intimacy and love do blossom. There are no Hasidic marriage statistics but the divorce rate, by all accounts, is tiny,

---

* Author's interview with Nechuma Mayer.

far less common than with most American marriages, where one of every two end in divorce. Deen told me that in his class of 50 adult students in the Yeshiva of Skver only five men have gotten a *get*, a Jewish divorce. And the numbers of men and women who end up as lonely, childless singles is minuscule.

Deen's narrative of his own marriage, which ended in divorce, may explain why some of those slight divorce statistics may be misleading. For one thing, divorce would limit the options of their children in finding a mate, so couples endure loveless marriages.

"My wife and I were extremely incompatible," he told me. "But we lived together for fifteen years and I cared for her very deeply. It's because of the kids you have and someone you're very close to for a long time."*

Since neither the Hasidic man nor the woman typically has been well tutored in the mechanics of sex, let alone the acrobatics, an expert is often consulted. Most people in the secular world may not know much, either, before their first sexual encounter, but they pick information out of an ether filled with books, films, and gossip that Hasidim are never exposed to. Almost all Hasidic women go to *kallah* classes, classes for brides where they learn about the so-called laws of family purity, including the rules for bathing in the *mikveh*, covering one's hair and the proper times and atmosphere for intercourse (preferably at night, lights off, shades drawn, husband on top). Some Hasidim say the experts who run such

---

* Author's interview with Shulem Deen.

classes often spend too much time on the prohibitions around intercourse, like the days off for *niddah*, but not enough time on the choreography of sex itself. Obviously, most Hasidic couples figure things out so well that Hasidim have one of the highest birthrates of any subculture in the world. But there is ample literature, much of it hilarious, at how strange a Hasidic wedding night—the first chance for either emotional or physical intimacy—can end up being.

Deen, who now blogs under the pen name Hasidic Rebel but grew up in a Skver community where men and women were so separated they walked on opposite sides of the street, wrote on his blog about his experience as a new groom a month short of his nineteenth birthday.

"I knew nothing of female anatomy except that girls had no penises," he wrote. "I knew sex involved the male organ entering some crevice in the female body, and I imagined—perhaps just by intuiting a male-female anatomical symmetry—that said crevice was somewhere in the nether regions. Lacking anything more substantial, I spent most of my teen years imagining that point of entry to be what others considered only a point of exit. Needless to say, I had mixed feelings about the whole idea."

He got engaged to a girl he met for 15 minutes before the official engagement party and "wasn't even sure I was attracted to." A few hours before his wedding, he went to see a "groom instructor," an "emaciated-looking man with a very long beard" in a home filled with heavy religious texts. The instructor waded immediately into the laws of separation between the spouses during menstruation.

I freaked out. I needed the basics, not the religious laws on what comes afterwards. I needed to know what goes where, what to say to her, what or what not to wear. I wanted technical details of biology, perhaps some guidance on positions, and the like. But I was too stunned to say anything. Throughout the session he referred to sex as "the *mitzvah*," literally, "the commandment," which was also the term my friends and I later used on those rare occasions we dared mention it, a topic deemed so vulgar that even with the euphemism it felt taboo.

The rabbi concluded the hour with hand gestures that explained the positions of intercourse.

Hours later, with the wedding party over, the guests gone, and the gifts inventoried, my new wife and I began preparing for the *mitzvah*. Dressed in the requisite clothing (nightgown for her, nightshirt for me), with a heavy sheet hung over the window curtains to ensure total darkness, we fumbled our way into bed. Still virtual strangers, we moved about each other shyly, awkwardly adjusting to the unfamiliar intimacy. I did exactly as I'd been told: I gave her a kiss on the lips, said "I love you" in Yiddish (incidentally, a language most unsuitable for amorous expression), and we both lifted our clothes as I moved on top of her. Something was definitely wrong. A piece seemed missing. I was sufficiently erect, she claimed to have no anatomical peculiarities, but something didn't fit. Hard as I tried, I couldn't get my penis into any kind of body cavity.

At four in the morning, he called the "groom instructor," who told him to tell his bride "to lubricate her area with some water."

We tried that. Nothing doing. I called the rabbi again. "Tell her to take your 'organ' with her hands and direct it to the position." After many more tries, my penis long flaccid by the unerotic disaster the whole business had become, we determined that I must have already penetrated, and we called it a night. Owing to the intricacies of Jewish law, we couldn't have sex for the next two weeks. After which we tried again, and pretty much the same thing happened. After another two week interval we tried it again. Given our track record, the whole thing was turning into a drag. Expecting another frustrating round of fumbling in the dark with vague guesses as to whether it had "worked" or not, we braced ourselves and looked forward to getting it over with. But this time something was different. As soon as my erect penis put just a little pressure against her vaginal area something magical happened. Something gave way, and all I felt was the overwhelming violence of my throbbing penis, a sensation I'd never felt before. I can't say my wife felt as much pleasure as I did, but she was definitely relieved to know that it finally "worked." We felt like congratulating ourselves; it was our first challenge as a married couple, and we'd pulled it off. It would be a long time before sex would come to resemble anything like the pleasurable experience intended by nature. It took months before I dared to caress her back, touch her breasts, put my hands on her butt, and suggest we get fully naked. But when those moments came—as we navigated this new carnal territory, finding our own rhythm in the act previously considered so animalistic and therefore, best avoided— they carried an erotic energy that would be unmatched by anything later on.

We would go on to be married for fourteen years, and eventually moved on to have sex like pretty much everyone else. But the innocence of those early days and weeks is still something to be remembered.*

---

* Shulem Deen, "My First Time," *Nerve*, February 16, 2010, http://www .nerve.com/love-sex/my-first-time/male-19-years-old-brooklyn-ny.

THE UNKOSHER VARIETY

Given the lack of knowledge of so many young Hasidim, both as children and later as adults, outside experts are not surprised by the recent explosion of publicized incidents of sex abuse in the Hasidic community, incidents that had always been covered up and handled within the walls of the sect. Shtreimel, one of the pen names of the Hasid who wrote the blog "A Hasid and a Heretic," told me that the groundwork for abusive sex is set early when many adolescent yeshiva boys engage in homosexual play because, in a world where boys and girls are rigorously segregated, they have no other outlets for their sexuality.

"The gay experience stays on forever in some kids," he wrote in one blog.*

Some teachers and rabbis who have a predilection for sex with young boys can in all-male yeshivas use their authority

———

* Shtreimel, "Sexual Promiscuity," *A Hasid and A Heretic* (blog), December 25, 2004, http://hassid.blogspot.com/2004/12/sexual-promiscuity.html.

to prey. The daily obligation of *mikveh* before study—where naked men dip together in a small pool of warm water—also seems to offer a relatively convenient location for such abuse. Back in 2009, Joe Diangelo, a 28-year-old defector from the Satmar Hasidim originally known as Joel Deutsch, told National Public Radio about an incident in a *mikveh* that happened when he was just seven years old.

"I was in the tub and I had my back turned and somebody raped me while I was in the water," he said. "And I didn't know what happened. I couldn't make sense of it really."*

He said he never saw the man who raped him, but Joel Engelman, another defector from the Satmar Hasidim, who heads the Jewish Survivors Network, a group that hosts an online support site for men and women who were abused as children, is suing the man he says regularly molested him for two months when he was just eight years old. He was a student at Satmar's United Talmudical Academy in Williamsburg and was called to the office of an administrator, Avrohom Reichman, who told him to close the door.

"He motioned for me to get on his lap, and as soon as I got on the chair, he would swivel the chair from right to left, continuously," Engelman told NPR. "Then he would start touching me while talking to me. He would start at my shoulders and work his way down to my genitals."†

He told no one until he was 18 years old and then only

---

* Barbara Bradley Hagerty, "Abuse Scandal Plagues Hasidic Jews in Brooklyn," NPR, February 2, 2009.

† Brad A. Greenberg, "Sexual Abuse in Brooklyn's Hasidic Community," *Jewish Journal*, February 2, 2009.

his parents, and in his early twenties, the parents, who said they learned from other school parents that Reichman was molesting other boys, told the school. At first school officials gave Reichman a polygraph test, and when the results indicated Reichman was lying the officials told Engelman's family Reichman would be fired. But a few weeks later, the officials seemed to dawdle, asking Engelman to describe the severity of the molestation on a scale of one to 10. Since there was no skin-to-skin contact—perhaps an important point in Jewish law but not much of a psychological consolation for Engelman—the school hired Reichman back. Satmar officials deemed the charge not credible and Reichman was still teaching there as of April 2014. Engelman sued Reichman and the school, but the suit was dismissed on grounds that the statute of limitations for the abuse claims had long expired. Reichman's lawyer, Jacob Laufer, told me his client "vehemently denies that he ever abused any student.

"He enjoys an excellent reputation," the lawyer said. "Parents are vying to have children put into his class. Engelman obviously is a person who has chosen a different path in life, and his suggestion that Rabbi Reichman was part of that choice is wrong."

Stories like these started emerging in the Jewish press—the *Jewish Daily Forward*, *Jewish Week* and the *Baltimore Jewish Times* among them—around 2005, echoing a series of revelations about sex abuse by Catholic priests of children, mostly boys, under their supervision. The stunning idea that two pious religious groups could be tainted by such scandals soon became front-page news in the secular press because the incidents they depicted smacked of breathtaking hypocrisy and challenged the wisdom of the groups' imposing so restrictive a sexual climate. The charges in the Hasidic community set off a feeding frenzy, and within a few years major news organizations like the British newspaper the *Guardian*, the *New York Times*, NPR and others were acquainting their readers with this once-insular world. How many readers had ever heard of a *mikveh* before? But what was also salient in the news stories was that rabbis were hushing up the crimes or denying them outright, leaving victims feeling even more powerless and badly treated. Mordechai Jungreis told the *Guardian* and the *Times* that when he reported the molestation of his mentally disabled teenage son to the law enforcement authorities, he was shunned on the streets of Williamsburg. Anonymous messages appeared on his answering machine cursing him for informing on a fellow Jew to secular authorities, a crime known as *mesirah*.

What's more, rabbis, both Hasidic and those from the *Yeshivish* black-hat world, insisted, publicly so, that victims and their families must first report any allegations of abuse to a competent rabbi before going to the authorities. The Brooklyn district attorney's office, led from 1990 through 2013 by Charles J. Hynes, who as an elected official had been close to several of the Hasidic leaders in Brooklyn, even worked out a system with rabbinic authorities—one observed for almost no other crimes, not even rape. The office agreed not to publicly identify those arrested or convicted for abuse, on the theory that revealing the names would, in a tight-knit community, identify the victims. The decision, which was a blanket one for the ultra-Orthodox community and did not exclude cases where a disclosure of a victim's identity was unlikely, was widely criticized. Marci Hamilton, a professor of law at Yeshiva University, told the Jewish newspaper the *Forward* that "what the DA's office is doing, unfortunately, is playing right into the hands of the abusers." Identifying abusers, she pointed out, encourages other victims to come forward.[*]

But Hynes and his subordinates defended the policy, contending that they were able to bring almost a hundred criminal cases within the Hasidic community, far more than the handful they brought before they instituted the protocol. And in June 2012, Hynes, perhaps defensively trying to resurrect his tough-prosecutor image, charged four Hasidic men with bribery and intimidation for trying to silence a witness in a high-profile molestation case—that of Nechemya Weberman, an unlicensed therapist. The four were accused of offering the witness and her boyfriend a $500,000 bribe, threatening the kosher certification of the boyfriend's restaurant and urging the pair to flee to Israel to avoid testifying.

"I'm hoping that this will be a message to those who are intimidated that they should come forward and help us," Hynes said at a news conference announcing the charges of bribery and intimidation against the four Hasidic men. "No one can engage in this kind of conduct and feel free that, based on prior experience, nothing can happen to them."

---

[*] Paul Berger, "Orthodox Abuse Suspects Get Exemption," *Jewish Daily Forward*, May 4, 2012.

Despite the natural inclination to be dismayed by the Hasidic community's handling of all such cases, it is worth understanding that, as with most matters Hasidic, the community's decision to keep sexual abuse within the tribe is not just a matter of protecting its own and its reputation but is also a long tradition grounded in its interpretation of Jewish law. The prohibition against *mesirah* arose in a world where the public authorities were virulently anti-Semitic, and it was one that made eminent sense until the latter half of the 20th century, when Jews began to assimilate and be accepted more fully into democratic societies and achieve rights and even parity in many spheres. Hasidim themselves are torn over how much secular authorities can now be trusted. Moreover, reporting any crime has a reservoir of scriptural and Talmudic fine points. The Torah, for example, requires two witnesses for a crime, and abuse is rarely witnessed.

"Circumstantial evidence is something Hasidim have a problem digesting," Alexander Rapaport told me. "You might not want your kids hanging around an abuser but it doesn't mean he's going to go to jail."*

Requiring an abuser to present his charges to a leading rabbi would also not surprise ultra-Orthodox Jews. They check every important decision with rabbinic leaders—whom to marry, what career to follow, what house to buy. A Hasidic woman unsure whether she has finished menstruating so she can resume sexual relations with her husband will bring

---

* Author's interview with Alexander Rapaport.

a cloth with an ambiguous stain drawn from her vagina to a seasoned rabbi so he can make certain it is not blood.

"You can destroy a person's life with a false report," Rabbi David Zwiebel, the executive vice president of Agudath Israel of America, an umbrella group of Orthodox organizations and rabbis, explained.*

Against this background, Hasidim for generations have chosen to handle accusations of abuse within the fold. A teacher might be reprimanded and watched more closely or fired. Or the matter might be referred to a *bes din*, a rabbinical court, which could demand a payment from the accused to the accuser. Seldom would the government authorities be informed. When they were, pressure was often put on the families of victims to back off. Others were ostracized or shunned.

In 2009, Justice Gustin Reichbach of the New York State Supreme Court in Brooklyn publicly admonished the Hasidic community at the sentencing of Yona Weinberg for molesting two boys who were under 14 years old.

"While the crimes the defendant stands convicted of are bad enough, what is even more troubling to the court is a communal attitude that seems to impose greater opprobrium on the victims than the perpetrator," he said.†

Even those who have attempted to call attention to the problem of intimidation by rabbinic authorities have found themselves ostracized. Rabbi Nuchem Rosenberg, a

---

* Sharon Otterman and Ray Rivera, "Ultra-Orthodox Shun Their Own for Reporting Child Sexual Abuse," *New York Times*, May 10, 2012, pp. A1, A24.

† Ibid.

Williamsburg Satmar, operates a call-in line that, in Yiddish, assails rabbis for hushing up cases. He told the *Times* that he has been banned from Satmar synagogues and denounced and ostracized by rabbinic authorities, who urged that Jews stay away from him "until he returns from his evil ways." After his public role in the Weberman trial, a Hasidic man threw bleach in his face.

Shulem Deen, the rebel blogger, told me that "the Hasidic community has a huge problem when it comes to sexual abuse. In general they tend to dismiss it. They don't know what the harmful effects on children are. They know it happens, but they don't recognize the impact on the victim. They see it as some perversion. They don't realize that sexual abuse is abuse."

Still, it should also be noted that there is no evidence that sex abuse is any greater in the Hasidic community than it is among other Jews or gentiles. The daily crime ledgers are replete with charges of abuse but the ones that get prominence in the newspaper are those involving celebrities, public and private school teachers at dozens of public schools and elite private high schools, like Horace Mann School and Poly Prep Country Day School in New York, or devout religious figures like Catholic priests. The non-Hasidic Jewish world has not been spared, either. Yeshiva University is the flagship of the modern Orthodox movement and in 2013 a lawyer for 19 former students at the university's high school for boys filed a federal lawsuit accusing a former teacher and an administrator of dozens of acts of sexual abuse during the 1970s and 1980s. The former teacher, a rabbi, was accused of sodomizing a

16-year-old student with a toothbrush. The longtime administrator was accused of groping students while checking whether
they were wearing *tzitzit* and forcing them to wrestle with him
in a sexually charged way. The lawsuit said that the university's
leaders squelched the incidents, did not report them to prose-
cutorial authorities and simply forced the two accused rabbis
to leave. The administrator even went on to work at a Jewish
day school near Miami.* Amid the revelations, Dr. Norman
Lamm, who had been president of Yeshiva University from
1976 to 2003, issued a letter of apology for his "ill-conceived"
responses, saying he submitted "to momentary compassion in
according the individuals the benefit of the doubt."

When they look at the Hasidic scandals, psychologists and
social workers point to endemic aspects of that world that
may need rethinking. Just as Catholics debate the wisdom of
celibacy for priests and its possible contribution to abuse, Hasidim may need to look at the ironclad segregation by sex until
marriage, the lack of any outlets for sexual urges, the absence
of any real instruction about sex, the refusal to deal with outside authorities about charges of sex abuse, the triumphalism
that suggests that Hasidim are immune to the failings that
plague other people.

Perhaps they should take some bittersweet comfort in a
message from Engelman's mother, Pearl.

---

* Al Baker, "Lawsuit Says Two Rabbis Abused Boys at Jewish High
School," *New York Times*, July 8, 2013, p. A17.

"There is no nice way of saying it," she said. "Our community protects molesters. Other than that we are wonderful."

There are indications that attitudes are changing and that some self-examination is taking place about how Hasidim have been dealing with the issue. Shortly after the Leiby Kletzky killing in Borough Park—a case that, as best as is known, did not involve sexual abuse, although it did end in Leiby's dismemberment—I spoke to Ruchama Clapman, who runs Mothers and Fathers Aligned Saving Kids, a small agency that deals with drug and alcohol abuse and sexual molestation largely within the community. She recalled that when she started her agency in 1997 she encountered tremendous resistance simply talking about the problems, "and it took many years before the community was accepting that we had these issues in our community."

"It was hanging out dirty laundry," she said.[*]

People were afraid that if a victim sought help and a problem became widely known, parents might find it difficult to find matches for their sons and daughters and social and business relations would be hurt. Dov Hikind, the local assemblyman for Borough Park and an Orthodox, though not Hasidic, Jew, received a backlash similar to Clapman's on a radio show he hosts that for several years has highlighted the issue of sexual abuse by people in the Orthodox community. He believes that several dozen victims have shown up at his office as a result of the show, but wonders about how many

---

[*] Author's interview with Ruchama Clapman.

are still afraid to come forward because of community pressure.

"People were upset at me," he said. "People were furious. They would say: 'You're embarrassing us. We're dealing with it ourselves.' They were not dealing with it."

But they have been more willing to alert the authorities when crimes are committed by Hasidim or Orthodox Jews. In a spate of cases between October 2008 and October 2009 alone, Brooklyn prosecutors arrested 26 ultra-Orthodox men—rabbis, teachers and camp counselors among them. Others have provided names of abusers to Jewish news media. By 2012, the numbers surpassed 100. In March 2012, the Satmar leaders issued what many said was an unprecedented edict urging Hasidim to stay away from a community member who, the edict said, was molesting young men and was "an injurious person" and "a great danger to your community." The police were not called in but the sign alone was evidence of a shift in attitudes. Thus a comment from Clapman indicating that Hasidic abusers may be influenced by the louche atmosphere of the surrounding culture can also be read paradoxically.

"We have problems that the outside world may have," Clapman told me, "and the outside world is seeping in."

In December 2012, after a trial in which both he and his accuser testified, a State Supreme Court jury convicted Nechemya Weberman, the unlicensed therapist, then 54, of repeatedly sexually abusing the young girl who sought his counseling. The abuse started when she was twelve, and the girl had accused Weberman of groping her, forcing her to perform oral sex and insisting she replicate the actions in pornographic videos.

"The veil of secrecy has been lifted," District Attorney Hynes declared after the verdict. "As far as I'm concerned, it is very clear to me that it is only going to get better for people who are victimized in these various communities."

The case drew more newspaper and television attention than perhaps any other abuse case involving Hasidim. However, it was the first time that Hynes' office had won a sexual abuse conviction of a prominent Satmar. On January 22, 2013, a judge sentenced Weberman to 103 years in prison for his abuse of the girl. In the statement she gave in court before the sentence was delivered, the girl, by now an 18-year-old married college student, told the court of how "she would cry until the tears ran dry" and look in the mirror and see "a girl who didn't want to live in her own skin."

"You played around with and destroyed lives as if they were your toys, without the slightest bit of mercy," she told a stone-faced Weberman.

But now that he has been convicted and was bound for jail, she said, she can look at herself and see a person "who finally stood up and spoke out" on behalf of herself and "the other silent victims."*

Hasidim now are more willing to seek out psychological help for their troubled members, willing to bare their inner-

* Sharon Otterman, "Therapist Sentenced to 103 Years for Child Sexual Abuse," *New York Times*, January 22, 2013, p. A17.

most problems to secular Jewish and gentile psychologists and psychiatrists. A Manhattan psychiatrist told me how she was called in to treat a case of postpartum depression and soon had a roster of such cases.

"A lot of times men would come in with their wives," she said. "That was interesting because the women had to get permission from the rabbi to go on birth control. The rabbis didn't want them to get pregnant while they're depressed and wanted the women to get better before they have a baby.

"One Satmar woman who came to me three years ago had had a fifth child and was psychotic. She couldn't get out of bed. Her job was to take care of kids, get them to school, clean up and make their dinner. She was a perfectionist and when she couldn't keep up the perfectionism she fell apart. She couldn't do anything. They had to farm the kids out to relatives. But she asked the rabbi if she could have another baby on an antidepressant and the rabbi said yes, and she was fine afterwards. This was a person who had a sister who died. But you couldn't get very psychological. They are not about unconscious motivation. They are much more about getting things fixed and getting things done and not wanting to probe deeply. She was terrified of her own mind. When she realized her mind could do fine on medication, she felt safer and safer and even if it ever happened again she could be okay." (Research shows that many types of antidepressants are generally considered safe during pregnancy.)

The psychiatrist, who spoke to me if I guaranteed her anonymity because the publication of her name might reveal her patients' identities, encountered many of the sexual idiosyncrasies of the Hasidic community. Married women are allowed to fantasize about sex with other men because Hasidim believe it is harder for women to get aroused. But men, oddly enough, are forbidden to fantasize about other women because this might lead to an unwanted "spilling of the seed." Yet more than a few Hasidic men, she told me, go to gentile prostitutes in the belief—one that many rabbis scorn—that sex outside marriage with a gentile woman is not a sin. Several Hasidic women she has seen over the years came because they were not sexually attracted to their husbands yet had to perform frequently. Some developed various anxiety disorders after ritual bathing in the *mikveh* because they felt they were obligated to have sex.

Hovering over every sexual problem is a deep-seated fear of the whiff of scandal, and not necessarily because scandal will lead to shame. That fear is amorphous. Rather it is fear that it may be difficult to marry off the children of a tainted family. The psychiatrist told me of two cases where that issue arose. The first was of a mother she was treating for depression who asked the psychiatrist to treat her daughter as well. The daughter, she told the psychiatrist, often made her way to downtown Manhattan in short skirts and told the family she no longer wanted to be Orthodox.

"Her brothers were telling her, 'If you're caught your sister won't get married.'"

The second case was of a Hasidic woman brought in by her husband for postpartum depression. The psychiatrist found her to be virtually psychotic, paranoid about how badly she was neglecting her newborn and mouthing bizarre expressions.

The woman was hospitalized. Still, her rabbi called the psychiatrist wanting to know if the woman was crazy. The motive was not out of compassion for the woman but fear that exposure would impede future marital matches for the children.

"The family was trying to cover up the psychotic nature of the problem," the psychiatrist told me. "There's lot of covering up. A number of patients say to me, 'Is your waiting room public?' The idea they would be seen is terrifying. They wanted to hide. Any disability had to be hidden."

11

REBELS WITH A CAUSE

Call him Shtreimel. That is what he styled himself on the Web, using the Yiddish word for the round fur hat that Hasidim wear on the Sabbath, when he operated an inflammatory blog called "A Hasid and a Heretic," and before he used other pseudonyms for other blogs. But almost everyone who knows him thinks of him as just another bearded Brooklyn Hasid, a mid-thirtyish man with a growing family that he supports by working as a businessman. The blogs are his deep dark secret, his confessionals, his not-so-private diaries. There he can admit to the whole world—or as much of it as tunes in—that, as the subtitle of the Shtreimel blog says, he is "a conflicted soul torn between two worlds, the world of Hasidim and the world of reason. It is two different worlds yet I'm in both of them at the same time, acting like a Hasid but thinking like a Heretic."

On these blogs, Shtreimel not only reveals some of the hypocrisies he observes in his corner of the Hasidic world, like the willingness to beat up adherents of a rival sect; he also confides his grave doubts about keeping kosher, observing the Sabbath, believing the reality of the stories in the Old Testament. For years, he has occasionally grabbed a hamburger at a McDonald's, watched a Yankee ball game on television on the Sabbath and snatched a snack on Yom Kippur when he should be fasting. Yet he remains in the fold, letting only his wife know that he is the blogger who calls himself Shtreimel. (His wife is not happy about his decision but has agreed to keep the matter to herself.)

One of his early blogs in 2004 should give outsiders a sense of how subversive his messages can be to the Hasidic self-image:

A couple of years back, during the summer I went out with my friends one night. We went to the water on the west side of Manhattan to relax and possibly have some fun. We met there a few college girls who had a shared apartment not far from there. They intrigued us as much as we intrigued them. For them it was our exoticness that made them sit with us and talk for hours, and for us it was the simple presence of their feminine being. For one of my friends it was the first time he engaged in talk with a female companion. I saw that he was enjoying the idea of him doing something wrong more than he enjoyed the conversation, I was happy for him. Soon enough he felt that he had the courage to ask her if he can touch her breasts, while making the motion with his hand as if he was ready to actually act on his idea. She slapped him on his face, his glasses went flying and so did his newfound ego. It was the first and so far the only time I've seen a woman slap a boy for being stupid just like you see in the movies. It was novel, but it was my friend we were dealing here, plus I felt as if we have to save the awkward situation. So one guy took her aside and tried explaining to her that it was his upbringing and lack of common knowledge that made him act out like that, while I tried convincing him to apologize. He was too stubborn to apologize and she wasn't willing to forgive without it. The next night I came back with just one of my friends, and from that night on I got hooked onto the city. As a young teenager I knew that on the outside—the non-Orthodox world— every woman is promiscuous. It was a sad fact known to us young boys who on one hand longed to join the undiscriminating young ladies out there, but on the other hand we took pride in our puritanical way of life. Sometimes the pleasure of feeling purer and better of ones way of life is stronger then sexual or otherwise earthy pleasures. It wasn't only me of course, it is something shared by Chasidim in general, that is until one reaches maturity and/or sees a little bit outside of his confined ghetto. It's a combination of the education one gets in *Cheder* or Yeshiva combined with the fact that boys don't mingle with girls from a very young age. The schools are all proudly segregated, at the age of nine-ten it becomes unaccepted to play with girls even in the shared backyard or while roaming the streets after school. After the bar-mitzvah it becomes the norm to not even greet anybody of the opposite sex. Not even first cousins. Some would see the beauty in it.

There's certainly something to a society in which the youngsters aren't occupied the whole day whistling to passing girls or starting up with them. There's something nice in a community where you'll find no open gays or registered sex offenders. However, quite something else is really happening behind the scenes and any Chasid could testify to this. Boys who don't see a girl since the age of 10 become involved in anything sexual that they could lay their hands on, in a yeshiva that means that a lot of the boys are homosexuals. Of course it is only the boys who would otherwise be the ones who run after the girls, the good boys don't do this either, but the gay experience stays on forever in some kids. I've been to a few yeshivas in three continents it's a universal problem. Don't get me wrong I've nothing against gays, I truly think that if they want to get married so be it. My own sexual preferences or one's religious preferences should not be imposed on anybody. But, it's funny for a religious community to instigate homosexuality. The other problem is even a bigger case. We don't talk about sex we don't teach them in school and therefore some perverts have pretty easy access to our young ones. If there's no knowledge of what is right and what is wrong how can you watch out for those old perverts lurking in the *mikveh* or wherever? The pervert himself has no problem either, since in ninety-nine percent of the cases the issue will be closed within the community without involving the authorities thus the violator has no fear of the law. This is where the idea that the other gender is for sex and sex only comes from. It is hard for one to

grasp that a female is anything other then a sexual object.
It takes time and knowledge which my friend didn't have at
that time and neither did I at one point.*

When Shtreimel and I first met in a Starbucks on the
Upper West Side—a true Hasid would never drink its not-
strictly-kosher coffee since the milk was not *cholov Yisroel*, milk
produced under the supervision of an observant Jew—he told
me his actual name, but asked me not to use it nor to identify
his Hasidic sect or the specific neighborhood he lives in. Yet it
was clear he was an active Hasid by the way he looked. He had
a stereotypical Jewish *punim*—pale face and dark eyes—and
he wore the Hasidic summer uniform of a tieless white shirt,
dark woolen pants, *tzitzit* fringes dangling over his belt and a
black yarmulke that did not conceal the sidecurls he tucked
behind his ears. He proceeded to unspool for me his life story,
how he grew up in a Hasidic home with a dozen siblings, studied at Hasidic yeshivas in Brooklyn and Israel, including two
years of advanced post–high school *kollel*, and, still in his teenage years, married a young woman about his age with whom
he had spent less than three hours getting acquainted. He told
me about the four children he and his wife had raised so far
in standard Hasidic fashion. He told me about how gnawing
doubts mutated into a desire to communicate with the rest of
the world through a blog.

I took many of his views as the eruptions of a jaundiced
single soul, and did not give everything he said full credence.

---

* Shtreimel, "Sexual Promiscuity."

After all, only a tiny minority—probably less than 2 percent—of Hasidim actually break away and reestablish themselves in the wider world as secular Jews. These rebels, of course, have achieved prominence by writing books published to considerable attention, like Deborah Feldman's 2012 memoir, *Unorthodox: The Scandalous Rejection of My Hasidic Roots*. But the quantity of such works must be balanced against the inalterable fact that true Hasidim do not write books for the secular world to read. Nevertheless, Shtreimel gave me a cautious perspective on Hasidic life that may spur a bit of skepticism about the storied cohesiveness of Hasidic ranks and is certainly worth some reflection.

He offered me a rather sensible explanation of how, after a conventional Hasidic upbringing, he was casually seduced into the sometimes risqué netherworld of the Internet. It started with radio, he said. In the Hasidic world, radio, television and secular newspapers are discouraged by communal pressures; indeed, some yeshivas, Shtreimel told me, will kick students out if they discover they are watching television. But many Hasidic men have cars and long ago began listening to the dashboard radio for traffic reports. Traffic reports escalated to talk radio. "A lot of Hasidim are hooked on talk radio," Shtreimel told me. In a similar fashion, Hasidim who started using computers and exploiting the Internet for their accounting, real estate businesses or other work soon gravitated to other Internet functions. Shtreimel told me his wife has an email address, shops online for clothing and often checks the weather websites, something that more rigid Hasidim might frown on. And Shtreimel found himself surfing widely on the

Web, exploring many sites he knew to be forbidden because of their philosophical and deeply secular content.

"It gave me a glimpse of a different world," he told me.

Around 2004 Shtreimel found himself reading blogs by other Jews who confided their own misgivings. One was titled "Hasidic Rebel: Off the Cuff Musings of a Hasid Gone Astray," and Shtreimel started posting responses to those musings. By 2004, he used an AOL account at work to set up his own blog. The blog is flawed by grammatical and spelling errors, and infelicities of language, flaws for which Shtreimel is more angry than defensive. "I stopped learning English when I was twelve years old," he protested. It was a backhanded condemnation of the Hasidic yeshivas, which, it must be said, teach only the most basic English and math and stop even doing that early in high school. Still, Shtreimel has hundreds of followers—1,200 to 1,300 read his blog every week by his count—and dozens of them write comments, including, he said, several rabbis. But what makes him different than many Hasidic bloggers is that he remains an active Hasid, down to the uniform of sorts, letting the community think he is a faithful follower.

"I don't believe in nothing—why then don't I leave," he told me. "I've got a wife and kids. It's a paradox. When I realized my doubts I had two kids, I waited and stayed and then I had three kids, and then I had a fourth kid. The more kids you have the harder it is to get out."

But he does believe in the power of the Internet and it seems he is on a mission, a halfhearted one perhaps, but a purposeful one, or so he says.

"People can get connected to each other and once ideas that are not yet implanted by the establishment spread they can explode. Life as they know it is not going to be the same. Once you get someone into thinking, a large percentage of them are going to leave or start to doubt. I've also discovered I enjoy it. When I get a comment from a person and he says he likes what I wrote, that's good."

The Internet permits this kind of secret communication because when he is online with the door closed, no one knows what he is doing. Before he confessed to her, his wife would open the door, see him at his computer and figure he was just surfing the Web for business. Privacy is one of the glories of the Web.

"Buying a book at a bookstore is much harder," he told me. "If you are on the street, people will see you. You bring it home, your wife will see it and the kids will see it."

Many Hasidim, he speculates, are exploiting the Internet in even more illicit ways.

"Guys find girls," he said of Hasidic men. "Married guys meet married women, which they have no way doing in real life. If she emails me she's not the good person she claims to be. Every guy wants sex and every woman wants friendship, just like in the real world. We're real people. I have friends who while their wives are in the country are in chat rooms twenty-four hours. Some use it to hook up socially."*

When we first met in 2005, Shtreimel took a wicked enjoyment in knowing that people in the Hasidic community

---

* Author's interview with Shtreimel.

did not know his secret, that he was writing underground and inflammatory blogs as Shtreimel. His first smile during that conversation, a guilty bemused one perhaps, came when he told me about an incident that had him gulping nervously.

"I was once with my wife," he recalled, "and this Hasidic guy started talking to me about this blog he just found out about. He said it was called 'Shtreimel.'"

But when we spoke more recently—in the summer of 2012—more people had learned of his blogging and within his family, relatives, even if they did not know of his blog, knew he was less than passionate about Hasidic practices. "I'm the black sheep," he told me. "It's pretty easy to know who is very much into it and who is lapsed. I don't know if other people know about me, but people have an inkling of where I stand and what I believe. It doesn't reflect well on the family."

Nevertheless, he has made a firm decision to stay within the community "and make the most of it." "Some people do know my beliefs and lack thereof," he said. "But there is no need for me to leave. I will live out the rest of my life living like this." The reason, he said, is that people his own age and younger are "much more open-minded. They do not agree with what I think but they are accepting." Indeed, a younger generation, shaped by its contact with Twitter and texting, is more questioning and less submissive, he believes. "They just don't care enough to start a revolution," he said. That is why, he said, the rabbinical leadership of Hasidic sects has been issuing edicts against wanton use of the Internet. Those pro-

nouncements reflect a rising panic that the entire Hasidic ed-
ifice could crumble if such exposure continues.

Shtreimel exaggerates the scope of the rebellion in the
Hasidic world, but there is no doubt there is one, however
budding and inchoate. Indeed, with the Jewish zeal for organization, there have arisen in the last decade at least two
associations of defectors, one called Footsteps, which caters
to disenchanted ultra-Orthodox Jews, and the other Chulent,
which hosts a more eclectic mix of Jews, including modern
Orthodox and secular skeptics.

Footsteps, the more prominent and established of the two, is
about a decade old and claims to have served 800 Hasidim and
other *Haredim* since it was founded—men and women who had
enough doubts about their culture that they chose to attend a
meeting that could jeopardize their communal esteem. Still, the
ranks of active members, acknowledges Lani Santo, the organization's executive director, total about two hundred and fifty,
about 20 percent of whom are current or former Lubavitchers,
Hasidim who as a matter of philosophy insist on mingling with
the secular Jewish world, and 30 percent are from the non-
Hasidic but ultra-Orthodox *Yeshivish* crowd. Obviously two
hundred and fifty is a tiny sliver of a faith universe with several
hundred thousand adherents, but the number is worth noting
because it does give Hasidic leaders some pause.

Footsteps was founded in 2003 by Malkie Schwartz, a
Lubavitch woman from Crown Heights, Brooklyn, who had
left the sect three years before while still a teenager to live
with a secular grandmother. That grandmother encouraged

her to enroll in Hunter College, where she met other defectors from ultra-Orthodox communities, many of whom were too ashamed to admit they had left. It dawned on her that these disenchanted souls could help one another. and Footsteps was off the ground. (Schwartz has since left the organization for a legal career with a southern Jewish organization.)

Footsteps has drop-in sessions three times a week at a center in lower Manhattan. In what are called "peer-support groups" shepherded by trained social workers, regulars and newcomers sit around and talk about their unhappiness with the Hasidic way of life, their fears about breaking away, the challenges they might face if they were to do so—like finding suitable jobs without a college degree or simply getting along in less than polished English. Footsteps seems to lessen the isolation many members feel within their Hasidic circles, where they are afraid to express any misgivings, worried they might be shunned if they do or be unable to marry or, if they are older parents, marry off their children. Both through these sessions and individual counseling, Footsteps tries to help its members work on the not surprising issues that doubting stirs, like advising those who need to tell a spouse of their skepticism but can't find the right words. About 30 percent of those who come to Footsteps are unhappily married, Santo said. Perhaps 10 to 15 percent are couples and 30 percent are parents. "But the majority are singles who haven't gotten married or are about to be married and haven't believed in the system and are about to complicate the life of another person," she told me.

Footsteps offers them all a number of programs, including scholarships ranging from $500 to $5,500 to finance their studies in secular colleges. It has been able to dispense more than $200,000 in scholarships since its inception because it is supported financially by liberal Jewish foundations, mainstream organizations like UJA Federation, and very heavily by a Wall Street executive and iconoclast, Steve Eisman, who grew up as a modern Orthodox Jew. Footsteps also offers GED classes and even lessons in basketball to work on a sport most Hasidim never quite grasp. Santo says that the organization scrupulously avoids urging the disenchanted ultra-Orthodox young men and women who visit to leave their sects.

"What we stand for is the individual freedom to choose," she told me. "We take a nonjudgmental approach although we do believe in the individual's freedom of choice, including that of a person who will end up standing in opposition to a community which says it's not about individuals. It's about a collective and a community. The Hasidic system works for many but it doesn't work for everyone, and those for whom it doesn't work should have a space and support."

Santo, who is in her early thirties, grew up in a *Haredi* but non-Hasidic community in Kew Gardens, Queens, and studied at the Yeshiva of Central Queens. She frankly volunteers that a major turning point for her was when her mother came out as a gay woman, confronting the restrictive conformity in her community. As her daughter, Santo too found that "I couldn't become my authentic self."

She told me that some of those who go through the Footsteps programs forsake Jewish observance altogether; others choose some less encompassing identity; the Jewish polity, after all, is made up of a motley spectrum that ranges across Reconstructionist, Reform, Conservative, modern Orthodox, ultra Orthodox, New Age renewal, humanistic, unaffiliated, entirely secular, and even identification with a different religion like Buddhism. But for someone who has grown up Hasidic, any lifestyle less rigorous will set off conflict and bitterness with family members and friends, so even deciding to keep a yarmulke but shave off a beard and sidelocks can throw down a provocative gauntlet—become a family casus belli.

So it is not surprising that, Santo said, about one of every four visitors to Footsteps ultimately decides to remain within the Hasidic fold, either reconciling themselves by squelching their doubts, or concealing them like Shtreimel and baldly living a duplicitous life—a choice that has revived the term *marranos*, originally used for the hidden Jews created by the Spanish Inquisition. Another 25 percent are, she said, "in the process of making a plan on how to leave and want help in thinking through the consequences."

"We tell them to slow down, not make an extreme break; otherwise they'll put themselves in real danger," she said. "They don't have a sustainable way of making a living and need to build up a plan for self-sufficiency. Sadly, if someone is married, there is usually a separation or divorce process going on."

The Hasidic community has had to face up to these defections and so far the two approaches they have taken are to tighten restrictions on the use of the Internet and offer more counseling and therapy to doubters. Many if not most defectors are ostracized or at best continue a private relationship with their families. Even the ostracism has its shadings. In 2012, I was surprised to see rebels—teenagers or young twentysomethings—passing out leaflets for candidates in a primary election in Brooklyn in which two factions of Satmar were fighting for rival candidates for Democratic district leader. Faithful young men were not allowed to pass out leaflets, for some obscure reason I never understood. But since some of the young rebels remain close to their Hasidic families, the political strategist for each faction felt it would make sense to hire them rather than strangers and pay them each $320 a day for the work.

Still, the price of leaving the Hasidic world can be colossal, and it becomes palpable to me when I talk to Shulem Deen. A self-taught computer whiz who is in his late thirties, Deen commands a blog of disillusion titled "Unpious" in which he uses the pen name "Hasidic Rebel," though he publicly outed himself around 2011. In the early 1990s, he was a full-fledged Hasid living with a wife and children in the exclusively Hasidic village of New Square. What happened to transform him is complicated, but in brief he began wrestling with philosophical and existential questions he could no longer shrug off.

"I had been searching, speaking to rabbis and trusted friends about issues on my mind about religion and the life-style," he told me. "Then slowly it came spiritually to me that the underlying principles of the life I was leading were just not reality."

One time, he found himself chatting with a Skverer friend about a mutual acquaintance who had renounced Orthodox Judaism as irrational, and the friend said: "Doesn't that *tipish* [dummy] know that the Rambam [Maimonides] has already answered all the questions." The idea that a medieval scholar had addressed all possible challenges seemed silly to Deen. So did his friend's argument that there is proof that God revealed himself to the Jewish people at Mount Sinai.

"I became furious but originally resisted," he told me. "I was too tempted by the idea that someone can prove things that are inherently unprovable, so I said, 'Let me hear it.'"

He found the friend's argument "ultimately inadequate," and it only led to more questions and more questioning. Soon he performed his first seditious act—he filled out a library card and began taking out books on biblical archeology. These, he said, made him realize in salient fashion that the biblical narrative that he had taken for granted as literally true could not be proven. There was no evidence to back up the famous miracles, and the archeological evidence even seemed to contradict the more mundane biblical stories, like the chronicle of the Israelites' conquest of Canaan.

"It started becoming more and more ludicrous. And I fell apart. I began to realize I did not want to live in a world I so fundamentally disagreed with. It was something I could not do."

His wife witnessed Deen's transformation and was not happy. She was upset at the books and newspapers he was reading. "If I did read the *New York Times* she didn't want me to bring it home where the children might see it," he told me.

"I tried to be respectful, but she would discover charges at a nonkosher restaurant on my credit card. On the Sabbath I would switch off the light in my study so nobody would see me checking my email, but she discovered me and asked me, 'How can you violate the Sabbath?'"

In the aftermath of their Jewish divorce, Deen came to realize he and his wife had been "extremely incompatible." "I care very deeply for her, but it's hard to say I loved her. It was the kind of love you have for someone you are very close to for a long time." So now he lives an irreverent life out of an apartment in hipster Brooklyn, eating and doing what he wants, when he wants, no matter the day of the week. He may go to synagogue on Yom Kippur for what he describes as "cultural reasons" but he does not fast. He is working on his blog and on a memoir of his Hasidic rebellion that will join what is fast becoming a genre, and a popular one at that. Feldman's memoir, *Unorthodox*, about her departure from the Satmar sect, made *The Times* bestseller list despite criticism of its accuracy and truthfulness and the fiction-like compression of characters.

Deen's wife and children have remained firmly in the Skverer sect and are bound by its code, both written and unwritten. So his defection has made his ties with his family quite awkward. After the arrangements were finalized in family court in 2008, his children, then ages six to 14, "grew withdrawn in my presence, eating dinner in silence and refusing the books and games I bought them." On their visits to his home, they inspected the labels on his foods to make sure they were kosher and ate everything reluctantly.

"Mommy says you want to turn us into *goyim*," he said a son told him.

By the time we spoke again in 2013, he had not seen his three oldest daughters for five years. For a time, he would pick up his two boys in New Square and they would dine at a kosher restaurant or, if the weather was nice, spend the day in a park. But after his bar mitzvah, the oldest of those boys did not want to see him any longer. His youngest son—now 11—sees him grudgingly.*

For the estrangement, he blames his wife and the pressures from the sect. His efforts to ameliorate the distance through the courts have so far not borne fruit.

"Occasionally," he told me, "I have some doubts about whether I did the right thing by leaving, whether I wasn't putting my own interests ahead of those of the people I care about. My children have been seriously affected by my leaving in ways that I had not anticipated, but it was my hope that my wife and I would be able to protect them. She chose not to have contact."

Still, he says, perhaps contradicting himself but ever the rebel, "I have not the slightest regret."

Once someone leaves a sect, he or she becomes a pariah, virtually disowned by parents, siblings, even children. There are stories of teenage rebels sleeping in the streets of Borough Park, of families conspiring with the large Hasidic commu-

---

* Author's interview with Shulem Deen.

nity to keep children away from a wayward parent. And sometimes this ostracism can turn deadly.

On September 27, 2013, a formerly Hasidic woman was found lifeless on the floor of her New Jersey bedroom, propped up in a sitting position against her bed. Underneath her body lay a half-drunk bottle of vodka and a Ziploc bag with an assortment of the pills that apparently killed her. Nearby were photographs of her three increasingly estranged children, ages 10, 11 and 13.

The body was that of Deb Tambor, a 33-year-old dark-haired and round-faced woman with a radiant dimpled smile. She was the daughter of a prominent Skver family; her father was the principal of an elementary boys' yeshiva in Monsey. She was one of 16 children but she was the outlier. She had left the Skver fold and was living with Abe Weiss, another former Skverer Hasid and the man who found her body, in their home in Bridgeton, New Jersey, an hour south of Philadelphia near Delaware Bay. She was no longer keeping kosher, no longer observing Sabbath, had become an avid Yankees fan—certainly an aberration for a Hasidic woman or man.

Although she left no note, telling entries in a diary she was keeping and that Weiss found made clear her death was a suicide.

"I'm done living. I can't take the pain," said one entry two weeks before her death. "People say give it a shot. But it's not working. I'm done."

What had driven Tambor to this point? The immediate cause seemed apparent to her friends outside Skver. Tambor had lost custody of her three children after an earlier suicide attempt four years before, when she was still a Skver member in good standing. In the aftermath, her husband, Moshe Dirnfeld, got her to agree to a divorce and obtained legal custody of the children in Rockland Family Court. By the summer of 2013 she was restricted to seeing them twice a month at her sister's home in Monsey—a two-and-half-hour drive away—with her sister there. The Tambor family and the Skver community had collaborated in minimizing contact with an apostate mother who might become a subversive influence on the children, her friends told me.* New Square, after all, is an enclave of 7,000 residents, all Hasidim who venerate a rebbe whose lineage goes back to the Ukrainian village of Skver, and it was established as a New York State village in 1961 to maintain its insularity. It is a place of mores mainstream Jews might find stringent, a place where, for example, men and women by their own consent walk on opposite sides of the street to avoid mingling. Tambor's renegade status would have made it difficult for her to maintain friendships and family relations even had she continued living there, and that was certainly true after she left. And so the community would have sought to keep the children within the fold, even if that meant alienating the children from their mother.

That alienation had begun emerging with heartbreaking clarity. Her oldest son was barely speaking to her, answering her questions about how he was doing with a resentful yes

---

* Joseph Berger, "Outcast Mother's Death, and Questions about Jewish Sect's Sway over Children," *New York Times*, November 22, 2013, p. A23.

or no. All three children called their stepmother "Mama" in Yiddish and they sometimes called Tambor by her first name, Devorah. She felt humiliated.

"Do you know how it hurts to hear your kid say they don't want to see you?" Ms. Tambor wrote on Facebook.

The final straw, as Weiss called it, came when the oldest daughter, Chaya, lied about her graduation date so her mother would not be there to watch her receive her diploma. When Tambor found out and showed up anyway, Chaya refused to take a bouquet of flowers from her. That was the proximate cause of the hopeless diary entry.[*]

But there was a deeper cause as well, according to Weiss and Tambor's friends. For years, they told me, Tambor had been sexually abused by a relative in her extended family as a teenager and married mother of three, when, at her family's insistence, she went to work for him as a typesetter of advertisements. It was the failure of her family and rabbis to address her complaints about the abuse that, Weiss told me, drove her to her first suicide attempt and led to her hospitalization for several months at Rockland Psychiatric Center, a state hospital for the seriously disturbed. Her husband, Weiss said, refused to believe her. She even asked for an audience with the sect's rebbe, Rabbi David Twersky, and told him of the abuse, making clear that she wanted to move out of New Square but not leave the Skver sect. The Rebbe, Weiss said, urged her only to leave the job but did nothing to discipline the relative and asked her not to repeat the story of the abuse.

---

[*] Author's interview with Abe Weiss.

"The Skverer Rebbe has blood on his hands," Weiss told me, his comment perhaps reflecting his anger rather than his belief in the Rebbe's actual culpability.*

Weiss could not elaborate on the degree of the abuse and whether, as he put it, there was penetration involved. "But every time he came around she jumped," Weiss said. Then why didn't she quit working for the man? I asked Weiss. He suggested that the question was naïve, betraying a lack of understanding of Hasidic mores.

"A woman should make a decision who to work for and who not to work for?" Weiss replied, incredulous at my asking. "That's not a woman's decision."

While she was at the hospital, Tambor learned that Dirnfeld had won custody of the children. A onetime roommate who spoke confidentially told me she was deceived into signing the divorce papers. Weiss suggested that Dirnfeld chose the hospitalization period for the divorce because "if she takes it hard, she still is in a safe place."

Of course, the Tambor and Dirnfeld families have different perspectives on the events. No one from the family would speak to me but Yeedle Melber, a first cousin of Dirnfeld who had spoken to close family members, said Tambor began to have mental problems several years before after she was struck by a car at a bus stop. Her erratic behavior culminated in the attempt to take her own life and her hospitalization for five months at Rockland Psychiatric.

"She became unbalanced," Melber, who is also Hasidic,

---

* Author's interview with Abe Weiss.

told me. "Her husband tried everything in his power to hold things together. She started going in a bad direction. He realized she wasn't capable of normal relationships at all. There was a feeling the kids are not safe with her because of mental issues."*

Weiss, though, laughed off the possibility that the car accident Melber mentioned was the cause of her psychological problems. She injured her leg, not her head, he told me with the vocal equivalent of a Talmudic raised thumb for emphasis.

"It's all part of the cover-up of sexual abuse," he said.

Weiss, who is thirty-eight and manages a Monro muffler repair shop in Bridgeton, met Tambor on Facebook about eight months before her suicide. She was recommended as a friend, and when it turned out they had 42 mutual friends, he realized she too must be a former Hasid. They were soon living together, though he cautioned me that she only let him in on "bits and pieces" of her story, finding the details too painful.

"She was a beautiful woman with a heart of gold and we really loved each other," he said.

Weiss and friends of Tambor said that whatever psychological issues she had were exacerbated by the way people in New Square circled the wagons to deny her full access to her children. After she left the hospital and moved out of New Square, she was permitted one visitation a month with her children at an Orthodox therapist's office, a visit that cost her $150 each time. She was not permitted to take the children out of New Square, and sometimes the infrequent visits

---

* Author's interview with Yeedle Melber.

were canceled because the children had to attend a bar mitz-vah or wedding. Only later did the visits increase to twice a month.

Weiss blames the Skver community for pressuring the family court judges making the decisions to limit Tambor's visitations. But an official in the state's court system familiar with the case said that the entire custody decision was based on Tambor's mercurial behavior and the fact that she had made a previous suicide attempt.

"She had mental problems," this official said. "The fact that she tragically took her own life is the clearest indication that what the experts said about her psychiatric problem was right."

Yet if Shulem Deen's experience offers a precedent, Weiss may also be right about the impact of the estrangement from her children. Tambor was a casual and Facebook friend of Deen—the community of Hasidic exiles stays in touch for support—and he wrote a moving article about Tambor's death for *Tablet*, a Jewish affairs online magazine. Deen, whose writ-ing reflected how well he has educated himself since leaving Skver, said that when he faced his similar custody ordeal he was unaware that in Rockland County—where Jews are one-third of the population and *Haredim* the majority of Jews—"custody battles required rabbis, community leaders and Orthodox family therapists on your side."

"I was unaware that that family courts were also part of the local political machinery and that elections and constit-uencies were never far from a judge's mind," he wrote. "I was unaware that my relatively meager resources were no match for a powerfully resourceful community with an ideological stake in he future of my children. Most of all, I was naïve about the powers of religious extremism to control the minds of children themselves."

When we spoke about Tambor afterward, Deen added this point: "It's clear it's not just two spouses battling each other. The community has a stake. They don't want Shulem Deen's children to be in touch regularly with Shulem Deen. They see it as problematic. Uniformity of behavior and out-look and worldview is so important that they think the child is damaged if he sees two competing worldviews. They think the child will have a breakdown."*

Hasidim, of course recognize that it is important for a child to know a mother or father, but Deen told me they think they can remedy the absence "by getting the religious spouse to remarry. They keep the nonreligious spouse out and con-tain the problem." It is not the divorce that creates a stigma; Deen's ex-wife, who remarried, was welcomed back into the fold. It is the abandonment of Orthodoxy and the Hasidic way of life.

By the time Tambor met Weiss, she was living in New City, not far from New Square, had obtained a driver's li-cense (a no-no for Skver women), was supporting herself through Social Security payments for the disabled—in her case the disability being the mental issues that had gotten her hospitalized—and was taking courses at Rockland Commu-nity College. When she would visit her children at her sister's

---

* Author's interview with Shulem Deen.

home, she would dress as modestly as she could by Monsey standards, wearing a long-sleeved shirt and a net over her hair. But her children's coldness anguished her.

"That was what killed her," Weiss said.

One of the photographs found alongside her body, one that she had been gazing at before she succumbed to the pills, was of Chaya's graduation two weeks before. That was the event that Chaya had tried to conceal from her and where she would not accept her mother's gift of flowers.

12

A MODERN MENSCH

The place took his breath away.

Mendel Werdyger was six or seven years old when his broad-bearded father, a synagogue cantor, brought him along to a recording studio in midtown Manhattan. His father was there to make a recording of songs favored by a grand rabbi famed for the original melodies he spun for *Shabbos* and holiday prayers. This was 1963 or thereabouts, so the sound waves were being etched into the grooves of a 33 rpm long-playing vinyl disc. Still, there was Mendel's father, Duvid Werdyger, a survivor of the Schindler's List slave laborers and several concentration camps, standing in front of the Jackie Goldstein Choir belting out a new version of the traditional Sabbath morning prayer, "*Yismechu B'Malchusechah, Shomrei Shabbos*" ("Those who keep Shabbos delight in your realm"), in his lyric tenor. Mendel was dazzled by his father's virtuosity and by the stately choir. But just as mesmerizing was the studio itself, outfitted with the kind of electronic hardware he had never seen before.

"It was like Alice in Wonderland," Werdyger, a tall and broad-shouldered 53-year-old father of six, told me. "You saw all the big machines and a lot of lights and tubes. They still had tubes then! And there was this huge room with a mike and a big stand. The mike stand alone cost fifteen hundred dollars. Today it goes for a hundred dollars. They recorded the whole song on a mono track, the choir and cantor, all in one room, on one track. No stereo. No nothing."

This was a world that was especially novel for young Werdyger because in his Hasidic home—the family allies itself with the Gerer Hasidim—there were few of the electronic devices that in the early 1960s might be found in a typical American home. Like most Hasidic families, their home did not have a single TV set. Young Mendel did not go to Saturday movies the way many American children did—verboten on *Shabbos*—and could not have seen the many movies about Al Jolson or Glenn Miller, or the Kirk Douglas movie *Young Man with a Horn*, that featured entertainers in recording studios. So this visit to a studio provided some splendid new sights for this young boy with *peyes*.

Still, cantorial music—the Jewish Sabbath and holiday liturgy that is sung with individual flourishes by a musically trained prayer leader—was not a novelty for the Werdyger family. Performing as a cantor was partly how Mendel's father put food on the family table. He led the Sabbath and holiday prayers at a widely respected Orthodox synagogue in the East Flatbush section of Brooklyn, Congregation Meir Simcha Hakohen. The synagogue was led by Rabbi Jacob J. Hecht, who was known for both his translations of Menachem Schneerson, the Lubavitcher Rebbe, and for his commentaries on a weekly Jewish radio show on WEVD, *Shema Yisrael*.

And Mendel was not entirely a performing novice. When he was not yet two years old, his father placed a microphone in front of him that was attached to a tape recorder and directed him to sing—not nursery rhymes but chirpy Hebrew liturgical songs that Mendel was already learning, like "Adon Olam," a concluding Sabbath prayer. Within a few years, Mendel, with a tender soprano, was singing in his father's *shul* as part of the 10-person choir that backed up his father on *Shabbos*.

"Every child wants to follow in his father's footsteps," he told me years later.

He remembers the choir leader was not as strictly religious as some because on Yom Kippur he flashed their salary checks in his jacket pocket and told them, "If you don't sing well, you don't get the checks." Observant Jews do not carry money on Yom Kippur, *Shabbos*, or most holidays.

His father had given the same cantorial encouragement to his older brother Mordechai, and Mordechai was to become the Frank Sinatra of the Hasidic world, by some estimations the "King of Jewish Music." Today, Mordechai performs as Mordechai Ben David at concerts and on recordings popular with Orthodox fans. He can be seen on YouTube in elaborate MTV-style videos that blend classic religious hymns and Torah passages with American pop–like tunes played by a full orchestra with trumpets and guitars. He has adapted the music of Cab Calloway, Bobby Vinton, and Andrew Lloyd Webber to cantorial hymns. Like Michael Jackson onstage, he even dances as he sings, almost as spirited if a good deal less flamboyant and acrobatic. Some rabbis in Britain have assailed him for "polluting" the Torah and hurting "the morals of our young people," but he has nevertheless sold more than one million records.

But Mendel has his own cantorial saga—if one that took a every different path. I was drawn to Mendel's story because it offered a striking contrast to the standard impressions people have of Hasidim. They are certainly provincial in their appearance and practices, but unlike, say, the Amish, there are ways in which they venture into the modern world while maintaining their Hasidic traditions. And Mendel's odyssey, so different than Yitta Schwartz's, captured that important adaptive resourcefulness of Hasidic culture without which, arguably, it too might have ossified and begun to lose members and wither. In an insular society that discourages college education, indeed education of any kind in many secular subjects, he taught himself the intricacies of sound engineering. He did so for one simple reason: with Hasidic zeal and single-mindedness, he wanted to record a much finer version of the works of the man considered the greatest cantor of the 20th century, Yossele Rosenblatt, who died before the era of long-play records, let alone digital recordings.

Mendel was a fairly typical Hasidic boy—immersed in the study of Torah and the weekly rhythms ascending toward Sabbath that defined Hasidic life. He too was kept apart from the neighborhood youngsters in denim and sneakers who might tempt him into the everyday mischief that could subvert his family's traditions. Mendel was born in Crown Heights in February 1958, a few blocks from Ebbets Field,

the fabled home of the Brooklyn Dodgers. Indeed, Mendel
has a gossamer memory of glimpsing the vacant stadium just
before it was torn down in 1960 to make way for a housing
complex. Crown Heights in central Brooklyn, a mix of plain-
spoken apartment buildings, limestone row houses and blocks
of grander town houses, had at the time a substantial Orthodox population, including Hasidim, but it was also peopled
by more mainstream working-class Jews, Irish, Italians, Ja-
maicans and other immigrants from the Caribbean. Today,
the Jewish portion is almost entirely made up of members of
the proselytizing Lubavitch Hasidim, but then it was far more
diverse.

Mendel's education was typically Hasidic. He went to the
Gerer yeshiva in Crown Heights, Yeshiva Yagdil Torah, led by
Rabbi Israel Olewski. (The yeshiva eventually moved to Borough Park, joining the gradual exodus of non-Lubavitch Jews
out of the neighborhood as a result of the crime wave of the
1970s; the Lubavitcher Rebbe, however, proclaimed that his
followers must stay and weather any conflicts with their neighbors and he proved prescient in preserving his tribe.) In elementary school, Mendel spent a half day in Hebrew studies and
a half day in secular studies—English, social studies and math.
In his early grades, he studied *Chumash*—the Five Books of
Moses—and general Hebrew but by fifth grade he was already
burrowing into the fevered arguments of the Talmud, starting
with the tractate Baba Metziah and its famous dialectic called
Matzah clí B'Ashpah: What should a person do if he or she finds
a vessel of some sort in a garbage heap? Should he assume it
was discarded or make an effort to return it to the owner? Like

other boys, Mendel translated and debated the Aramaic text in Yiddish, often chanting the words with a singsong and an animated thumb. That was the European style that had easily been transplanted to America. The back-and-forth arguments among the great rabbis kindled a fire in Mendel's brain, sharpened his thinking, whetted his ardor for study.

"Every single *halacha* is usually put through the dishwasher," Mendel says now. "Everybody says maybe it should go this way or go that way until we come out with a clear position. It teaches us how to think. We know how to tackle life's issues—hopefully better than other people."

The Gerer Hasidim to which his father and grandfather belonged like to single themselves out among the crowd of Hasidic dynasties by their stress on the study of Torah. Other sects might accentuate joy in prayer, but the Gerer Rebbes put their emphasis on impassioned learning of Torah and Talmud and the tomes of commentary that followed. The Gerer were spin-offs of the Kotzker Hasidim, whose leader died in 1859. When his successor, Rabbi Yitzchak Meir Alter, moved to the town known in Polish as Gora Kalwarya and in Yiddish as Ger, a town on the Vistula River 15 miles southeast of Warsaw, the sect became known as the Ger court. The most famous Gerer Rebbe, popularly known as Sfas Emes when he died in 1905 at the age of 57, composed commentaries on the Bible and Talmud that are revered as masterpieces by almost all Hasidim. And his successors were also esteemed for their scholarship. In prewar Poland, Mendel's father, Duvid, sang for one of the rebbes, Rabbi Avraham Mordechai Alter.

At the start of World War II, the Gerer numbered 200,000 by some estimates, composing one of Europe's largest Hasidic groupings, but they suffered the same fate as Poland's Jews—almost all perished at the hands of the Germans. In the Gerer case, most wound up first in the misery and hunger of the Warsaw Ghetto, and those who survived were murdered in the extermination camp of Treblinka. Rabbi Alter, however, managed to escape and rebuilt the movement in what was then British Palestine, where 15 years before, while living in Poland, he had established a yeshiva in Jerusalem. Some of his followers chose to settle in New York and created a significant satellite in Borough Park, though today most Gerer Hasidim and the movement's Rebbe, Yaakov Aryeh Alter, live in Israel. The Jerusalem yeshiva is the movement's flagship.

Though he enjoys a quite modest Hasidic life, Mendel has what is know as *yichus*—a prestigious pedigree. However, it is a heritage that is laced with pain and sadness. Duvid, his father, was born in 1919 to a prominent Ger clan that had gained a reputation for musical talent passed from father to son. The family settled in the great Polish cultural center of Cracow shortly after Duvid's birth, and at the age of six Duvid became the soloist in the choir of the Eizik Yeikeles Synagogue. At the age of 12 he was invited by the legendary Ger composer Yankel Talmud to be a soloist in the choir that sang on Rosh Hashanah for the Gerer Rebbe of that era, known as Imrei Emes, and thousands of his followers.

In September 1939, the German army rained bombs down

on Cracow and then occupied the city, looting the Jewish quarter, beating and murdering inhabitants and confiscating their possessions—as Mendel put it to me, "anything that caught their fancy." They immediately set a 6 p.m. curfew for Cracow's 70,000 Jews on pain of summary execution and demanded that Jews wear identifying yellow armbands, hand over all radios and fur coats and limit their own holdings to 500 zlotys. The Germans were aided by Polish peasants, who sadistically enjoyed torturing the very identifiable Hasidic Jews by cutting off their beards and *peyes* or making them grovel.

After a year of terror, Duvid, his parents and an unmarried sister—Yettie, who was a close assistant of Sarah Schenirer, founder of the movement that sought to educate Jewish girls—went to live with an Uncle Elisha. They witnessed or learned of barbaric killings, like the brutal slaying of the hamlet's Jewish leader after he was forced to watch his five sons being executed. So they built a bunker behind their uncle's plumbing and hardware warehouse that ultimately housed 20 people. The only warmth came from the quilts stashed in the bunker, but the occupants entertained themselves with tales of the great Hasidic rabbis.

When a Polish laborer who was providing them with food stopped doing so because he felt the risks were too great, they were forced to return to the ghetto in Cracow. Duvid was pressed into one of the labor battalions that emptied Jewish homes of their furnishings. He managed to survive a nearly fatal bout of typhus. But within the ghetto, Hasidim tried to maintain their way of life at great risk. Duvid saw groups of young "gaunt, hollow-eyed men" men bent over their Talmuds, engrossed in intricate *sugyas*—the argumentation and analysis that follows a rabbi's legal hypothesis—in cellars and attics. As Duvid said in his autobiography, *Songs of Hope*, they were tenaciously clinging to their faith as their own form of resistance.*

Still, there were some Nazi decrees that were virtually impossible to disobey, such as one forcing Jews to shave off their beards. One of the autobiography's most poignant scenes is when Duvid is commanded to shave off his father's white beard. Tears roll down his father's cheeks and his mother weeps at the sight of her husband's naked face.

"I had never seen my parents break down and cry," Duvid writes. "Somehow it was the removal of my father's beard that brought home the full extent of the tragedy that had befallen us."

In Duvid's memoir, he recounted how he was next dispatched to the Płaszów concentration camp, on Cracow's outskirts, where he and other men were looked over by the camp commandant, who was deciding, often arbitrarily, who would live and who would die. Duvid sensed his fate was likely to be a firing squad. But the commandant, Amon Göth, asked him what type of work he did, and he replied:

"I am a professional singer, and I have a trained soprano voice. Would you like to hear something?"

"Sing the song you Jews chant when you bury your dead," Göth ordered.

Werdyger sang the verse heard at all Jewish funerals, *El*

---

* Duvid Werdyger, *Songs of Hope* (New York: CIS, 1993).

Molei Rachamim ("God, Full of Compassion"), and did so with such piercing tenderness that Göth, visibly moved, ordered him back to the camp. Duvid eventually spent time in seven concentration camps, including the notorious Mauthausen, where he lay on a hard wooden bunk, starved and chilled, and vowed one day to write a chronicle of his experience if God spared him.

"Even in the valley of the shadow of death, we maintained our joyous spirit and our unwavering trust in *HaShem*," he wrote in *Songs of Hope*. "The enemy could break our bodies but the strength of our faith made us invincible."

Duvid's name appears on a list compiled by Oskar Schindler, the German industrialist, of Jews whose work was essential for his enamelware and ammunition factory near Cracow, a listing that saved 1,100 from the gas chambers. Duvid worked as an electrician, though he was not particularly skilled. Like other Jews at the factory, Duvid was able to pray every morning in a *minyan*, argued Torah and Talmud and sang *zmiros*—special songs for *Shabbos*. There was none of the wanton killing that took place in Płaszów concentration camp, which was next door, or in the other camps to which Duvid was then transferred.

"He didn't talk about it until recently," Mendel told me. "It was too painful for him. He does tell me that on Passover he did not eat any *chametz* and he managed to keep his *tefillin* with him until shortly before he was liberated. He knew how to hide stuff. He managed to put on those *tefillin* in the concentration camps until the last couple of months. Why they took it away from him he never told me."

In perhaps the memoir's most revealing passage, Duvid explains how he went about absorbing and reconciling his faith to the genocide of Poland's Jews. "He recalled the passage where the Bible describes Aaron's reaction to the death of his two sons: "And Aharon [Aaron] was silent."

"Like Aharon, I would abide by *HaShem*'s infinite wisdom," Duvid wrote. "I, like Aharon, would remain silent."

Two of his brothers and three sisters perished, but after the war Duvid reunited with a brother and sister, and on a journey to his brother's wedding in Russia he met his wife-to-be, Malka Goldinger. They and their first child, Yisrael, came over to the United States in 1950 and settled in Crown Heights. Duvid was clean-shaven for much of the 1950s, when Orthodox Jews still retained anxieties about being identified as Jewish. "The resurgence happened later," Mendel told me.

Duvid went to work in a sweatshop in the Garment Center that made socks; his job, his son Mendel remembers, was to tease out the irregular threads, a job known as "scratching." While doing that for three years or so, he led prayers at a series of synagogues on the Lower East Side and in Brooklyn. A prominent rabbi heard him sing and offered him a hundred dollars to lead the service at his synagogue on Rosh Hashanah. His singing was so sublime that he received an offer of a thousand dollars for the following High Holidays. That was Rabbi Hecht's synagogue, where Moishe Oysher, another great cantor of the 20th century, had sung and where Duvid's American cantorial career was born. Rabbi Hecht, a Lubavitcher rabbi, invited Duvid to sing on his weekly radio program.

"Reb Duvid, there's only one way that you can make it in today's world of popular singers and children's choirs—you've got to make a record," Hecht told Werdyger.

So Duvid in 1959 rented a studio for his first album, *Tefillah L'David*, which was sold through the small but established House of Menorah label on Eldridge Street on the Lower East Side. While playing records on an old needle phonograph to hear other cantors performing the traditional melodies, Duvid realized that there was little music available for Hasidim. There were none of the Gerer *nigunim*, or melodies, he remembered from his childhood in Europe. Duvid started recording albums featuring the music of the Ger dynasty but also other dynasties like Bobov, Skulen, Boyan and Radomsk. He also recorded 30 albums of himself singing. Those early recordings became the germ of the Aderet Music label, which he founded and which today is a major wholesaler and producer of Jewish recordings.

Meanwhile, Duvid's son Mendel was growing and by high school he was sent to the Gerer yeshiva in Tel Aviv, the Yeshivat Chiddushei HaRim, named after the honorific title of the first Gerer Rebbe. For four years, on the narrow jostling streets of the neighborhood, he was surrounded by teeming crowds of Gerer boys and young men, all spending six days a week studying, with scarcely a moment for exercise or sports. Though there were other Hasidic factions around, the Gerer stood out by the nuances of their Hasidic garb. On *Shabbos* they wore their dark pants tucked into their black socks and Mendel did, too—and still does today on Saturdays and holidays. On *Shabbos*, they wore a *spodik*, higher than the Hungarian *shtreimel*. At 19, he returned to Borough Park and started studying in the adult Gerer yeshiva. Any thoughts he had about going to college were easily discarded.

"It's not really acceptable in our circles because of the coed situation—men don't mingle with women," Werdyger explained to me. He acknowledged that today Touro College provides some opportunities for Hasidim to attend college because men and women can go on separate days, but said he never regretted missing out. "I'm fine. I have Google. It's almost as good as college."*

In Borough Park the dominant language was still Yiddish. The weather, of course, was far cooler than in Israel, but the scene was similar to Tel Aviv's Hasidic ghetto. To Mendel the switch was painless—like ending up in a cloistered American colony in, say, Jakarta might be for a midwestern American. He polished his Talmudic studies in preparation for three years of *kollel*. As is common in the yeshiva world, his father paid his bills.

Meanwhile, he married a Borough Park girl, Dvora. They were set up by a matchmaker who knew that Dvora used to babysit for his older brother Mordechai's family. Mendel spent time with his intended just twice before the marriage, and found her congenial and a promising mate. (They have been married ever since—for 35 years.) He also started singing in a local *shtibl*, which allowed for greater intimacy, camaraderie and intensity then a grander synagogue. He seldom doubted his Hasidic life or questioned the lack of the freedoms that he

---

* Author's interview with Mendel Werdyger.

saw among the New Yorkers he passed: freedom of dress, of casual association among the sexes, of activities like watching television and going to the movies.

"The question is how you define freedom," he told me. "Freedom can be defined as doing what the heck you want. Freedom can be defined as being totally absorbed by earthly things. But there's a famous saying in the Talmud: 'There's nobody as free as someone who learns the Torah. He's free of all earthly desires.' It basically means to feel humbled, to feel submissive to a higher authority."

In the early 1980s, after completing his Jewish studies, Mendel went to work for his father's music business, then just a label that produced about five recordings a year that were cut and distributed by House of Menorah. Mendel soon understood that his father and he could earn more money by wholesaling records themselves—selling not only their own Aderet label but others as well—from his father's Brooklyn offices to the scores of Judaic bookstores and shops that were then scattered in big cities around the country. He asked the owners of the few bookstores that bought the Aderet label what would appeal to them and along the way learned about the other Jewish bookstores that were then selling just books. He encouraged these stores to stock Aderet music as well as their books and in time compiled a comprehensive list of such potential customers. Aderet (which means "glorious" in Hebrew) slowly grew into a major worldwide distributor of Jewish music. Today it is something of an Amazon of the Hasidic world, and business profiles put them in the category of enterprises that sell more than $500,000 a year, though that figure seems absurdly low. Mendel also opened a music store on Borough Park's main drag, 13th Avenue near 48th Street, operating Aderet from the second story of the store with a half dozen employees. He called the new store "Mostly Music."

By about 1990, Americans were beginning to buy computers not only for their offices but for their homes as well, and word was filtering into the businesses in Borough Park that this device, with a monitor that looked suspiciously like a television set, could greatly enhance the calculating, word processing and graphic designing functions for an enterprise dependent on advertising its wares and toting up revenues. Word reached Mendel, too. With great entrepreneurial instincts, he decided to investigate; a computer might speed up his bookkeeping, he figured. So where else would he and his accountant go to but to the Mecca of cheap, if curtly sold, electronics, 47th Street Photo, which was then, luckily enough, run by Satmar Hasidim from Brooklyn (though it was a few years away from declaring bankruptcy because it could not pay back its loans). Werdyger wandered through the crowded aisles and looked at a computer with a twenty-megabyte hard drive—ludicrously small by today's gigabyte standards—and was captivated by the other equipment around him, such as a fax.

"What is a fax?" he asked the bearded salesman in Yiddish.

"You put it in one end and it comes out the other," the salesman told him.

Werdyger, to use his own words, was "totally awestruck" and "got hooked on technology." He bought the computer and later the fax. They did indeed enhance his business operations. But that visit also kindled his romance with other electronic gadgets, a passion that would blossom into a full-blown technological love affair with a long-dead cantor, the most famous of the 20th century and the one who had impressed himself on the wider American culture by appearing in the first talking movie, Al Jolson's *The Jazz Singer*.

13

JOSEPH IS YET ALIVE

He was called the Jewish Caruso. Indeed, aficionados of cantorial music sometimes referred to Enrico Caruso as the Italian Yossele Rosenblatt. Standing barely five feet tall yet casting a commanding and pious figure in his heavy dark beard, pillbox yarmulke and well-tailored frock coat, Rosenblatt was indisputably the greatest cantor of his time. But his time was the end of the 19th century and the first three decades of the 20th century, and that was an era when music was first being recorded on discs made of heavy shellac or celluloid, whirring at a speed of 78 revolutions per minute. The quality of those recordings was never that faithful in the first place, and it grew worse with the wear and tear of time. Scratches, hisses and pops were inescapable. Still, among those who fell in love with Rosenblatt's recordings was Mendel Werdyger. Like a teenager infatuated with Frankie Avalon or Connie Francis, he listened over and over to CD reissues of Rosenblatt's "Kol Nidre," of Rosenblatt's powerfully rendered Sabbath prayers, of Rosenblatt squeezing the pathos out of warhorses like "My

Yiddishe Momme" and animating the great operatic arias. As a cantor himself, Werdyger could appreciate the sweet timbre of Rosenblatt's tenor, his extraordinary range of two and a half octaves, his flair at hitting accurate notes at high speeds, his ability to shift from the tenor to a falsetto without a pause, and a plaintive "sob" that drew the tears out of a melancholy passage. Most of all, he was moved by Rosenblatt's spirit, what in Hebrew is called *ruach*.

"The key to Yossele Rosenblatt's kingship is he knew how to light a fire under the soul," Werdyger said to me as we sat in his small music distribution office. "When he sings you know what he's singing. He captures the meaning of every word. If he's crying, you know he's crying."

Still, for Werdyger, listening to his singing was frustrating. Those sonorous melodies were marred by the crackling and other distortions that were embedded in the old 78s and that had never been properly cleaned away when the records were remastered or reissued on C.D. "They were duplicates of the 78s and the sound was not what I wanted—with every generation it deteriorates greatly," Werdyger told me.

He wondered if he could do better. Partly he was driven by Rosenblatt's life story. While other cantors like Richard Tucker and Jan Peerce catapulted to wider fame in the opera and the entertainment worlds, they were not as rigorously Orthodox as Rosenblatt and quickly forsook cantorial careers for that of the stage, returning perhaps to the synagogue world just to lead services on the High Holidays. Rosenblatt remained firmly Orthodox and, until financial problems proved too burdensome, he always remained a cantor, whatever detours he took onto the American stage. And, significantly for Werdyger, Rosenblatt actually came from a Hasidic background.

Rosenblatt was born in 1882 in a Ukrainian *shtetl* to a father who was a Ruzhiner Hasid—a sect whose members were known for their regal ways because of their purported descent from King David himself. The father hailed from a long line of cantors and was delighted that Yossele, his first son after nine girls, was blessed with a crystalline voice and a natural flair for delivering a song. "He was born for the *amud* and he will stay by the *amud*," his father said of Yossele, referring to the pulpit behind which the cantor stands to lead prayers. To supplement the family income, the father began touring synagogues in the region with Yossele, for it was the son everyone wanted to hear. By the age of 18, Yossele was named the *hazzan*—the cantor—at the synagogue in Mukachevo, then a Hungarian city that was the seat of the Munkacs Hasidic dynasty, which traces its lineage back to Hasidism's founder, the Baal Shem Tov. Those Hasidic roots were to give Rosenblatt extra cachet among Hasidim. Then in 1911, after leading a congregation in Hamburg, Germany, and winning wider fame through his first recordings, Rosenblatt was invited to move to the United States to become the *hazzan* at Ohab Zedek, a Hungarian-rooted synagogue then on 116th Street in Harlem.

His penetrating bell-like tenor, his gift for the runs, trills and leaps of coloratura, his ability to squeeze the pathos or elation out of every prayer began drawing the attention not just of other New York cantors but of Toscanini, Carnegie Hall and the Chicago Opera House. His talent led to meetings with luminaries like Charlie Chaplin and a kiss from Caruso him-

self (at a rally to raise money for the allied campaign in World
War I). Rosenblatt would consider the temporal offers if they
did not conflict with his Jewish observances; despite promises
of kosher food and Saturdays off, he ultimately turned down
a role in the Chicago Opera's production of *La Juive*, possibly because its story is about the love between a Christian
man and a Jewish woman and would require him to perform
in close contact with women. But having to support eight
children and charities that regularly called on him, "Cantor
Rosenblatt," as he was billed, let himself be shepherded by
the legendary impresario Sol Hurok. He took many offers of
solo concerts, operatic arias, even vaudeville, and had a fertile recording career on labels like Columbia Graphophone.
"Thomas Edison recorded Yossele Rosenblatt and said he had
never heard a voice like his," Werdyger told me. Most memo-
rably, he took a cameo singing role in the 1927 talkie *The Jazz
Singer*. The renegade son, played by Al Jolson, having rejected
his father's wish that he become a cantor, hears Rosenblatt
sing a sacred song on a Chicago stage and is inspired to return
home to take his ailing father's place at Kol Nidre, the solemn
Yom Kippur prayer that is the high point of the cantor's year.

Rosenblatt died of a heart attack in Jerusalem in 1933 at
the age of 51. So esteemed was he that 200 cantors sang the
mournful "El Molei Rachamim" at a memorial service at
Carnegie Hall. But he died while shellac 78s were the state
of the recording art and later generations were never able
to fully appreciate his talent. So what could Werdyger do to
make Rosenblatt's recordings sound better? Like almost all
Hasidic men, he had never gone to college or taken a physics

class, let alone study sound engineering at graduate or professional schools. But he knew what sound waves were from his long experience in recording studios and, through his work distributing Jewish music, he was fully aware that recordings were becoming more sophisticated and exacting. The words "restoration" and "remastering" were becoming ingrained in the argot of the Jewish music business, and advertisements were urging people to buy recordings of old-time performers without the hisses and crackles of the originals.

"There was less tolerance of the noise that was coming from the old LPs, especially ones copied from the 78s," Werdyger told me. "Restoration was starting to become in. In the 1990s, they were restoring all the secular artists."

At a time that Larry Page and Sergey Brin were PhD students at Stanford University and working on the research project that would become Google, Werdyger went online to search for some restoration experts who might be able to help him reinvigorate old music. He found engineers in France and Canada. He made a long-distance call to the Frenchman—a man he remembers only as Andrew.

"I told him 'I'd like to send you some records. Tell me what we can do with it.' He said, 'I believe we can do x, y and z, and we can come up with some pretty decent sound.'" They continued to communicate by email and telephone, and the Frenchman recommended some software programs and settings he himself was using. Werdyger bought an audio restoration program, called Soundsoap, that he could use on the ordinary computer in his ragtag office and he experimented patiently with cleaning stray or invasive sounds. By 2005, he had become practiced enough to start working on cantorial recordings made by his father in the 1960s and 1970s and seeing if he could enhance them. They indeed sounded better. He worked on 78s his father had of great cantors like Moishe Oysher and Moshe Koussevitzky, the Lithuanian who had been cantor at Temple Beth-El in Borough Park.

"Every time I took the next album I tried to hone my skills," he said. "I was very pleased with the results."

Then he latched onto an even more important mentor, Alan Silverman, who runs Arf! Mastering in Manhattan, which specializes in high-resolution recording and remastering. Music is recorded in a sound studio, but before it can be copied thousands of times for CD or other forms of distribution it often needs to be "mastered"—tweaked and polished to bring out the best in a piece of music for a particular medium like LP, CD or MP3. The tones have to be bright, distortions have to be cleaned away and the sounds of each individual instrument enriched and elevated. Silverman, who on the side is an instructor of music technology at New York University and runs workshops on his arcane skill, has worked with such artists as Billy Joel, Judy Collins, Paul Simon and the Rolling Stones, both on originals and remasterings, and has applied his talents to films for Francis Ford Coppola and Martin Scorsese.

More important from Werdyger's standpoint is that Silverman understood the Hasidic world. The bespectacled Silverman had grown up Orthodox in Jersey City and went to a yeshiva for a few years before studying mathematics at Brown University and discovering the Greenwich Village music scene of the 1960s, where he developed a passion for sound recording. In those days, sound engineering was learned apprentice-like in the studio, not in university classrooms. Werdyger had heard of him because Silverman had mastered the Hasidic pop recordings of Werdyger's brother, Mordechai Ben David, and the two met for the first time at a concert of cantorial music.

It was Silverman who advised Werdyger on how to make transfers from the old Rosenblatt 78s. Silverman then guided Werdyger through the first remastering. Silverman was amused to hear Werdyger and his bearded, dark-suited Hasidic buddies conversing in a hybrid of their Brooklyn Yiddish and techno-speak, dropping terms like "midrange balance" and "compression" amid their Yiddish slang.

"It was as if they were discussing a point in the Talmud, with their vernacular mixed in with the jargon of recording engineering," he told me.

Wherever Werdyger went in the music business seeking help, he struck people as an anomaly, a broad-shouldered, lush-bearded grandfather who like many Hasidim daily wore the same long double-breasted *rekel*. Nevertheless, people agreed to spend hours helping this visitor from seemingly another planet.

"People are very open-minded to the man who does the best job," Werdyger told me. "It doesn't matter if he's Indian or Swahili as long as he does it correctly. That's the beauty of the Internet and of engineering."

And how could a Hasidic man who had never been to college not only pick up the skills of engineering sound that today are taught in universities but also do an expert remastering of a famous cantor?

"Mendy was no layman," Silverman pointed out. "He ran a recording label. He had a good ear. He committed himself to rolling up his sleeves." The analogy, Silverman told me, "is to studying Talmud," explaining that Talmud is first imbibed from teachers and mentors one seeks out and then requires the commitment of rehashing a passage until its fine distinctions emerge.

"He did have a sense to turn to people who were more experienced," Silverman said. "He had the vision and he realized he wasn't going to reach that vision until he put in the time, and that he was the person to do it. He listened to criticisms and commentary and little by little he got there."[*]

Curiously enough, Silverman later learned from an aged aunt that he and Werdyger might be related. The aunt's mother, who came from Ukraine, was also named Werdyger, an uncommon name, though the spelling was slightly different. When he passed this information on to Werdyger, Werdyger said that now he would have to invite Silverman to his children's weddings.

Werdyger was ready to tackle his Everest, Yossele Rosenblatt. It dawned on him that he needed better originals of the Rosenblatt recordings than the ones he was using. So he searched out collectors willing to lend him their 78s. There were people like Charlie Bernhaut, the host of a Jewish radio and Internet program on WMCA and a cantorial aficionado who has a collection of 10,000 albums. There were institutions like Florida Atlantic University, which has one of the

_____
[*] Author's interview with Alan Silverman.

largest libraries of Jewish music. He bought even more so-phisticated equipment—a fancier turntable, soundboard, and a state-of-the-art restoration programs like iZotope RX. He estimates he spent $50,000 on equipment. Silverman also sent him to an engineer at the Rodgers and Hammerstein Archive of Recorded Sound at the New York Public Library, which not only has 700,000 recordings but develops tech-nology to enable the transfer of sounds from obsolete to con-temporary formats. That engineer, whom Werdyger does not want to identify because he is his secret weapon, told him that to best capture the sound off the old 78s he needed to use old-fashioned needles or their equivalents with curves pre-cisely designed for the way grooves were cut in Rosenblatt's time. The engineer had 50 different styluses and he offered to use these needles to make the transfers for Werdyger. He then gave Werdyger CDs that he could work with, some-times taking the same piece of music off a half dozen 78s so Werdyger would be able to extract the clearest passages with the fewest scratches and digitally splice them together. Always there was the urgency to take great care in not marring or blemishing the originals. The engineer also pointed out what amplifiers would best equalize the tone of those old record-ings and taught him to put the 78 recordings into a 24-bit digital format.

Sitting at his computer using his new software and his turntable and his four-foot-tall Infinity speakers, Werdyger transformed Rosenblatt's voice into electronic bits. The iZo-tope RX restoration program broke each song into frequencies ranging from 100 hertz to 20,000 hertz, which appeared as waves on a computer screen. Such programs make the crackles and hisses implanted by the original recording equipment or by the ravages of old phonographs visible as anomalous patterns. With a few clicks of the mouse, Werdyger could strip those away, and the restoration program filled in the voids, much as a Photoshop program patches in the missing color. Still, it was painstaking work, requiring hours at the computer for each song, five to 10 hours for a three-minute song. Werdyger estimates that he spent 350 hours for the first three albums of Rosenblatt songs—or 35 days working 10 hours each day. It also took taste and restraint. Silverman compares the effort to "restoring an old painting."

"There's not a shortage of programs," he said. "What there is is a shortage of people who have the skills and talent and dedication to use the software to good effect."

To Werdyger, the new sound was deliciously satisfying. "It sounded better than when it was recorded in the room," Werdyger told me. "I don't think Rosenblatt would have recognized how well we preserved and enhanced the original recording."

The eventual result: five compact discs with Rosenblatt singing more than 50 tracks, including prayers and even a folk chestnut, "Mein Yiddishe Momme." The first CD sold 15,000 copies. "That's a gold record by Jewish standards," Werdyger said. The total for all five—30,000 buyers. That would make 30,000 people who would hear Rosenblatt's music as clearly as the day he sang those songs more than 80 years ago. And thousands more downloaded the music off the Aderet website.

Experts in the cantorial field were impressed.

"It never sounded so clear," Bernard Beer, director of the Philip and Sarah Belz School of Jewish Music at Yeshiva University, told me. "I was brought up with this music and I know those recordings from childhood, and I listened to it and I told a colleague there's no comparison to anything that was done before."

The title of the Rosenblatt series is *Od Yosef Chai*, which means "Joseph is yet alive" and echoes the patriarch Jacob's words in Genesis about the son he had thought was dead. The double entendre suggests that Rosenblatt, whose formal first name was Joseph, has been brought back to life.

The Rosenblatt restorations occurred at a time when the right stars were aligned. Cantorial music was having a revival among Hasidim. Hasidic prayer services typically emphasize ardor rather than vocal flourish; the prayer leader is someone who can bring emotion and intent to the words of the prayer book rather than a fine baritone, and few synagogues have a true cantor. "When I started in the 1980s, cantorial music was totally dead," Werdyger told me. But today, according to Werdyger, "there's been a major resurgence—more Hasidim that follow cantorial music than anyone else." They prize the work of active cantors like Yitzhak Meir Helfgot, the Israeli-born *hazzan* who sang for Pope Benedict XVI in 2008 when he visited Manhattan's Park East Synagogue, a modern Orthodox house of worship. Hasidim have learned to make fine distinctions between Helfgot's brilliance in the high register and the soulfulness of someone like Koussevitzky or Rosenblatt. Hasidim like Werdyger's friend, Menashe Silber, some-

times sneak away from their own synagogues to hear sonorous
chanting of the prayers by a cantor like Benzion Miller at
Young Israel–Beth El of Borough Park, an Orthodox but not
Hasidic house of worship. Silber has downloaded 1,300 cantorial songs onto his BlackBerry. He says of Werdyger, "By doing
this work, he's bringing back cantorial music to his generation."
More recently, in February 2013, Cantor Helfgot, accompanied by Itzhak Perlman on the violin, an 18-piece orchestra and
a klezmer band, sold out the 6,000 available seats at the Bar-
clays Center in downtown Brooklyn with cantorial chestnuts
and folk tunes. Most of the audience, paying between $80 and
$250, was made up of men with black hats or black yarmulkes
and their wives, many of them Hasidim. The impresarios made
sure there was a section of separate seating and lots of kosher
pastrami and corned beef sandwiches for sale.

After the albums were released, Werdyger was swamped
with letters, emails and telephone calls. "People are extremely
touched by it," he said, turning the praise to Rosenblatt's
singing, not his remastering efforts. "He had a unique way of
touching people. There's a certain message he's conveying. It
brings people closer to *HaShem*."

Among those sending valentines to Werdyger were the
grandchildren and other relatives of Yossele Rosenblatt, who
expressed their appreciation that he had made their patriarch's music accessible to new generations of listeners. "The
sound is spectacular," a grandson, Josef Rosenblatt, who lives
in Baltimore, wrote him after Werdyger sent him some of the
new CDs. "My grandfather died ten years before I was born,
yet through these CDs I feel that he is in the room with me."

For Werdyger, the effort was, of course, deeply gratifying. "I was able to accomplish something you have to learn in college how to do—taking something that sounded terrible and making it sound great." But to that gratification there was an extra layer of Hasidic satisfaction, that he accomplished a *chesed*, or righteous act, a mitzvah of sorts. What does a *chesed* do?

"We can use the analogy that people are born and have *neshamas* [souls]," he explained to me. "During the course of a lifetime they get tainted. We try to restore them to their pristine state."

Through his work and his own singing, Werdyger is extending his cantorial DNA into the next generation. When Mendel and his four daughters and two sons sit around the dinner table on the eve of Sabbath, the men sing *zmiros*—the special Sabbath songs—while the women listen or putter around the table cooking and serving. (Whatever modern Jews and gentiles think of this allocation of labor, it is the Hasidic way; ultra-Orthodox men, after all, will not listen to a woman's singing voice.) One of his two sons, Yisroel, showed a particular delight as a young boy in singing along with his father and had a voice whose timbre matched his enthusiasm. He also enjoyed striding alongside his father toward synagogue (Mendel's wife and daughters seldom go to synagogue, but spend the morning hours reading or preparing lunch) and listening to Mendel sing the Sabbath melodies along with a 10-man choir. The son has also accompanied his father on several trips a year he makes to Israel to be with his rebbe—Yaakov Alter—in the main Gerer synagogue in Jerusalem. Father and son sit at the Rebbe's Friday night and Saturday afternoon dinner table—the *tish*—and imbibe his "electrifying, charismatic" presence and sometimes his wisdom. More than once the Rebbe has asked Werdyger to sing. All in all it is an intoxicating experience.

"I get a high," said Mendel. "It's like you have to gas up every once in a while and this is gas for the *neshama*."

It has also been an intoxicating experience for the son. That son is now in his early thirties and is a Hasidic journalist, writing and editing for the Orthodox newspaper and website called Hamodea. But when he gets off from work he frequently heads to his second job—as a wedding singer—and in the Hasidic community there are weddings every night. He has produced a couple of CDs as well and can be seen on YouTube, wearing a foot-high fur *spodik* or singing at a *melaveh malkah*—the meal held at the conclusion of the Sabbath that in this case was just at the start of another wedding.

The revived music of Yossele Rosenblatt has particular resonance for earlier generations. Not long after I first met Werdyger, I happened to be in Mostly Music, Werdyger's small retail shop on 13th Avenue, to check out their cantorial offerings. As I was looking around, in walked a wizened old man named Yosef Klein, wearing a rumpled fedora that he confided dated back to World War II. He came to buy the latest Rosenblatt CD. He was in his early eighties and vividly remembered when his grandfather took him to hear the great Rosenblatt sing. Now, he told me, he would hear Cantor Rosenblatt again, the voice as true as when he was a little boy.

14

SACRED WORK

Since devotion to the Torah dominates a Hasid's life, the work that forges an identity for most mainstream Americans takes second fiddle for all but a few Hasidim. Work is not done for self-fulfillment, to earn a fortune, enact high-minded ideals, outperform a rival or any of the multitude of reasons that many Americans toil at their occupations. In the Hasidic world, work is done for the purposes of *parnossah*—the financial earnings that put food on the table and sustain a family. The Bible seldom mentions work. "On six days work may be done, but on the seventh day you shall have a Sabbath of complete rest, holy to the Lord," Exodus tells Jews (Exodus 35:2–3). Work then is mostly as an afterthought to the Sabbath, a day devoted to God. The sages have expanded this idea with a diminution of work that would startle American careerists. Work should be done with one's hands, but the heart and mind, the intellect and spirit should be foremost dedicated only to the study of Torah and to the performance of *mitzvos*—good deeds and other religious obligations. Work is seen almost as a distraction from these priorities. While many Orthodox Jews observe this hierarchy of values, Hasidim do so in spades. Work is not there to make one happy. Indeed, devoting one's heart and mind to work means that they are not as fully focused on Torah. Work as a be-all and end-all amounts to a sacred cow, and sacred cows are a form of idol worship denounced by the Torah.

When a Hasidic man finishes his formal studies in Torah and Talmud—though study is lifelong and never finishes—he will look to do something to secure that *parnossah*, usually a job in the community serving its residents in a store or other business or as a teacher. Nehuma's husband runs a yeshiva and she writes children's books in Hebrew that are published within the Hasidic world. Werdyger owns a music store that has blossomed into a major distributor of Jewish music. The Hasidic blogger Shtreimel is a traveling salesman for a Hasidic retailer. Those are occupations where the uncommon Hasidic appearance draws no stares and where there are accommodations for early departures on Friday to observe the start of Sabbath. Their work also allows for a dozen extra days off during the year for the smorgasbord of Jewish holidays—as many as four days for Passover, four days for Succoth, two days for Shavuot and three days for Rosh Hashanah and Yom Kippur. If works results in earning a fortune, that person has *mazel*, or luck, or God has shined down a particular blessing, and the good fortune must be shared with the community to some extent. But earning a fortune is not the primary purpose of the work.

Akiva Kizelnik, a slender Vizhnitz Hasid in his mid-thirties, told me that "every Hasid dreams he's going to stay in *kollel*, staying at learning, or going to become a rebbe. But unfortunately not everybody can. Still, you don't typically hear in school kids talking about careers. That's not the philosophy because everybody is going to have a career in studying." Indeed, after he got married and spent a year in *kollel* and his wife gave birth to their first child, the agreement his and his wife's parents made to support him and pay the rent expired, and so he had to search for work. He found a job as a salesclerk at B&H Photo Video, the huge camera and digital gadget store on Manhattan's West Side. "I don't have any background or education so the easiest thing to do was to go to B&H photo and ask for a job," he said.*

Isaac Abraham, a leader in the Satmar community, told me that in his father's time employment was limited to a few fields: garments, textiles, diamonds and other jewelry. "My mother used to operate a textile machine in one-hundred-degree weather," he said. "She came home exhausted. But that was a major part of the Jewish industry, and it went down the tubes. Everything went to China and Bangladesh."

But over time Hasidic businesses that started small—real estate, insurance brokerage, accounting practices, groceries—have grown large. "Now you can find employment in anything you can think of from cradle to the grave, from ceiling to floor, ceiling tiles, floor tiles, insurance, real estate, travel agencies."

---

* Author's interview with Akiva Kizelnik.

The various opportunities for employment are evident
in a ramble through Borough Park or other ultra-Orthodox
neighborhoods. Travel agencies arrange yearly trips to Jerusalem or Amsterdam or Sydney for Hasidim to visit fellow
Hasidim or their rebbe or to make a pilgrimage to the tomb of
a sect's founder in the Ukraine—the way Yeedle Melber did
in 2012. Specialty food emporiums like Gourmet Glatt and
Midwood's Pomegranate (which sells kosher cheeses from
Italy and France, wasabi herring, dairy-free cheese puffs for
eating with meat and even precut tablecloths so scissors do not
have to be used on the Sabbath) rival Fairway supermarkets in
scale and variety and employ dozens of ultra-Orthodox Jews
in sales, shipping and supervision. With hundreds of babies
born every year, stores that sell baby clothes, strollers and
cribs have burgeoned and employ hundreds more Hasidim.

But Hasidim do not just stay in the neighborhood. Buses
ferry them into midtown Manhattan, where thousands work
in the bustling warren of shops, booths and offices of the city's
Diamond District, a single 600-foot long block of 47th Street
between Fifth and Sixth Avenues where 80 percent of all the
diamonds entering the United States are processed. There are
so many Hasidim among the diamond dealers, cleavers, saw-
yers, cutters and setters that the street has been christened
the Rue de les Payess, a pun that plays on the Yiddish term
for sidelocks while also echoing the street in Paris, the Rue de
la Paix, where the Cartier family had its signature shop. Deals
for hundreds of thousands of dollars are conducted here in a
dozen languages—Hebrew, Yiddish, English, Flemish, French,
Russian and increasingly Chinese and Spanish—and usually

sealed without paperwork, just a handshake and the Hasidic blessing "*mazel* and *brucha*," a code of honor that has its roots in the Talmud. Of course, these paperless deals raise the issue of unreported income, which may explain why the Internal Revenue Service is also sniffing around the street.

In 1977, on the eve of Yom Kippur, Pinchos Jaroslawicz, a 25-year-old, slightly built Orthodox Jew from Borough Park who worked as a middleman between the diamond owners and the retailers, was beaten and strangled and robbed of more than $600,000 worth of diamonds. His body, nearly every bone broken so it could be stuffed into plastic bags and then into a packing crate, was found a week later beneath a workbench in the office of a diamond cutter, Shlomo Tal, an Israeli who told police that the murder was done by two masked men who invaded his office. The case was not solved until members of the Diamond Dealers Club, many of whom tended to spurn the secular authorities, broke their rules against informing and gave police tips that led to the conviction of Tal and a friend.

And then there is B&H Photo Video one block west of Madison Square Garden on Ninth Avenue and 34th Street, which claims to be the world's largest retailer of imaging products. It started life in 1973 as a small storefront on the Lower East Side opened by Herman Schreiber, a Satmar Hasid, and his wife, Blimie, and then moved to West 17th Street in Manhattan. It took its name from the initials of the Schreibers' first names. By 1997, the Schreibers moved to their current location at the corner of 34th Street. Every day except the hours between Friday afternoon and Saturday night—that's

Shabbos, after all—professional photographers, artists, hobby-ists and computer geeks stream there to buy their camera and video equipment. Its Internet operation, beloved by Google founder Sergei Brin, is even larger. The business now employs 1,500 people, most of whom are Hasidim who, while some-times shunning taking pictures themselves, have developed an expertise in the merits and shortcomings of hundreds of cameras. A bus service even transports many of its employ-ees from the Hasidic village of Kiryas Joel, 50 miles away in Orange County, New York.

A large proportion of Hasidic men and women—25 per-cent by some informal estimates—work as teachers, the men in boys' schools, the women in girls' schools. Another cohort work in other religious institutions—as inspectors of kosher meat and products, as arbitrators in a *beis din*, a rabbinical court, as suppliers of religious objects like the *shofar*, or ram's horn, or *tefillin* and *talesim*—phylacteries and prayer shawls.

"God in Borough Park is like steel in Bethlehem," Alex-ander Rapaport tells me, using a perhaps outdated metaphor since the last time I was in Bethlehem, Pennsylvania, the steel mill had closed down. But there is no doubt that religious ob-ligations generate much of the neighborhood's jobs.

If a young Hasidic man or woman wanted to investigate a profession suited to his drive and intelligence, say medicine, law or engineering—he could not. Each of those professions requires attendance at college and graduate school, and Ha-sidic culture discourages both. The ban is not absolute, and in recent years a handful of colleges have sought to accommo-date Hasidic idiosyncrasies.

The champion in this field is Touro College, founded more than forty years ago by Bernard Lander, an Orthodox Jew, with an original emphasis on appealing to Orthodox Jews, though it now counts 19,000 students of a variety of faiths and ethnicities and offers a full range of undergraduate courses. Yet it has a campus in Midwood, Brooklyn, where it alters attendance days by gender, with men attending on, say, Monday, and women on Tuesday to allow separation of the sexes. Some courses are offered exclusively for men and others for women. Most of the students are from the ultra-Orthodox but non-Hasidic world of Lithuanian or *Yeshivish* Jews who subscribe to many Hasidic traits, like somber clothing, but value intellectual scholarship as well. A program Touro started in 1998 in Borough Park to prepare students for community college degrees is aimed directly at the Hasidic market, and 300 students attend those. It calls itself, tellingly, Machon L'Parnassa—preparation for the livelihood—avoiding any pretensions of intellectual challenge or stimulation.

The courses at Touro's Lander College for Men in Queens are exceedingly practical—geared toward a sustaining livelihoods in accounting and business, computer science, health-related fields like pharmaceutical science, occupational therapy, psychology and politics and government. Talmud lectures are held in the morning and evening, college classes in the afternoon. While the school offers bachelor's degrees and there are surveys of Western literature and history, there are few of the courses found at a typical liberal arts college, no classes in the modern novel, art history or the Renaissance. Similarly, Touro started the Lander College for Women on

Manhattan's West Side, where the primary focus is on Judaic studies and practical courses in accounting, psychology and computer science. Nevertheless, unlike the men's college, it does offer a menu of courses in the humanities. Women, it is believed, do not bear the same obligation for Torah and Talmud study and, within limits, can fill their minds with such frills.

15

SCHOOLS OF THOUGHT

The word "yeshiva" means a place of sitting, yet few out-siders visiting a Hasidic yeshiva would find it a restful spot. There is, to be sure, a lot of sitting on worn benches in front of battered volumes of Talmud. But the air in a yeshi-va's often run-down study hall is clamorous with young men explicating ambiguities and enigmas, analyzing texts in ex-quisitely penetrating fashion, arguing over superfine distinc-tions. As they study, the students or scholars rock back and forth with single-minded ardor, as if the vigor of their sway-ing could concentrate their minds and help clarify a particular elusive passage.

This is the manner in which Jews have studied for 2,000 years as they have tried to master the laws of Torah and Talmud that govern their faith and the rhythms of daily life. In the yeshiva they are being prepared for a lifelong dedica-tion to *Torah lishmo*, study for its own sake, a concept practically unique to Judaism among the world's religions.

In most Jewish communities, the synagogue is the central institution of Jewish life. In Hasidic and ultra-Orthodox communities, it is the yeshiva, its largest enterprise and usually its biggest employer. Since studying Torah is the uppermost obligation of the Jewish man and basic Judaic knowledge is also required of women, Hasidim put enormous effort and money into operating schools. They make sure to educate even the most disabled. There is nothing quite like it in any other religion because no other religion emphasizes daily study to the same extent for all its adherents, not just its clerical elite. If a sect's main synagogue is Buckingham Palace, the royal seat of the tribe's monarch, the Rebbe, then the yeshiva is its Parliament, the place where Jewish law is argued over, sharpened, illuminated, and sometimes enhanced, though the rules are never actually honed into finished form because in yeshiva, study never finishes and nothing ever seems final. Indeed, all such governmental comparisons really don't apply because— despite assumptions by many secular Jews and non-Jews— there is nothing like any official communal authority for Hasidic and other forms of Orthodox Judaism, and almost everything is up for grabs and fair game for dispute. (Yes, Hasidim do revere a rebbe but officially he has no police powers or any enforcers, so his authority derives largely from communal pressure. That pressure, however, can sometimes be quite powerful in sects that have shadowy modesty committees, those self-proclaimed enforcers probably operating with the rebbe's tacit approval, who may scold a woman for wearing a turban that does not conceal all her hair or a young man for visiting a secular museum or reading a secular newspaper.)

The origins of the yeshiva go back to the rabbinical academies that arose during the first millennium in Babylonia and the Holy Land. Jews struggled with creating a portable, migratory institution that would forge some form of authority in the wake of the destruction of the Second Temple and the dissolution of its priestly class, one that would also hold their tribe together. The synagogue replaced the Temple as the site of worship and Judaism focused on Torah and Jewish law as ruling daily life rather than empowering a political or priestly elite. A loose, ad hoc leadership structure emerged of wise men—the rabbis—and what distinguished the rabbis from the rabble was their scholarship and insight. This shift enabled Jews to survive as a people and a faith because Judaism was no longer rooted to a place and an authority; rather, Torah study and personal or communal worship allowed it to flourish in exile however oppressive the conditions.

The objective of study as a strategy for enriching the faith filtered into the general populace—or at least the male half of it. The *Mishnah*, the first compilation of Jewish law and the foundational six books of the Talmud, states that every Jewish community should have three times as many students as rabbis. It also asserts that every Jewish male should devote two entire months to study, one before Succoth and one before Passover. Over the centuries those pursuing deeper study found themselves clinging to sages and mentors whose particular towns and villages gained a reputation for advanced learning. The yeshiva itself was formalized as an institution toward the end of the 18th century by Chaim of Volozhin, a disciple of the anti-Hasidic Vilna Gaon, who created a protocol of study, exegesis and analysis adapted from the methods of his master. Though Volozhin became the model of all the great anti-Hasidic Lithuanian yeshivas, its methods were also absorbed by a kind of osmosis into the Hasidic world—to such an extent that the nuances would be indistinguishable to an outsider.

In much of the so-called *haredi* world, the yeshiva has evolved into an institution with many levels—all of which may take the name yeshiva. There is the elementary yeshiva where boys and girls—separately of course—begin to study the classic Bible stories and the basics of Hebrew writing and grammar and slowly move up to intense study of Torah. By fifth or sixth grade, boys—seldom girls—study *Mishnah* and afterward boys delve whole hog into *Gemara*. In some schools, boys may get as little as an hour of English studies a day, so paramount are the Hebrew and Yiddish subjects. Girls usually end their studies at Jewish law—educating themselves for the roles they will play in life as wife and mother, roles that *Haredim* feel do not require the arcane and coiling knowledge of the *Gemara*. However, the girls in most yeshivas will learn English, history and mathematics, and some carefully vetted science (no evolution), but they emerge from high school better prepared for grappling with the secular world than boys might be.

For boys, the study of Talmud broadens and deepens after bar mitzvah in a high school setting known as a *mesivta*, but the study of secular subjects virtually stops. Boys are expected to learn any science, mathematics or history on their own. The New York City yeshiva system is bigger than the Boston public schools, yet some schools offer almost no secular instruction after fifth grade, others after eighth grade, others no more than an hour or two a day.

That may not be kosher according to state law, which requires private schools to offer "equivalency of instruction" in fundamental subjects like English, history, math and science. When you ask a headmaster of a yeshiva whether omission of these subjects violates state education law, he will tell you that the rabbis provide lessons in geometry when they probe the Talmud portion about the architecture of the Temple and lessons in astronomy when they hash over the questions of what constitutes daybreak and sunset for purposes of daily and Sabbath prayers and what constitutes a new moon for counting months in the Jewish holiday calendar. The state and city authorities have seldom cracked down on what seem like clear-cut violations of state law, partly for political reasons—the Hasidim are a potent force and stepping into a possibly constitutional quagmire of church and state is particularly tricky—and partly because the state's sprawling public education system fails so many children that officials have bigger fish to fry.

"The authorities understand they're not a burden to society," Rabbi Hertz Frankel, the principal for English studies at Bais Rochel d'Satmar, a yeshiva for girls, told me. "So they don't learn English. They study *Gemara*. They stay in school. You don't find them in the streets selling drugs or hurting people." Using the example of his own son, a successful investor who learned economics through correspondence schools and did not go a conventional college, he said: "He's not sitting on a stoop drinking beer." He also argues that government policy makers also realize that each student in a yeshiva is saving taxpayers and the public school system an average of $10,000 in educational costs, not to mention hundreds of million of dollars in capital costs for additional school buildings.*

Nonetheless, the paucity of English learning has consequences. The yeshivas may operate at an equanimity that public schools could only envy, yet they barely teach many young men to speak, read and write English. It is as if English were a foreign language they were learning, treated no differently than French or German might be in a public school, and Americans are familiar with how poorly most students master a foreign language. Of course, Hasidim can justify the deficient English instruction by pointing out that it is Yiddish that is the everyday language in their neighborhoods.

A psychological therapist who works in Rockland County, where Hasidim form a substantial slice of the population, told me that she frequently encounters teenage boys who have trouble casually writing their names in English, let alone full grammatical sentences. Yet when she mentions the problem to parents, they tell her, as one European-born mother did, "You need to understand that he's going to marry a woman who's going to take care of these things for him. She's going to do the banking and his job applications while he studies *Gemara*." The therapist told me she was struck by how beautifully the mother spoke English, a result, she speculated, of the fuller grounding girls get in English subjects. Indeed, the

---

* Author's interview with Rabbi Hertz Frankel

therapist said she once met a principal of a Satmar elementary school of 300 students who admitted he could not read or write English well. "I'm very literate in Hebrew and Yiddish," he told her. The helplessness of so many Hasidic men in English and basic secular concepts helps keep them in the fold—leaving the Hasidic community feels frightening when someone is so ill-prepared—and that may be the sly rationale for the lack of instruction.

The labyrinthine complexity and hairsplitting nuances of *Gemara* are not for every boy, and those who don't have the mental acuity or discipline to grapple are often lost; schools don't know how to manage them. Nevertheless, the therapist thought it important to also point out that the atmosphere in most of the yeshivas she has worked in is strikingly supportive, with each child valued and encouraged to achieve the peak of his or her talents, even if those are not talents the outside world may esteem. She said she was struck by the "beautiful acts of *chesed*, of kindness" she sees every day working with Hasidic schools. If a student is troubled, the school may swamp him or her with tutors, anything they can do to help. She told me of the principal of a Satmar school of 1,500 boys who knows every single boy.

"If I say I'm calling about Shapiro, he knows all ten or fifteen Shapiros in the school. He might tell me, 'You're not going to be able to do anything for him. He's just like his father.' But he knows the family well."

The Skverer Hasidim, she said, have made a specialty of taking in all developmentally disabled children that families from other Hasidic groups cannot manage. "The amount of *chesed* in the *haredi* community is astonishing," the therapist said. "I have learnt so much from them—and when the community works, and when the children can function within the parameters of expectation, their lives are very rich."

Study never stops. The young men and fathers and grandfathers in the *beis medrash* ("house of study") or *yeshiva gedola* ("supreme yeshiva") revisit passages they may have pored over in high school, but delve more deeply with commentaries not only by great by sages like Rashi or Rambam (Maimonides), but more obscure ones as well. The idea is to gain new insights or detect new facets they may have missed in the way that rereading a Henry James novel is a different experience at 30 or 50 than it was at 18.

From adolescence onward, the standard template for study is a *shiur*—a lecture by a rabbi on a passage of Talmud—followed by and sometimes preceded by independent study sessions with a learning partner—a *chavrusa*. A student in the *beis medrash* will not only review a text with his partner but point out errors in his partner's reasoning or gaps in his knowledge and be vulnerable to the same critiques from the partner. In the process, understanding is sharpened, points are elucidated, ideas are more precisely articulated—or so is the hope. This is not done through emails or murmurs but through vociferous conversation, often in a traditional singsong. A stranger walking into a Hasidic study hall filled with scores of or sometimes even a few hundred young men would find a very noisy place, filled with rambunctious argumentation, pounding of fists, upraising of thumbs when a point is notched, and he would hear snatches of a few whining melodies that have become the background music of the yeshiva.

The stranger might wonder how anyone can concentrate in such pandemonium, but Hasidim will tell you that the opposite is true. Learners focus entirely on their dialectic with their study partner and block out the rest. The clamor seems to foster more intense focus on the subject at hand in the way that the score of an adventure movie heightens the excitement.

The Talmud is a formidable body of work: 63 volumes of rabbinical discourse and disputation that form Judaism's central scripture after the Torah. It has been around for 1,500 years—its compilation was completed around 540 CE—and is studied every day by tens of thousands of Jews. Indeed, a peculiar phenomenon has come into being in recent decades called *Daf Yomi*, in which tens of thousands of Jews around the world commit themselves to studying the same *daf*—both sides of a page of Talmud—every day until all 5,422 pages of the 63 volumes of Talmud are completed, a cycle that takes seven and a half years. Then they begin all over again. Some 90,000 people attended the *Daf Yomi* graduation of sorts in August 2012 at MetLife Stadium in New Jersey.

Daniel Retter, a lawyer and Talmudic scholar who compiled what he believes is the first true index to the Talmud's passages, one that has been accepted by many scholars and rabbis, told me for an article I wrote on his index that the Talmud "was designed to be mysterious, designed to be locked—I call it the 'book of mystery.'"

"The Talmud was written in exile, and it was the thread that kept Jews together," he said. "It had no punctuation, no paragraphs; it was a book that was to be transmitted orally from father to son."

Rabbi Benjamin Blech, professor of Talmud at Yeshiva University, in explaining why there had been no index, also gave me an insight into what the perpetual study is all about. The rabbis he said, believed that study should not be made too easy. "We want people to struggle with the text because by figuring it out you will have a deeper comprehension," he said. "They wanted a living index, not a printed index."

The *Gemara* student, Hasidic or otherwise, analyzes arcane matters—the more arcane the better—like how one should handle a lost object found in a garbage heap, when in the morning is the precise time that that the iconic prayer of *Shema Yisrael* can be uttered and whether one can remarry a former wife after she has been betrothed to another. Questions, sometimes improbable, even incongruous, are broached: What if a man is engaged to be married in 12 months but finds for whatever reason that he cannot wed in time; is he still obligated to take care of his intended's need for food and shelter? One rabbi, say Hillel, puts forward his hypothesis, another, say Shamai, counters with a different interpretation or solution, a third, a fourth, a fifth and a sixth rabbi venture other opinions and angles and before the Talmudic scholar realizes it the issue is lost in a maze, with pathways leading to byways leading to offshoots that sometimes end in culs-de-sac. Along the way, as the young scholar sits hunched over reading the dog-eared Aramaic text, his voice rises and falls in that Talmudic singsong, his eyes glittering with delight at the saga's oddities.

I spent a day at a Hasidic yeshiva high school—this one run by the Chabad-Lubavitch Hasidim. It is the only Hasidic

group that proselytizes, though it does so only with assimilated or lapsed Jews, not gentiles, often asking them to don
a pair of *tefillin* and say a blessing, or, during Succoth, to wave
the ritual palm branch known as a *lulav*. At Oholei Torah in
Brooklyn's Crown Heights neighborhood, I discovered that by
high school boys are already spending 14 hours a day at study
starting at seven thirty in the morning, grappling most of the
day with the conundrums of the Talmud. (Chabad-Lubavitch
Hasidim also get a good dose of the philosophy of their group's
sages, particularly the venerated leader, Menachem Schneerson. He died in 1994 but is believed by one faction in the now-
schismatic sect to have been the Messiah and to eventually
return as the Messiah.) After breakfast the boys, all wearing
similar outfits of white shirt, unbuttoned at the neck, and dark
slacks, pack a bright but shabby second-floor study hall, three of
whose walls are covered in drab wood paneling and the fourth
lined with tall volumes of Talmud and commentary surrounding a Holy Ark, where the Torah scroll is kept (like many study
halls, this *beis medrash* doubles as a synagogue). Each boy sits
with his *chavrusa*, his study partner, at a tightly clustered bench
around a long table and begins poring over a Talmud passage,
often one that is going to be the subject of a rabbinical lecture.
During my visit, Shlomie Chein, then a slender 16-year-old
youth with wisps of facial hair, and his study partner, Zalman
Marasow, a stockier young man with the beginnings of a black
beard, were hunched over a page of the *Gemara* tractate known
as Baba Kama. The question before them: if a person gives
wool to be dyed and it comes back the wrong tint, how much
should the craftsman pay the aggrieved customer?

Well, the two boys discovered, the answer, as with all Talmudic riddles, is far from simple. A ruling depends on whether the worker was a professional or just a helper, whether the badly dyed wool can be sold and whether the profit on that sale exceeds the cost of the wool. It is on such nuances that many decisions in law and life ride.

Ask Shlomie why at 16 he should be learning such fine points of law instead of science or history, and he responds: "It sharpens the mind. The book of laws tells you what you do, but the *Gemara* takes everything apart. There are two sides to every story, and every sage will hold a different side. You can sit with a page of *Gemara* for weeks."

The lecture at eleven thirty that morning was given in a classroom by Rabbi Nachman Y. Twersky, a burly figure with a curly black beard draped over his blue three-quarter coat, and it was on a different topic. Quoting such commentators as Rashi, the 11th century French rabbi whose elucidations of passages in Torah and Talmud are a bedrock of Jewish study, he talked in Yiddish to his rosy-cheeked teenage scholars about an ancient rite known as *pidyon haben*: the redemption of the firstborn son. Because Pharaoh condemned the firstborn of Egypt's Jewish slaves to death, every firstborn is regarded as belonging to God and in God's service like a priest. That firstborn must be redeemed by a payment of five silver dollars to a temple priest within 30 days of birth (children born through a Caesarean section or the children of Levites and Cohanim, the priestly class, are excluded). Today it is largely a festive rite, but the Talmudic study of the topic in Rabbi Twersky's class was quite serious.

What if the child is stillborn or dies before 30 days, does the obligation persist? What happens if the boy is born with two heads? Does the father pay twice or nothing since the baby is likely to die?

As he lectured, Rabbi Twersky's right hand spun arabesques in the air that seemed to trace the looping intricacy of what he was arguing. "What if the child lives?" one boy asked Rabbi Twersky.

"A child with two heads can't live more than twelve months," the rabbi retorted.

The school's principal, Rabbi Wilhelm, told me that the Talmud's cases, though they may be considered outdated, nevertheless form precedents for adjudicating modern conflicts. The Talmud may speak about the damages that must be paid when a farmer's ox chews up a neighbor's field, but the case may be applicable to an accident in which a car's tire strikes a piece of wood that hits a passerby in the eye. In common law, too, real-life cases are decided on specifics that vary from incident to incident, but parallels can be drawn from seemingly unrelated situations and some general principles stated. It is no wonder that the legal profession is peopled by a disproportionate number of Jews.

After the lecture, students return to the study hall to review the lesson. They go to lunch, come back for afternoon prayer then spend the next two hours delving into Talmud on their own. After supper, which the neighborhood youths eat at home, there is a return to the *beis medrash* for a final review of Talmud and a study of the week's Torah portion that lasts until 9:30 p.m.

Although they do not watch television or go to movies, the students seem to take pleasure in this dense daily routine. Their eyes twinkle at a particular insight or finessing of logic. Many are rather pale, as if they have not had enough time in the outdoors, though they will vigorously contend that they find time for exercise in their own ways. During the lunch period, a half dozen boys improvised a rough game of hockey in a third-floor classroom, using their legs as sticks and a flattened soda can as the puck.

At Oholei Torah, which means Tents of Torah, many of the youths in the high school and those in the advanced yeshiva situated on the building's first floor plan to seek rabbinical ordination even if they will not work as conventional rabbis. That is because after they make their arranged marriages they want to spend several years as emissaries of the Lubavitch tribe, settling in far-off Jewish communities and working to expand the commitment of the assimilated Jews there. But Hasidim in other sects also seek rabbinical ordination, even though few will actually lead congregations. A rabbinic ordination is almost as ubiquitous as a driver's license because being a rabbi is helpful in all sorts of lines of work—teacher, kosher inspector, social agency administrator. But even those who do not choose ordination subscribe to the communal ethos that study of Talmud is a lifelong occupation.

Indeed, the students at Oholei Torah told me that whatever careers they will choose, all will devote much of each day to the study of Talmud.

"There's a saying," Shlomie Chein told me. "Teach a child

when he's young, and then when he gets older he'll do it by himself."

Hasidic schools, private, isolated and insular as most are, have often embroiled the Hasidim in acrimonious disputes with the wider American public. In a few years in the late 1980s when I was writing about religion for the *New York Times*, there were a half dozen dustups involving Hasidic schools. In Williamsburg, Hasidic girls of the Satmar sect were receiving federally subsidized remedial education programs in a partitioned-off section of a public school so they would not have to mingle with boys from the public school itself, something disallowed by Hasidic codes of conduct; they were in a public school building because the United States Supreme Court decision had barred public school districts from sending their teachers into religious institutions even for remedial education. The partition was built and maintained by the New York City Board of Education as a way of accommodating Hasidic groups in the wake of the Supreme Court's ruling. But then a federal appeals court banned the partition and the girls had to receive their remedial programs in yeshivas, requiring administrators there to quickly train teachers in the specialty.

Congress has long tried to provide some services to Roman Catholic and other religious schools without violating the constitutional strictures against establishment of religion and over the years the courts have permitted subsidies for discrete services like food, transportation and remedial programs for the disabled. In the early months of 2013, Hasidic exploitation of these permitted services was one of the issues in an explosive budget crisis in the East Ramapo Central School District, which embraces several of the Hasidic villages and hamlets in Rockland County. The district is one of the more unusual public school districts in the United States. It has 29,000 schoolchildren, but only 9,000 attend public schools, with the rest choosing Hasidic or other Orthodox Jewish schools and a handful of Catholic schools. The Hasidim and other Orthodox Jews have to support the public schools where they do not send their children and are upset by rising property taxes to fund services like athletics, music and art they do not have in their yeshivas. The public school children come largely from poor and working-class Haitian, Hispanic and African-American families and want to get the same educational services that their neighbors in other districts get. But the Hasidim dominate the school board because they turn out in droves in school board elections on issues crucial to them; in 2013 Hasidic or other Orthodox men occupied seven of the nine seats on the board running the public schools.

An inordinate slice of the district's budget is dedicated to expensive special education services for mentally or physically disabled Hasidic children, who mostly receive the services on yeshiva property so Hasidim won't have to intermingle with secular children or mix sexes. But the state aid formulas for education are constructed in such a way that they count only the number of public school children, not the special education children in yeshivas and private schools that the district is legally obligated to serve, which means a district like East Ramapo is badly shortchanged. To find new ways to balance

THE PIOUS ONES   257

the perennially starved budget—400 jobs were cut in the five
years before 2013—the Hasidic-dominated school board has
had to trim programs in art, music and gym and has elimi-
nated social workers. The members even threatened to eliminate kindergarten, though that threat was ultimately dropped.
One tactic was to sell a shuttered public school for $6 million
for probable use as a yeshiva property, an act that stirred new
resentments.

As a result of these tensions, some of the board's actions
have led to expressions of anti-Semitism, the Rockland
County therapist, who asked me not to use her name to protect her ability to practice, told me.

"You don't care about our kids, you're just a Jew," the therapist, who is Orthodox herself, said she heard at one meeting.
Teachers in the public schools have told her of high school
teenagers who complain explicitly: "The Jews are taking everything away from us." Matters got so bad by May 2012 that
Daniel Schwartz, the president of the school board and a
modern Orthodox Jew, warned that the district was facing
a "terrible, terrible crisis" of anti-Semitism. He said community activists were repeatedly saying that "the board members cared more about money and taxes than they do about
people.' Such statements, he said, repeated the hoary stereotype of Jewish obsession with money that, he said, "paved the
way to Auschwitz."*

"I won't have it, I simply won't have it," Schwartz declared.
"To suggest that we lack the moral authority to sit in these

---

* Benjamin Wallace-Wells, "Them and Them," *New York*, April 21, 2013.

seats is absolutely un-American and wrong." When his statement was shouted down by someone in the audience, he told
dissenters that if they didn't like what he had to say, then "find
yourself another place to live." He concluded by urging that
the district's schools design a curriculum to educate children
"about the evils of racism and anti-Semitism."

No educational incident has received the national attention
that was garnered in the 1980s and 1990s by the upstate
New York village of Kiryas Joel, which is populated entirely
by Satmar Hasidim, culminating in a major decision by the
United States Supreme Court and a long series of state court
rulings interpreting that decision.

The surrounding school district of Monroe-Woodbury
had long tried to provide remedial and special education services while accommodating Hasidic mores but it found that
tailoring the program for Hasidim—by, for example, providing only male drivers for buses—ran afoul of other provisions
of state and federal law. Meanwhile, sending the Hasidic children into a public school environment had its own drawbacks.
With their spiraling earlocks or long-sleeved dresses and
odd accents for rural New York, the Hasidic children were
often ridiculed by their public school classmates. Eventually,
the state legislature was asked to intervene, and in 1989 it
carved out a special school district—the Kiryas Joel Union
Free School District—so that instruction and other services
the village's handicapped children receive could be provided
within Kiryas Joel.

I visited the squat brick schoolhouse, which is inside a village of 20,000 residents, virtually all of them Hasidic and more than 40 percent of whom are poor enough to receive food stamps. Black-suited men and bewigged women pushing baby carriages scurry through the spiraling streets of ample but tightly clustered houses in scenes that seem to be taken out of an album by Roman Vishniac, the great photographer of prewar Jewish life and of the *shtetl*. My guide was the district's superintendent, Dr. Steven Benardo. He told me that about 80 Hasidic children—the most severely handicapped or developmentally disabled by such ailments as cerebral palsy—were attending full-time. But another 500 or so of the students who attend Satmar yeshivas, he said, were pulled out for up to three hours a day for remedial lessons geared for those with learning disabilities, for English-as-a-second language instruction for those who have learned only Yiddish or for counseling, physical therapy or other services financed by the federal government. The program cost the public about $6 million in the early 1990s.

Since they receive regular visits from federal and state monitors, there were no clear-cut violations of the church-state wall. The school's kitchen is kosher and on those Jewish holidays when work is forbidden, the school is only nominally open. And Benardo acknowledged that he made sure older children honored the Satmar prohibition against mingling boys and girls. Still, Benardo took pains to point out that there were no religious classes in that building, and during Chanukah, no menorahs or holiday decorations are visible even though such symbols are common in public schools.

"Since we're being scrutinized I've got to be glatt kosher,"

Benardo, a former New York City school administrator who is Jewish but not Orthodox, jested.

While most teachers' aides are Satmar members of the village, none of the 18 licensed teachers and 30 therapists came from Kiryas Joel. Satmar residents could not qualify as teachers because licenses require a college education. Many of the teachers are from more lenient Orthodox communities in nearby Monsey.

Still, some critics—like Louis Grumet, then the executive director of the New York State School Boards Association, who brought a suit challenging the school district's creation—expressed concern that the district might eventually be used to provide all yeshiva students with their English and secular programs under the fiction that that these were all special education and bilingual services. After all, almost all students can qualify for English-as-a-second-language classes since they grow up speaking Yiddish, so why would the village need to spend its own community's money to teach English in the yeshivas?

On my visit I could see how that might come to pass. In one English class I saw, which, as required by law, was given in a trailer outside the yeshiva, not in the yeshiva itself, Chavy, a nine-year-old girl, was sitting at a computer working on past tenses with exercises like "Did Jean want an apple? Jean wanted an apple." That was her English class for the day.

To concerns like those held by Grumet and others, Benardo and Abraham Wieder, the president of the school board and a Hasidic industrialist whose wire factory makes cables for navy submarines, pointed out that parochial school children are entitled by law to such government-assisted programs. Indeed, Wieder told me, the biggest problem he faces is getting villagers to trust the public school and enroll for services to which they are entitled.

"Lots of children are going without special education and who knows what effect it has," he said.

Moreover, he contended, the villagers are finally receiving some benefit for the $1,500 the average yeshiva-going family has always paid in school taxes each year but for which they have historically seen little return.

Still, critics view the entire arrangement as violating the Constitution because of the way the village's temporal government intersects with its religious leadership. All members of the seven-person school board are chosen by the Rebbe. When dissidents have tried to run for the school board, they have been ordered to withdraw by the Rebbe and afterward widely denounced. Joseph Waldman, a Satmar dissident, told me that for opposing the village leadership on some fine points of how the school was being administered, his family has been banished from the village's main synagogue, Congregation Yetev Lev D'Satmar, and his children—Waldman had six at the time—were expelled from the principal yeshiva, United Talmudical Academy.

"Why should my children suffer because someone is trying to use the democracy of this country?" Waldman told me.*

---

* Author's interview with Joseph Waldman.

And there was one more indignity: the family has been barred from entering the village cemetery to visit grave sites let alone for any burials they might need.

"There's a total intertwining of church and state," said Michael Sussman, the lawyer for Waldman and his allied dissidents, describing Kiryas Joel as a theocracy.[*]

In conversations we had, the leaders of the village shrugged off all such charges and argued that they had been scrupulous in keeping the school district free of religious influence. The dissidents had been ostracized not because they had challenged the school board slate, but because they had been disrespectful to the Rebbe. "Respect for elders precedes the learning of Torah," Wieder told me, quoting an ancient proverb. "And that is why we have no crime, no drugs and the largest village in New York State without a police force."

Wieder, who went on to become the village mayor as well as its synagogue president and raised substantial funds for such politicians as Governor David Paterson, claimed Waldman and others were denied the use of the cemetery because they had violated the congregation's bylaws.

"Whoever works against the interests of the congregation, we ask that they no longer be a member, and cemetery rights is one of the membership privileges."[†]

Still, it was hard to discount some of the publicly visible attacks the dissidents suffered. Windows were broken, rocks hurled, tires punctured and condemnations posted on banners

---

[*] Author's interview with Michael Sussman.

[†] Author's interview with Abraham Wieder.

across the village main shopping center. A dissident's house was burned down.

"They are using their power exactly like Khomeini," Waldman told me.

It was against this background that the United States Supreme Court took up the matter of whether the state legislature could legally carve out a school district especially for the Hasidim of Kiryas Joel. The court was aware that the petition was supported by the larger Monroe-Woodbury school district, which didn't want the hassle of accommodating the curious needs of the Hasidim and didn't want the Hasidim on its board exerting influence over how much money could be spent on public school children. The court was also aware that its earlier 1985 decision forbidding public school teachers from entering parochial schools to give lessons to handicapped Catholic and Jewish children had created the problem that led to Kiryas Joel's designation as a school district.

Nevertheless, in 1994 it ruled that the district's creation in 1989 constituted an establishment of religion because it amounted to a favor for a single religious group, the Satmar Hasidim. It did not say that the legislature could never carve out such a district, but that the way it had been done in Kiryas Joel's case was wrong. It told the state legislators to go back to the drawing board. The legislature did—four times—prodded on by a Democratic governor, Mario Cuomo, and then a Republican governor, George E. Pataki. First, 11 days after the Supreme Court decision, it passed a law that did not name Kiryas Joel but whose demographic characteristics—population, per-pupil wealth and the like—suggested that it was tailored exclusively for it. Then it fashioned two other laws whose demographic characteristics applied to one or two other villages. Each of those efforts was thrown out by lower and appellate state courts. At bottom the courts saw all these laws as a favor to Satmar, though one dissenting judge said that as long as other municipalities might be entitled to the same favor, the legislature did nothing wrong. The Hasidim were doing nothing more than other "supplicants walking and working the corridors of power in the Statehouse," the judge wrote. It is not "un-American or unconstitutional to refuse to be absorbed into the melting pot."

Finally, in 1999 the legislature, with Assembly Speaker Sheldon Silver, a Democrat and an Orthodox Jew, leading the charge but with the full support of Governor Pataki and the Republican leadership, took a chance and wrote a broader law, allowing any municipality of 10,000 to 125,000 inhabitants that is contained within a larger school district to petition for the creation of a discrete school district of its own, essentially to secede—and still receive state education assistance. Twenty-nine municipalities, including small cities and towns like Elmira, New Rochelle, Saratoga, Kingston and Westbury, could qualify under the new law, though none had evinced any interest in doing so. Still, the school boards association, which had led and financed the legal fight, threw in the towel.*

Many observers agreed with the dissidents that the state legislature's pursuit of the law in the face of so many court re-

---

* Joseph Berger, "Albany Tries Again to Aid Hasidic Village," *New York Times*, August 5, 1999.

versals testified to the power of the Hasidic vote, its ability to vote as a bloc of thousands of votes in support of a single candidate. But ultimately the legislative leaders also felt that the handicapped children of Kiryas Joel were entitled to the same benefits the state awarded to other religious groups, even if that meant providing the service in the curious and exacting ways that allowed the Hasidim to obey the strictures of their faith. Persistence paid off.

16

THE JEWISH ROSA PARKS

E very workday, dozens of commuter buses travel between the upstate *haredi* villages of Kiryas Joel, Monsey and New Square to Manhattan locales, like the Diamond District and the Lower East Side, where the Hasidim and other *Haredim* work. It is one of those astonishing phenomena that combines an 18th century lifestyle—that of the anachronistic bearded and black-suited and fervently pious Hasidim—with 21st century innovation: the sleek, streamlined, air-conditioned commuter bus. Most of these buses, though privately operated, receive government subsidies aimed at encouraging Americans not to drive, and receive franchises from the state or city for the routes they ply. But many of them come equipped with an amenity seldom found on a Greyhound bus: a curtain down the center aisle that separates the men and the women for Jewish prayers. The curtain allows Jewish men to fulfill their daily prayer obligations—mornings and afternoon—saving time during the otherwise boring and confined routine of commuting.

The curtain—known as a *mechitza* and similar in concept to the barriers separating men and women in Orthodox synagogues during prayer so they will not be distracted
by, say, sexual urges—has been a feature of these buses since
the 1950s, ever since Hasidim chose to settle in these rural
enclaves while needing to pursue livelihoods in the city. For
the most part they have not been a source of vocal objections.
Non-Hasidim who use the bus lines long ago reconciled
themselves to the peculiarities of Hasidic life and have toler-
ated even the curtain, congregating behind the driver along
with the Hasidic women and leaving the right side of the bus
to the Hasidic men.

Until one woman objected. In December 1993, Sima Rabinovicz, a 47-year-old Soviet emigrant and mother of two who
then worked as a supervisor of cardiology tests at a Lower
East Side clinic, was sitting in a seat in the back of the 49-
seat bus as it cruised up a crowded Manhattan avenue heading
back to Monsey. Rabinovicz, a slim, slightly built, dark-haired
woman customarily also sat in the front of the bus behind
the driver along with the other non-Hasidim. She did not
object to morning prayers—known informally as *minyanim*
after the quorum of 10 men preferred for certain prayers like
the mourner's *Kaddish*—because they were usually advertised
by the bus company on its schedule with the words "*minyan
on board.*" But she was irritated by the impromptu *minyanim*
spontaneously patched together in the afternoons on her way
home because they had not been advertised. She sometimes
would not move when asked, forcing the men to find another
spot for prayer or otherwise working around her. There was

also something in the way the men partitioned off the women and the way they spoke to the women that offended her feminine—and perhaps feminist—pride.

But on this early December day of the dustup one of the men told her rudely, "Move it!" and when she refused the men complained to the driver, who urged her to obey them. As the bus rolled northward, she held her ground, but the men persisted and she told them: "I'm going to move only if you call a cop." One of the men, she told me later, threatened her by saying he would, in her words, "stone her until she bled." Eventually, the men asked the driver to halt the bus and they murmured their prayers—which must be completed before sundown—on the sidewalk. Then they reboarded the bus and wound their way homeward.*

But an indignant Rabinovicz found her way to the New York Civil Liberties Union, which filed a complaint of sex discrimination on her behalf with the State Division of Human Rights and followed up with a civil lawsuit.

"I didn't move because I didn't feel it was right just because I'm a woman for them to tell me what to do," she told me later in a chat at the civil liberties union's office. "Today they can tell me to move my seat; tomorrow they will tell me to get off the bus. And they can tell me those things just because I'm a woman, nothing else."

Instantly, Rabinovicz's story became a minor cause célèbre in the Jewish and feminist worlds. The *Forward* newspaper, the

---

* Joseph Berger, "Discrimination or Discourtesy? A Woman Won't Leave Her Bus Seat for Hasidic Prayer Meeting," *New York Times*, September 9, 1994.

Jewish affairs weekly, christened her the Jewish Rosa Parks in homage to the black seamstress who in 1955 in Montgomery Alabama, refused to give up her seat on a bus to a white man, something she was required to do under that city's segregationist laws.

The New York bus company, Monsey Trails, operated by a Hasidic family that lives in the village of New Square, fought back, retaining the Becket Fund for Religious Liberty, a public interest group, to defend it against a possible lawsuit. What was at issue, it said, was not discrimination but simple courtesy. She was being asked to defer to fellow passengers performing a routine task—prayer—and she refused. The request, the company's owners suggested, was no more burdensome or different in kind than one passenger asking a fellow traveler to change seats so the first passenger could sit down next to a spouse or get up so they could pass by to go to the toilet. In short the company said, Rabinovicz was "a troublemaker," unnecessarily causing a rumpus in the daily routine of hundreds of passengers.

But Rabinovicz and the civil liberties union pressed on, pointing out that Monsey Trails received its license from the state to operate along a prescribed route and so must adhere to state laws that ban discrimination in public conveyances, housing and employment. For the NYCLU. the issue was another in the roll call of instances where the Hasidic way of life clashed with government prerogatives. It was in its way no different than the Kiryas Joel case, where Hasidim were asking the government to finance a school just for Hasidim. Indeed, it turned out on closer examination that Monsey Trails that year had received $650,000 in mass transit subsidies from New York State, a quarter of the company's annual revenue.

Ultimately, the NYCLU decided not to press the case further in the courts and, in yearlong negotiations, hammered out an out-of-court settlement with the Becket Fund. Why it did not go further was not precisely clear from its statements, though it is more than plausible that the case posed a dilemma for an organization that is also a strong defender of religious freedom and the accommodations governments have to make to see that religion thrives. It is also possible that Rabinovicz decided not to press the point too forcefully because the Hasidim are people she must deal with daily as a resident of heavily Hasidic Monsey.

The seven-page settlement, reached in March 1995, was a compromise of Talmudic subtlety, with the parties having different interpretations of what was agreed on and what it would require. Monsey Trails stipulated that it would no longer provide a curtain and the hooks and ceiling tracks needed to hang it for purposes of prayer. It also agreed to stop listing the availability of prayer *minyanim* on its timetables. After that, the implementation remained in dispute. Kevin J. Hasson, president of the Becket Fund, said passengers would still be able to fashion a makeshift curtain and hang it with, say, duct tape if no other riders objected and if safety was not compromised. However, Arthur Eisenberg, legal director of the civil liberties organization, said he understood that any curtain would violate federal safety regulations. However, he allowed that if the Hasidic men wanted to hang a coat up to prevent them from gazing at women during prayer, "arguably they can do that." And Jacob Lunger, the manager of the bus company, told me that the settlement boiled down to this: drivers may ask passengers to accommodate the wishes of other passengers as long as "they make sure nobody's harassed."

"The religious shouldn't be harassed, the secular shouldn't be harassed," he said.

But what, I asked him, will happen if some woman chooses to take a seat in the middle of the impromptu prayer service?

"I hope it never happens," he said.

As far as I can tell, not much has changed. The men find ways to drape a makeshift curtain and wall off an area of the bus for prayer, and when a certain feisty woman is on board they work around her seat. When the *Forward* revisited the Monsey Trail dispute in 2011, Lunger told the reporter that drivers are instructed not to put up or take down the dividing curtains, but the company "leaves it up to the passengers for them to decide what to do."

"Sometimes they decide and put it up, and we let them do what they want," he said.*

Not much has changed in a more recent case as well—after an initial commotion. There is a bus line in Brooklyn that few New Yorkers, other than Hasidim, would ever need to take. It plies a route between the Hasidic neighborhood of Williamsburg and the Hasidic neighborhood of Borough Park five miles away. It is called the B110 and costs the same as any city bus but it is privately operated by a company owned by

---

* Josh Nathan-Kazis and Sasha Chavkin, "Riding Together on Sex-Segregated Bus," *Jewish Daily Forward*, November 11, 2011.

Orthodox Jews under a franchise from the city, which has absorbed several private operators into its transportation system in Brooklyn and Queens.

A stranger boarding the bus would quickly notice that the men, almost all in standard-issue Hasidic garb, cluster in the front and the women, bewigged and wearing long-sleeved apparel, sit in the rear. Practically no one seems disturbed by this arrangement. That has been true since 1973, when Private Transportation Corporation acquired the route through a bid. The company even posts guidelines in the front and rear of the bus telling passengers "when boarding a crowded bus with attending passengers in the front, women should board the back door after paying the driver in the front." Another guideline speaks of "designated areas."

In 2011, the bus line's odd practices came to the attention of readers outside the Hasidic world. A Columbia Journalism School publication, *New York World*, described the curious seating arrangements and reported that a female rider was told she had to move to the back. Soon the blogosphere lit up with the story and then mayor Michael R. Bloomberg was forced to comment.

"Private people: you can have a private bus," he told a news conference. "Go rent a bus and do what you want on it." But segregating men and women is not permitted on city buses, he said, stating the obvious. The city's Department of Transportation followed up by asking the bus company's president, Jacob Marmurstein, to provide any complaints filed about the company's practices and to explain what the company was doing to prevent discrimination.

Weeks later, the guidelines were taken down but not much else had changed. Men still sat in the front and women in the back, and almost everyone observed the guidelines as unwritten law. These are people who are, after all, very familiar with unwritten law. Christine Haughney, my colleague at the *New York Times* who first wrote about the bus for the *Times*, took a ride and found no one who objected to the arrangement. The male photographer who accompanied her was told to sit in the front with the other men and she herself was urged to sit with women in the back—though no one ordered her to do so.

"It's such a normal thing for us that women and men are separate," said Gitty Green, a thirty-year-old mother who boarded the bus with her three children and a stroller and headed straight to the back. "Most of the ladies go to the back."

A male rider, Asaf Amitay, a thirty-five-year-old regular passenger who lives in Borough Park, told Christine that he doesn't like women to sit in front. "The women is in the back, the men are in the front," he said, as if the arrangement made perfect sense.*

Comments like that suggest the blinkered world view that many Hasidim have, which ignores the rules the wider society has adopted. A public bus is not where religious mores can be obeyed to the letter, particularly if they chafe against rules against discrimination by gender. Yet Alexander Rapaport, as cosmopolitan a Hasid as you will find, someone conversant with contemporary American culture and politics, argues that

---

* Christine Haughney, "Bus Segregation of Jewish Women Prompts Review," *New York Times*, October 20, 2011, p. A26.

some tolerance and latitude ought to be applied in this case because Hasidim simply "do not feel like sitting next to the opposite sex."

"Lots of Hasidim never go onto public transportation, never use a city bus or subway," he told me. "They're having a transportation headache all the time. A Hasid might say that he's taking away lots of liberties to live that holy life style. He would say, 'I live my entire life in the Williamsburg ghetto. It may be a narrow way of looking at the world, but I gave up the entire world.' That's where a lot of the tension ends up."

His views have some backing from some experts in the First Amendment. Cole Durham, director of the International Center for Law and Religion Studies at Brigham Young University in Utah, said that separate seating could be regarded as a an effort "to accommodate religious beliefs." Without the curtains, Durham said, Hasidim might feel unable to take public buses. "So you have to ask which is the greater form of discrimination," he told the *Forward*.

In New York City, the B110 is still operating pretty much the way it always has. In April 2013, I saw the bus stop in Williamsburg, and men exited from the front door and women from the back in two gender-determined groups. The rules of its riders, it seems, are implicitly understood and preferred.

Meanwhile, segregation of the sexes seems to be expanding into other public spheres as well. In October 2011, Yiddish signs appeared on many trees in Hasidic Williamsburg instructing women to be careful when approaching men on the sidewalk. "Precious Jewish daughter," one sign said, "please move to the side when a man approaches." Pictures of the sign were posted by a blog, called Failed Messiah, that is openly critical of many Hasidic practices, and city workers took them down for the simple fact that it is illegal to place signs on public trees. Yet the Williamsburg signs mirrored those in the upstate Hasidic village of New Square, where it is an ongoing practice—spawned by tradition as well as by the sign's commandment—for men to walk on one side of the street and women on the other. Samuel Heilman, the expert on Hasidic Jews, said that increasingly confident Hasidim are echoing practices in Israel—enforced not by the government but through unspoken communal pressure—where the genders are segregated on many city buses and on streets in Hasidic ghettoes.

"What is special about this isn't the segregation of the sexes, but the segregation in the public domain," Heilman told the *Forward*, speaking of the Williamsburg bus line. "That didn't happen before. They separated men and women but they never would have thought to do it on turf that isn't completely theirs. They are saying, 'We own the street, we own the bus, we own the public square.'"

17

THIS PROPERTY IS CONDEMNED

In no area of public life have more conflicts sprung up between Hasidim and their neighbors than on matters of private property. Sometimes the battles reflect communal hostility to the Hasidic way of life, sometimes the cavalier attitude Hasidim have often shown toward government regulations, often both. But land and housing issues offer a window into both the rising power of Hasidim within their communities and the dilemmas that these communities face. They are exquisitely caught between the pulls of religious freedom for one group in a democracy and the personal privileges and predilections of other inhabitants.

Twenty-five years ago, I visited a rabbi who was causing quite a stir in the suburban hamlet of Monsey in Rockland County, which had already grown into a teeming Orthodox and Hasidic enclave. His name was Solomon Rottenberg, an emigrant from Hungary who had a lush silvery beard, spiraling sidelocks and broad shoulders that gave him a strikingly distinguished air in his gray silk *kapote*. On the day I met him,

he also had on a *shtreimel*. Perhaps it was Chanukah or perhaps
a visit from the *New York Times* was a festive occasion. I never
asked. Nevertheless, Rottenberg, an émigré from Brooklyn's
Hasidic streets 50 miles away, was caught in peculiar cross-
winds. Orthodox Jews, especially Hasidim who lived nearby,
were eager to pray with him because of his reputation as a
devout and spirited rabbi. But his neighbors on the tranquil
suburban street resented the crowds of Hasidim suddenly
scampering along their sidewalks on quiet Saturday mornings.
A tableau of dozens of bearded Jews wrapped in prayer shawls
and walking among freshly cut lawns and aged oaks and wil-
lows was not the suburban picture they had had in mind when
they forsook New York City for Rockland County.

"When a man sits in his backyard on a Saturday afternoon
listening to the radio and his new neighbor comes along and
asks him to 'turn the radio down, you're interfering with my
Sabbath,' he doesn't like it," Herbert Reisman, then the town
supervisor of Ramapo, which embraces Monsey, told me.

Rottenberg had set up a *shtibl* in what had been the basement playroom of his ranch house. He furnished it with a
Torah and Holy Ark that had been among the possessions he
brought from Brooklyn in the early 1980s. In his Orthodox
Brooklyn neighborhood such *shtiblech* studded every block.
Not so in the suburbs. But observant Jews near his house
liked praying in that onetime playroom because the nearest
formal synagogue in this remote patch of Monsey was a one-
mile walk away, a burden on sultry summer days or snow-
laden winter ones. By joining Rottenberg, they were not only
able to pray communally with 10 or more Jewish men—the

preferred *minyan* for certain prayers—but they were able to do so with a rabbi steeped in the mystical and emotive Hasidic tradition.

Soon Jews were flocking to Rottenberg's *shtibl*—40 by the count of neighbors. So Rottenberg decided to convert the two-car garage attached to his basement into a women's prayer section. By doing so, he was allowing the *shtibl* to blossom into a literal house of worship. The neighbors were annoyed and distressed and they complained to officials of Monsey's governing entity, the town of Ramapo.

"What do they want?" Rabbi Rottenberg asked me. "That I should lock the door and not let anyone come in because they want to pray?"

Ramapo's zoning laws only allow synagogues on two-acre plots, not in typically small suburban tracts like the one-acre plots on Rottenberg's street. The town's fire laws require that spaces where so many people regularly gather must have appropriate alarms, exits, wiring and other safety features. Moreover, the neighbors felt that the rustic quiet of their block was being regularly disturbed, not just on Saturday mornings, but on Friday evenings, Saturday evenings, eight days of Passover, eight days of Succoth, the night and morning of Purim and many other days. There is, after all, no shortage of Jewish holidays.

"You're making a residential area into a commercial, heavily trafficked area," Leonard Weiner, a business executive who lived four houses away, told me. Weiner had moved to the suburbs years before and his idea of the sound of a Saturday morning was the whirr of a lawn mower's blades, not the murmur of Jews praying or schmoozing on the way to synagogue. Like many of the complaining neighbors, he was Jewish, so he could not be charged with anti-Semitism. But that logical hurdle did not stop the defenders of Rabbi Rottenberg.

"There's a species of anti-Semitism called anti-Orthodoxy," Mark Greenberg, a public relations executive who resided in the neighborhood and supports Rottenberg, told me.*

Indeed, it became evident to me that gentile neighbors were loath to complain precisely because they feared being accused of anti-Semitism, while their Jewish neighbors, who preferred the conventional, sedate synagogues of the Reform and Conservative movements, if they worshipped at all, were eager to be accepted as regular American Joes and were ready to take on the Hasidim. The subtext of some of the comments they made suggested they were embarrassed that they were being followed into the clean-cut suburbs by these throwbacks to the ghettoes and *shtetls* of Europe.

More than that, the Hasidim and other ultra-Orthodox Jews were beginning to dominate Monsey. What had been in the early 1950s a typical suburban landscape dotted with just a single yeshiva and a few woebegone shopping strips on Ramapo's main roads, containing kosher butchers and bakeries, had by the late 1990s mushroomed into an Orthodox settlement filled with 112 synagogues, 45 yeshivas, a number of ritual baths and thousands of Hasidim on *Shabbos* walking the rustic

---

* Joseph Berger, "Basement Synagogue Causes a Clash in Rockland," *New York Times*, December 8, 1986.

roadsides in full regalia. In 1997, the Hasidic and Orthodox population was estimated at 6,000 families, or more than 35,000 people in a town of 94,000 inhabitants. Monsey had willy-nilly grown into the world's third-largest Hasidic settlement after Israel and Brooklyn. There are entire kosher supermarkets, clothing stores sell the standard Hasidic black rabbit men's hats and long-sleeved dresses preferred by the women, and the hardware stores even stock prefabricated *sukkot*—huts used in the eight-day feast that commemorates the flimsy housing of the Israelites in the desert. The *Haredim*—as Hasidim and other ultra-Orthodox Jews are together known—have been pressing into areas of Monsey that were never *haredi*, like north Monsey, including Mr. Weiner's Forshay neighborhood, a subdivision of forty one-acre homes that at the time of my visit were selling for $200,000 each and today are probably triple that in value.

The resulting disputes have a way of becoming public— and in Monsey they did. The town of Ramapo—where all five board members in the 1990s were Jewish—took the rabbi to court, fining him $250 for persisting with worship services in the face of zoning and fire violations. In fact town building inspectors sat in their cars outside Rottenberg's home on the Sabbath, counting worshippers who streamed in, an insensitivity remarked upon by Rottenberg's lawyer, John F. McAlevey, a former town supervisor. Nevertheless, Barry Traub, the deputy town attorney, pointed out that the town had no choice: there were more than a dozen homes that had been illegally converted to synagogues and several months before the Rottenberg *shtibl* opened up, one of those illegal synagogues had burned down. The wiring there too had been inadequate.

Reisman, the town supervisor and a Conservative Jew, confided in a tour he gave me of his town that the accusations of religious prejudice were upsetting.

"It's obviously of concern to me that I might be accused of interfering with a person's right to practice religion, and the advice I got from rabbis and friends of mine is that I am not interfering with a person's right to practice religion, but that I am enforcing the law with the desire to protect the health and safety of the people."

In 1984, the town had in fact enacted a law to accommodate Orthodox Jews who wanted to pray in small groups with favored rabbis. The law even became known as the *shtibl* law. It allowed rabbis to designate half of their ground-floor space as a worship area. Rabbi Rottenberg's synagogue did not pass muster because its peculiar configuration uses almost all the ground-floor space.

The controversy eventually quieted down when Rabbi Rottenberg and his supporters spent $20,000 on contractors who installed fire-resistant walls around the furnaces, smoke and heat detectors, quick-opening exit doors and alarms linked to the town's fire department. And the issue of the zoning variance seemed to melt away; McAlevey told me many years later that he had "successfully argued that Rottenberg's use of the house was for a home occupation that was permitted under the zoning."

Nevertheless, the issue captured in miniature what has been happening in Rockland County and Brooklyn and almost anywhere Hasidic communities spring up: clashes, often fierce, about the application of municipal housing, zoning and land-use laws and codes. A few years after the Rottenberg controversy, Ramapo building inspectors had to close down two ranch houses used as a dormitory for 53 teen-age yeshiva boys because the houses were overcrowded and had no fire extinguishers or smoke detectors, wiring was exposed and gas lines were uncapped.

"It was a human firetrap waiting for a fire to happen," Reisman told me.[*]

In Ramapo itself and the surrounding towns, warring parties have gotten so stiff-necked and the conflicts insoluble that entire neighborhoods have seceded and formed their own villages so they can write or rewrite their own zoning laws. One Hasidic group, the Vizhnitz, created the village of Kaser in 1990 so its residents could build housing for its ever-flourishing community at greater density than Ramapo rules allowed. In the opposite camp, non-Jews and more secularized Jews have formed the villages of Airmont, New Hempstead and Wesley Hills to preserve the sparse *Better Homes & Gardens* ambience that attracted them to Rockland County.

"There are two reasons villages get formed in Rockland: one is to keep the Hasidim out and the other is to keep the Hasidim in," Paul W. Adler, chairman of the county's Jewish Community Relations Council, told me.

---

[*] Joseph Berger, "Growing Pains for a Rural Hasidic Enclave," *New York Times*, January 13, 1997.

In 1991, Airmont, a corner of Ramapo with 8,600 people, most of them secular Jews or gentiles but 250 of whom were Orthodox Jews, grew so frustrated with Ramapo's tolerance for home synagogues in basements and living rooms that it applied to wall itself off as a discrete village. It wanted to enshrine "strong zoning that would preserve Airmont's character." Ramapo approved the request. But the U.S. attorney general at the time, William P. Barr, and the U.S. attorney for the Southern District of New York filed suit against Airmont and Ramapo for discrimination under the Fair Housing Act for trying to exclude Orthodox Jews who needed to walk to a convenient synagogue on the Sabbath. The village responded by allowing synagogues on two-acre lots, but such properties are far too expensive for average Hasidim to acquire. A judge ruled that Airmont needed to revise that code as well.

From the Hasidic perspective, many of those laws that Hasidim are accused of disobeying amount to discrimination. Ramapo, Hasidic leaders told me, continues to forbid the construction of town houses, larger unattached houses and multiple family dwellings that the burgeoning Hasidic families need.

"You're putting a person into a corner to break the law," Mendel Hoffman, then the director of the Rockland County Development Council, an antipoverty group that focuses on obtaining grants for Hasidic families, told me. "We do not break the law in any other area. Why housing? Because you're forcing the community to break the law."

Approvals for housing developments cannot begin to keep

pace with the Hasidic birthrate. The Klausenberg Hasidim, one of the smaller sects, openly acknowledged they violated the zoning code in building three-family homes in an area restricted to two-families. They did so while suing Ramapo for $15 million and charging it with discriminatory enforcement that, the Hasidim said, gave them no choice.

Moreover, Hasidim come from an Eastern European tradition where they could set up a yeshiva or synagogue in a barn or in the basement of a large house—no questions asked. But in an American system where new laws are added every few years to ward off the latest well-publicized danger or demon, it can, for example, take two years to nail down the municipal approvals that a yeshiva needs to open, two years when students may have no place to study or live. Hasidim become impatient.

"If you do not give me the opportunity to do it properly, slowly but surely they do things without going through the proper channels," Hoffman said.

(It should be noted that in 2009 the Rockland County newspaper, the *Journal News*, and the Yiddish online newspaper *Voz Iz Neias* [What Is New] reported that a government-financed $7.3-million-a-year health center Hoffman runs, the Ben Gilman Medical and Dental Clinic, was closed for a time. The local board of health found that the facility was so badly contaminated by bird excrement and bird and mammal carcasses that patients were complaining about the stench and some employees wore surgical masks in order to breathe. Hoffman blamed the building's landlord. The clinic reopened after two months.)

As the Hasidim and other Orthodox Jews kept expanding, they also grew bolder. By 2002, Congregation Mischknois Lavier Yakov, a Hasidic congregation, purchased a 19.3-acre parcel on the north side of Hillside Avenue in Airmont, on what my colleague at the *Times* Peter Applebome described as "a narrow crooked street of eclectic homes, some dating back to the 1700s, towering oaks, wild turkeys and semirural repose." Twenty years before, the site had been considered as the location of a 950-seat church by the evangelical Church of the Nazarene, but after fierce resistance by neighbors, who complained about traffic and water issues, the church sold the site to the congregation, an obscure group of Canadian-based Hasidim. They were fiercer. The congregation said it wanted to build a 170-student dormitory along with 30 town houses for faculty that might house as many as 300 people. The neighborhood was again infuriated.

"Everyone's up in arms about it," Anthony Quattrone, who lives on the other end of the street from the site, told Applebome. "It's a quiet neighborhood, everyone's on well water, nobody thinks it belongs here."

Again the Hasidim managed to get the federal government on their side. The U.S. attorney's office argued that the dormitories were legal under a relatively new law passed unanimously by Congress in 2000, the Religious Land Use and Institutionalized Persons Act. The act overrides local zoning ordinances that unreasonably limit religious institutions unless an adverse effect on the health, safety and welfare of the community can be proven.

"I wouldn't want to say anything bad about another religious Jew, but to me this isn't about religion, it's about people
wanting their own space," Barry Kostrinsky, who had lived in
Rockland since 1987, told Applebome.*

Airmont's then mayor, John C. Layne, tried to settle the
conflict, knowing that a loss could cost the village's finances
hundreds of thousands of dollars. But he did not do so happily.

"I'm a practicing Roman Catholic," he said. "My children
go to religious school. My wife teaches at a religious school.
But I don't think it's the place of religion to change the character of a single-family neighborhood, and I don't think it's
the place of the federal government to take local land use decisions from local governments."

Airmont eventually had to settle in federal court, paying
a $10,000 fine and allowing the yeshiva to proceed with its
dormitories.

"The village of Airmont did the right thing by agree-
ing to amend its zoning law and by allowing Congregation
Mischknois Lavier Yakov to build a school and student housing
on land it purchased almost ten years ago," the U.S. attorney,
Preet Bharara, said emphatically. "As this case demonstrates,
we will vigorously enforce the federal civil rights laws against
those who discriminate based on religion."

Houses of worships—Christian churches, mosques, as well
as synagogues—and religious institutions perennially face
these obstacles in mature communities, particularly when the

---

* Peter Applebome, "Where Zoning Seems a Test of Tolerance," *New York
Times*, June 15, 2005.

religious group is alien to the majority of residents. In the affluent town of Millburn, New Jersey, a Lubavitch emissary,
like missionaries of yore, decided to establish a foothold so he
could proselytize among local less observant Jews and conducted Sabbath and holiday prayer services out of his standard suburban house. That alone did not make his neighbors
happy, but when he decided to expand—by tearing down his
family's home as well as a neighboring house and replacing
them with a full-blown 144-seat, Dutch Colonial–style synagogue and social center, with parking for 50 cars, more than
100 of his neighbors banded together to stop him. He needed
a zoning variance, but local zoning only allows houses of worship on three-acre lots and the opponents insisted the town
enforce that rule. The rabbi, the opponents said, could have
found a three-acre lot that size in a less residential section of
town accustomed to large institutions. Yet the rabbi, Mendel
Bogomilsky, argued that the landscape of the United States is
studded with churches in residential areas and it's clear that in
some towns the residents worshipping in these very churches
set up restrictive zoning to bar any other churches from invading. At last look, the case was still being argued before
town boards. But experience seems to indicate that Rabbi
Bogomilsky will eventually prevail. This is a country that was
founded by people who were considered religious zealots in
their home countries of England and France, and the very
first amendment to the Constitution bends over backward to
reject limits on the free exercise of religion. Hasidim are only
a contemporary specimen of religious zealots, no different
than the Puritans and Huguenots were in their time.

The strongest case that opponents of Hasidic developments can mount comes whenever health, fire and safety rules
are violated or paid lip service to, as often happens with Hasidim, who don't give laws on the civil books the same authority as laws in the Talmud. In 2007, the Skverer Hasidim,
its 7,000 residents choking on the limited housing in the
bounded village of New Square, dedicated what they hoped
would eventually become a satellite village in the Catskills
hamlet of Spring Glen, in the town of Mamakating. The 450-
acre spread, in a tranquil, verdant valley, was the former site of
a popular resort called Homowack Lodge, a place that had a
sprawling main building, 20 outbuildings, a golf course and a
pool. "We are talking about creating a city from scratch," a 12-
page brochure for the new village announced. It mentioned
yeshivas, *mikvehs* and a shopping center as features of the new
city. So heady were the Hasidim about this new opportunity
that 10,000 of them flocked to the camp for the festive dedication ceremony. The Skverer leaders even christened the new
enclave Kiryas Square, using a Hebrew name for settlement
and an Anglicization of the sect's name.

But neighbors quickly objected.

"What they want to do contradicts the goal of the master
plan of the town, which is to remain a rural community," said
Anita Altman, an official at the United Jewish Appeal who
owns a house adjacent to the former Homowack site.*

The opponents were able to find plenty of ammunition
for their case. The entire complex had been allowed to go

---

* Author's interview with Anita Altman.

to seed by several owners before the Skverer acquired it in 2006. That deterioration did not stop the Skverer Hasidim from establishing a camp for 300 girls and female counselors, Machne Bnos Square, while construction proceeded on the village itself. But in doing so, the Hasidim did not obtain the proper permits to run a summer camp. Moreover, a heating oil spill in July caught the eye of state environmental officials. Soon other regulators found dysfunctional fire alarms, pervasive mold and electrical hazards in waterlogged lines, and the health department issued a mandatory evacuation order. By August, when a judge interceded, the camp was evacuated, with the girls transferred by a fleet of school buses to a nearby Bobov camp so they could finish their summer vacations.

In July 2010, Congregation Ahavas Chaverim Gemilas Chesed, the governing Skverer religious group, pleaded guilty to four environmental crimes resulting from the incidents the year before and over the next few years the county revealed that the owners had not paid taxes totaling $453,000 for three years. Then in October 2012, a New York State appeals court upheld the town of Mamakating's denial of a property tax exemption for the Homowack property because the congregation had failed to prove that the property would be used "exclusively for religious purposes" and had not tried to get the necessary summer camp permits.

Unpaid tax bills and hefty fines have put the future of the site in jeopardy. In the spring of 2013, Altman told me the deal was dead, that the Skver Hasidim were facing foreclosure for nonpayment of $261,000 in taxes and fines and a public auction of the bulk of the property as early as the following spring. But other observers were not so ready to write the New Square II project off. If the Skverer sect can find the money to pay the tax bills, it will probably find some way to finesse the zoning, since American legal principles make it difficult to keep out religious institutions and communities. Or, as has happened elsewhere, the Hasidim might ask to have themselves declared an independent village and the surrounding town may submit and breathe a sigh of relief. It will be rid of the fights and squabbles that often come with having a determined, sometimes pesky group of Hasidim in their midst.

18

SCHOOLS FOR SCANDAL

Scattered throughout the Hasidic village of New Square in New York's suburban Rockland County are study halls where young men spend much of the day immersed in tall, yellowed volumes of Talmud, swaying and fidgeting as they almost sing the written words to an ancient melody. The men earn neither educational credits nor stipends for what they do, even though most of them are of breadwinning age. Studying is what these young men had been doing practically all their lives and what their tribe has been doing for centuries. (Yes, the Baal Shem Tov and his immediate disciples were famous for not extolling scholarship in the way the Vilna Gaon and his acolytes were to do, but when it came to the habit of daily study the two movements in time began to converge, and Hasidim will rhapsodize over their rebbe's command of Talmud.)

So it was not entirely surprising that in the early 1980s, the village accepted an offer by Rockland Community College to set up a Judaic studies program. Now they might get college credit for courses in Bible, Talmud, Jewish history and ethics. The course catalog offered such courses as Biology 140, the Anatomy and Pathology of Vertebrate Animals, where among other things they could learn the fine points of kosher slaughter, and where the *Shulchan Aruch*—the Code of Jewish Law, and not a textbook in modern zoology, was the required reading.

Hasidim like the Skverer have always resisted attending college, because it exposes them intimately to the temptations of the mainstream, requires them to mingle with the opposite sex and leaves them vulnerable to the ripples of confusing secular ideas. But this program would be different. The courses would be offered in New Square, a village four miles from the main college campus and where everyone is a Skver Hasid, not in the main college campus at Suffern, which has 8,000 largely secular students. Many of the courses were for independent study with mentors, a style of learning pious Jews have mastered for centuries even if is hard to monitor by public officials. And the students might earn two-year, community college degrees.

And there was another incentive, a financial one. Hasidim are under enormous pressure to lead a lifestyle that does not encourage young men to work until they have completed their yeshiva studies well into their twenties. They desperately seek ways of finding money to enable them to do so, and most receive support by in-laws or other family members. These Judaic studies students would be eligible for federal and state tuition-assistance grants geared to low-income students and worth as much as $2,400 a year. While that money would end up with Rockland Community College, the students themselves might qualify for federally subsidized Section 8 housing stipends and other antipoverty money. Women too could take the courses, though ways would have to be engineered to keep them separate from the men. Given the lip service often paid to secular legalities, Skver leaders clearly realized that the program's rules about accreditation, course content, degrees and other formalities of secular life could be fudged to make sure the students received the government financial support.

Rockland Community College was eager to enroll these students. Publicly, it said that it wanted to attract what it calls "nontraditional students" and that $2,400 a year would go into its own coffers and increase its revenues. Left unspoken, however, was the keen desire by college officials and political representatives to put them in the good graces of the Hasidic community, quite powerful in Rockland County, where the 90,000 Jews at the time, most of them Orthodox, represented almost a third of the population and where Hasidic groups like Skver vote in a bloc.

Starting in the fall of 1982 and over the next seven years, more than 3,000 students were enrolled in the Judaic studies program. The college even used recruiters to enroll the Hasidic students, promising them hundreds of dollars a year. But the gift turned out to be a curse, and again displayed how the attempts to mesh the Hasidic way of life with the secular world and its rules often leads to disaster. In 1997, six years after auditors for the state comptroller's office began raising questions, six New Square Hasidim, including leaders and founders of the Rockland County village, were indicted by the United States attorney's office in Manhattan on charges of fraud, money laundering and conspiracy growing out of the Judaic studies program. After many years all either pleaded guilty or were convicted. What was worse was the stigma arising out of the probability that the entire village was aware of the scheme and had condoned it.

The criminal charges described the study program as a fraudulent arrangement that obtained more than $11 million in federal subsidies, known as Pell grants, and state tuition assistance grants known as TAP. The sum constituted one of the largest cases of abuse of government educational aid at the time. In all those seven years, not a single student, it turned out, had completed a two-year associate's degree, which had been the purported goal of those who enrolled. That was because none of the 3,000 students actually took the 45 credits all students must—under state Board of Regents rules—take in general humanities, arts, mathematics and science courses that are given at the college's main campus at Suffern. And the courses they did take in Judaic studies, state auditors had earlier said, "provide Orthodox Jewish religious education with other Jewish perspectives sometimes included for contrast."* Thus the courses were "theological in nature," the kind

---

* Audit report of Rockland Community College, Office of the New York State Comptroller, 1991, pp. 5–6.

aimed at professional training and not eligible for government aid. The course in vertebrate anatomy was entirely a course in kosher slaughtering according to ultra-Orthodox principles, with other perspectives ignored. The students went along because their leaders told them to and it seemed to cost nothing, even providing housing and other benefits.

Many students, the indictment said, had been ineligible to receive aid because they were not pursuing degrees and some did not actually meet with mentors or take examinations. Even if they had met with their professors, officials said, those instructors held religious degrees in Orthodox education, not the required secular degrees. Registration for the program was so muddled—and often fabricated—that some students did not even know they were enrolled and some were enrolled in as many as five different yeshivas and other educational institutions in New York and Israel where they were supposed to be pursuing their independent study. Shulem Deen, the Skver defector, told me that some village officials came to him and asked him to sign some documents that were necessary for the yeshiva, but never explained he was enrolling in a college course. He remembers signing. Some students were listed as taking as many as 84 credits, and not those required for a degree. Some students did not even exist. According to the indictment, the six defendants— Chaim Berger, a village trustee and one of four Holocaust survivors who founded the village in 1957; his son, Benjamin; Kalman Stern and David Goldstein, administrators of a Brooklyn seminary; Avrum D. Freisel, the son of New Square's then mayor; and Jacob Elbaum—covered up the true nature of the program by submitting fictitious resumes, false minutes of meetings and faked "mentor logs." In 1985, Berger was made administrator of Judaic studies and eventually became chairman of the department, despite a lack of the required academic credentials.*

The program had to be accredited to receive tuition aid, and Abraham Berkowitz, the former dean of a Brooklyn yeshiva allied with New Square, eventually testified at the 1998–99 trial about how he faked resumes and other documents so that the rabbis, teachers and administrators supposedly working in the program could qualify under the guidelines needed for accreditation. He said the yeshiva he worked for in Brooklyn, Yeshiva Toldos Yaakov Yosef, had no courses, grades or semesters—it was an ordinary yeshiva—and so there really was no program in Judaic studies.† Nevertheless, he created one on paper in the government applications he filled out. Others testified that the only languages in the "courses" were Hebrew and Yiddish; any history of the Bible and Israel was taught through traditional religious texts. Documents were created for phantom students or laced with false information such as fake names and fake bank accounts to establish the eligibility of real New Square residents to participate in the programs. Many of the phantom names belonged to Russian immigrants who had no idea of how their personal information was being exploited. One name, that of Orit Riter, was used three times over five years

---

* Benjamin Weiser, "Six Indicted in Fraud Over Use of Grants for Hasidic Groups," *New York Times*, May 29, 1997.

† Eric J. Greenberg, "Witness: Yeshiva Faked Documents for Grants," *Jewish Week*, December 4, 1998.

to collect $8,600 in tuition assistance; but when the real Orit Riter applied for tuition assistance, she was turned down because state records showed she had already received it.[*]

The testimony raised the question of whether the yeshiva did anything differently than yeshivas normally do, except receive government financing. In other words, the government was subsidizing a theological and religious enterprise, not a strictly educational one. Investigators for the state education department had warned the college that the program "was indicative of religious education" and did not meet the college's own mission of offering students "a broad world view and cross-cultural experiences." Thus the program should not have been eligible for financial aid. But it was not until 1989—seven years after the program began—that the college suspended the program.

Indeed, as bad as the accusations against the Hasidic administrators were, the evidence contained in audits about the actions of college and county officials—none of them Hasidim—was almost as bad. A report by the county legislature in 1992 said the college, led by a "secretive" president and "ineffectual" trustees, had not monitored whether students were maintaining their degree status. They seemed to have conspired or turned a blind eye to the entire scheme. State education officials even said that the college had been given ample opportunities over several years to force the Judaic studies program to meet state standards but had chosen to

---

[*] Metro News Briefs, "Trial Begins for Four Tied to Stealing $10 Million," *New York Times*, November 17, 1998.

fight the complaints rather than fix them. The college's president, Thomas Clark, resigned in August 1992, claiming that the episode was a serious setback to attempts by colleges to reach nontraditional students. Another administrator, Elaine Padilla, who had championed the program from the start, raised the specter of anti-Semitism and wondered why state officials had not audited Christian study programs.* Whatever was said in the college's defense, the record shows that the college, as a result of the fraud, had to pay back to the federal and state governments at least $5.2 million of the $11 million in tuition assistance that was eventually disallowed (some payments were allowed by auditors). It took many years for the college to stabilize its finances.

Ordinary non-Hasidic county residents were also hurt. Much of the college's debts had to be repaid from county funds. "We were misled and snookered into believing there was no problem with the audit," John Grant, the county executive, said when news of the scheme first emerged in 1992. Of course, many residents disbelieved such statements and figured that county officials must have gone along with the scheme.

The trial in White Plains in 1998–99 lasted 11 weeks, and every day scores of Hasidim filled the courtroom to show their support for the defendants, claiming they were religious men who spent their lives doing charitable work.

"Am I going to stand here and tell you everything was one hundred percent kosher or forty percent kosher," one defense

---

* Jon Nordheimer, "College Plan Leads to Criminal Inquiry," *New York Times*, September 30, 1992.

lawyer said, before he laid the blame for the scheme on Chaim Berger, who along with Freisel had fled the country for Israel just before the indictments were announced and so could not be put on trial.

Nevertheless, Stern, forty years old at the time; Elbaum, thirty-eight; Benjamin Berger, thirty-seven; and David Goldstein, fifty-two, were convicted in January. Chaim Berger was arrested a month later in Israel, extradited to the United States, pleaded guilty in 2002 and was sentenced to six years in prison. He died of cancer in prison in 2004. Freisel, the son of the village's mayor, managed to stay abroad in Israel and Britain for more than 10 years until 2010, when he was extradited and pleaded guilty to embezzlement charges, which carried a five-year sentence.

While it may not be exculpatory, it is worth noting that there was little evidence that the state and federal tuition grants were used to lavishly line the pockets of any Hasidim. Rather, most of the money wound up in the Skverer yeshivas and rabbinical seminaries in New Square and Brooklyn. While those convicted have never explained or justified their actions, it is apparent that many Hasidim feel their community gets shortchanged in government funds—they pay taxes but don't send their children to public schools, for example—and so they may have felt they deserved this deal. And since the deal was offered to them by Rockland Community College officials without much interference or monitoring, the Hasidim may not have even felt that what they were doing was brazenly illegal—even if some faking of resumes to meet requirements was done.

One thing for sure is that the entire close-knit and *shtetl*-like village stoutly stood behind the six defendants and conspired to squelch the investigation as it progressed. FBI agents entering the community to deliver subpoenas found their cars surrounded by menacing Hasidim. One court-appointed administrator was locked in a room and intimidated into handing over teacher paychecks. Whatever one thought of such actions, they underscored the fortresslike cohesiveness of the village as it encountered the outside world.

Residents I spoke to shortly after the indictments were handed down contended that the defendants may have tried to shore up the village's hard-pressed educational institutions. "We believe very strongly that nobody pocketed any money," said Henry Braun, a Skverer Hasid who operates an importing business in Brooklyn.

A 53-year-old bookkeeper, who would give his name only as Mordechai C., said investigators did not appreciate that a degree program means little to a community that seldom encourages its members to study secular subjects and gives degrees only to those becoming rabbis. That is why not one of the thousands of students in the Rockland College program ever received a degree, a fact that astonished federal investigators but not the New Square residents. Gerald L. Shargel, a lawyer for the Yeshiva of New Square, now called Yeshivat Avir Yakov, even argued that "good faith is an absolute defense against fraud." Whatever justification there was for such feelings, it was clear in my conversations that people felt they were being discriminated against and saw themselves as a relatively powerless community. They recalled that just the previous April the office of United States Attorney Mary Jo White was willing to reach a $15.5 million settlement with New York University Medical Center on charges that hospital administrators inflated bills to increase federal reimbursements for research. No one was jailed. White, of course, rejected any accusations of discrimination and recalled how in 1995 a federal judge held the Yeshiva of New Square in contempt of court for defying a grand jury subpoena for bank records and other evidence, which led to a $1 million fine paid by the yeshiva. And legal experts said that improper use of federal subsidies constitutes fraud, even if the money never wound up in anyone's pockets.

One thing residents were unanimous about: the three-year investigation had shaken the village. They recalled FBI agents knocking on doors at dawn, frightening small children, "in a manner reminiscent to some of the Holocaust that many in this community endured decades ago."

"We feel watched over and followed all the time," David Gelb, a 35-year-old father of eight, told me. "I had to reassure my family all the time that it's just a few individuals and we're not going to be arrested."

And not all federal officials thought the actions of the Hasidic administrators was so egregious. President Bill Clinton, shortly before leaving office in January 2001, commuted the sentences of the four men—Stern, Elbaum, Benjamin Berger and Goldstein—who were convicted at the trial.

Of course, it was to some observers another glaring example of the reach of Hasidic political power: Just months
before, Clinton's wife, Hillary, had sought the blessings of the
Skverer Rebbe in her race for the United States Senate; she
got that plus a bloc vote of 1,400 votes that November by village residents (only 12 people voted for her opponent). Those
votes helped coast her to a victory in the election.*

---

* Randal Archibold, "Prosecutors Clear Clintons in Clemency for Four
Hasidic Men," New York Times, June 21, 2002.

19

CAIN AND ABEL IN BROOKLYN

On the bustling streets of Brooklyn's Williamsburg sits a large two-story, cinder-block building intended as a mega-synagogue, one that that could hold a breathtaking 10,000 Hasidim. Hundreds of black-hatted Hasidim scamper by every day, but no one stops in. Though $20 million was available for its construction, it is unfinished and has been for 10 years, its windows and doorways also filled in with cinder blocks to keep out thieves and mischief makers. It has yet to receive from city officials a certificate of occupancy that would allow people to pray there.

Nevertheless, just stagnating there, this ugly blight on an otherwise colorful patch of New York City makes a powerful statement, one that all those Hasidim breezing by recognize. It is a statement about the ferocity and endurance of feuds that until this day continue to tear the Hasidic world apart, even as its leaders are revered for their calm, moderation and wisdom.

To the world outside the virtual walls put up by Hasidim, the men and women in somber clothing who live such apparently spartan existences seem one uniform, cohesive group: they are all Hasidim. But not only is the Hasidic world broken up by sects, some two dozen sizable ones, and many smaller groups, but some of the sects have a history of enmity between them so bitter that it has sometimes erupted into beatings and kidnappings that have ended up on the police blotter. In the 1980s, one Lubavitcher teacher known for wooing Satmar defectors was grabbed by five Satmar men, pummeled and stripped of his clothes. The attackers even added the indignity of cutting off his beard.

Many of these battles have been prompted by two key issues that, more than fine nuances of daily observance, divide the Hasidic world: the central mission of the fedora-wearing Lubavitch Hasidim to persuade other Jews to become more pious, a proselytizing philosophy that no other sects adhere to and apparently threatens some of the black-hat sects; and the Satmar's fierce antagonism to the legitimacy of Israel as a state—absent the arrival of the Messiah.

Beyond the rivalries between groups, there are also fierce rivalries within groups—over leadership, control and real estate. What these antagonisms show is that Hasidim and their grand rabbis, despite their gloss of righteousness, wisdom and humility, are susceptible to the same jealousies and hungers for power and status as the rest of humankind, sometimes more so. Despite the lofty Hasidic immersion in Talmud and Torah, these rivalries are often played out on the quotidian, sometimes grimy battlegrounds of last wills and testaments, money, land and clubhouse politics.

When the Lubavitcher Rebbe, Menachem Mendel Schneerson, the movement's leader for 43 years, died childless in 1994,
his tens of thousands of adherents around the world divided
into two camps: those who believed he was the "Moshiach"—
the Messiah—and would return to lead the building of a Third
Temple and herald the Messianic Age, and those who believed the question should be left inconclusive. Even the non-
Moshiach side did not repudiate the notion that Schneerson
was the Messiah; they just felt it was indiscreet to trumpet his
messianic incarnation so publicly, that doing so would weaken
the movement's ability to promote a more Orthodox lifestyle
among college students and lapsed Jews around the world.

The Moshiach camp promptly flooded Brooklyn's Crown
Heights with signs proclaiming the Moshiach had arrived,
plastered their cars with Moshiach bumper stickers and sang
a Hebrew song proclaiming his arrival, which in English said:
"Long live our Master, our Teacher and our Rabbi, King
Moshiach, for ever and ever!" These enthusiasts could point
out that they had sung that song while Schneerson was alive
and that he had sometimes encouraged them with upward
hand motions. Nevertheless, the Moshiach skeptics refrained
from such outbursts.

The dispute had flared up even while Schneerson was alive,
with the two sides quarreling over what kind of medical treatment he should receive after his stroke. Why attend to the
physical needs of a man who as the Messiah was imbued with
a unique corporeal constitution? the messianic camp argued.
And after his death there was also a dispute over Schneer-

son's will, since two documents emerged. One was signed by Schneerson and filed in New York State court and ceded all the Chabad-Lubavitch property to the control of Yehuda Krinsky, Schneerson's onetime chauffeur and first assistant and eventually the de facto administrator of the Lubavitch empire, probably its most powerful figure. The Moshiach followers, however, unearthed a second will indicating that their leaders were the true heirs and giving Krinsky, who was agnostic on whether Schneerson was the true Messiah, only a minor role; the will, however was unsigned, though Moshiach advocates suspect that the signed version was squirreled away by Krinsky supporters.

The dispute broke into the wider public's consciousness rather theatrically in 2004 when several youths from the Moshiach camp ripped off a plaque honoring Schneerson from a wall of 770 Eastern Parkway, the neo-Gothic brick Lubavitch headquarters. The vandals did not like the plaque's referring to Schneerson with a honorific Hebrew acronym for a dead person—*zt"l* or *zekher tzadik livracha* ("may the memory of the righteous be a blessing"). The Moshiach camp, after all, did not believe Schneerson had died, just vanished temporarily to return one day. But the plaque-stealing incident exposed the battle within Lubavitch over who actually controls the cavernous synagogue in the building's basement. The community had elected Rabbi Zalman Lipskier as its head *gabbai*, the synagogue's chief administrator, in a 2005 election open to the Lubavitch community, and he hailed from the fiercely adamant Moshiach camp. He was able to point out that the Moshiach camp, led by among others Rabbi Leib Groner, a

longtime secretary to Schneerson and his major caretaker
during his waning days, had been able after Schneerson's death
to hang a long banner on the northern wall that proclaims:
"Live Our Master, Teacher, Rebbe King Moshiach Forever
and Ever." But Krinsky, the executor of Schneerson's will and
not disposed to emphatically and openly declare Schneerson
the Moshiach, maintained that the Rebbe effectively left him
the administrator of the entire building, the synagogue and
its plaques included.

Krinsky and the other administrators of the Chabad empire
sued in court over who controls the synagogue, and that dispute simmers on, along with a federal suit accusing Krinsky
of looting the publishing arm of Lubavitch. But it has always
been clear that more than property was at issue. As Lipskier
wrote, "the real issue in dispute involves conflicting views on
how our faith views the passing of the Grand Rebbe Schneerson and whether or not at this time he may be referred to publicly as the Messiah."*

Motti Seligson, a spokesman for Krinsky, contends that
the Moshiach battles have dissipated and that the Moshiach
faction does not hold any leadership positions, but he will not
say much more.† And Krinsky himself seemed to shrug off
the influence of the Moshiach camp in a 2010 interview with
Deborah Solomon of the New York Times Magazine: "There was
a group of people that felt that the Rebbe implied during his

---

* Samuel Heilman and Menachem Freedman, The Rebbe: The Life and Afterlife
of Menachem Mendel Schneerson (Princeton, NJ: Princeton University Press,
2012), p. 250.

† Author's interview with Motti Seligson.

lifetime that he was a Messiah. They became very vocal about it and sometimes more than vocal. They made a lot of noise, like a penny in a can; shake it, and it makes a lot of noise."*

The split within the Satmar movement offers another intriguing case study of unrest within the Hasidic world, one that merits comparison to classic dynastic battles within royal families. The feud opened an unusual window into a normally insular movement, with 150,000 followers worldwide, 60,000 of them in Williamsburg.

The modern Satmar movement, whose roots go back to the Hungarian/Romanian town of Satu Mare (St. Mary's in English), was patched together by Rabbi Joel Teitelbaum from the Satmar remnants after the Holocaust. He escaped Nazi-occupied Hungary in 1944 and arrived in New York around Rosh Hashanah 1946 with barely enough followers to form a *minyan*. But he saw them burgeon into the world's largest Hasidic sect, a movement of more than 100,000 followers. Joel died without any male descendants—he had had three daughters by his first wife, all of whom died in his lifetime—and the leadership was passed on to the male next in line—his nephew Moses Teitelbaum. But his widow Faige was not fond of Moses, felt no one then living could replace her husband and felt Moses might soften her husband's doctrinal stances. (Joel was very strict on matters of Jewish law, insisting on a *mechitza* that conceals women entirely, requiring married women to shave their heads and wear turbans, not wigs, and demanding

---

* Deborah Solomon, "The Rabbi: Questions for Yehuda Krinsky," *New York Times Magazine*, August 6, 2010, p. MM11.

that married men wear *shtreimels* so they could not be confused with non-Jews.) If a successor had to be named it should be a rival of Moses, Rabbi Nachman Brach, she was said to feel. Cynics told me she was mostly upset to be losing her position as the sect's queen for more than 40 years. Nonetheless, a significant faction of Satmar Hasidim agreed that Moses should not be installed as Rebbe. Calling themselves B'nai Yoel—the sons of Joel—they looked up to Faige as their spiritual shepherd, believing she could speak for her dead husband so that no rebbe was needed. They refused to accept Moses' authority. Even though she was a woman, Faige seemed to take on the de facto crown of rebbe, and she and a coterie of Joel's aides effectively set themselves up as a renegade movement.

The rebellion was centered in Kiryas Joel ("Joel's settlement"), the village about 50 miles north of New York City that was created as a satellite to handle the overflow of Williamsburg Hasidim who preferred a rural environment and was named after Joel Teitelbaum. By the 1990s it had become a bustling *shtetl* of 23,000 people—almost all Satmar Hasidim—living in tract homes built along looping streets that also contained grand Jewish institutions. I spoke to the anti-Moses dissidents there, such as Joseph Waldman, many times in the mid-1990s, and that is when they complained that their leaders were beaten, their tires slashed, their windows broken and at least one dissident's home set on fire. Their children, they told me, were barred from the village's yeshivas, and a breakaway synagogue they set up had been closed by the village on grounds of improper zoning variances and building code permits, even though other home synagogues flourished in Kiryas Joel. The incidents, they argued in court, amounted to a violent campaign of religious persecution by a village theocracy and blurred the constitutional separation between church—the village's religious leaders—and state— the village government. They even opposed Kiryas Joel's efforts to become a separate school district. That's how nasty that quarrel had become.*

The feud came to a head in 1997 when the leader of Kiryas Joel, Aaron Teitelbaum, one of Moses's sons and the reigning figure in Kiryas Joel, was subpoenaed to testify in a federal courtroom in New York. Entreaties came from Hasidic leaders around the world that the civil dispute be settled lest that insular world suffer the exposure—and possible embarrassment—of having a grand rabbi on the witness stand. Hasidim would recoil at the idea of hostile interrogation of a rabbi of Aaron Teitelbaum's stature just as Roman Catholics might chafe at the idea of a cardinal being placed in the dock. In this case, Aaron Teitelbaum might have been asked why in 1995 he did nothing to stop hundreds of students from Kiryas Joel's main yeshiva from throwing stones at dissidents' houses when a prominent Satmar dissident was speaking in the village. The rabbi might also have been asked about a contempt of court citation he received for failing to readmit six children of a dissident leader to the main village yeshiva.

---

* Joseph Berger, "Public School Leadership Fight Tearing a Hasidic Sect," *New York Times*, January 3, 1994.

Hours before his scheduled appearance, a settlement was announced between village leaders and the dissidents' synagogue, known as Khal Charidim (Congregation of the Devout). It had been hammered out by a neutral grand rabbi from a tiny Hasidic sect—Rabbi Usher Anshel Katz, head of the Weiner Hasidim—and was largely a victory for the dissidents, who received a payment of $300,000 for their troubles.

Joseph Waldman, by then a spokesman for the dissidents, celebrated the agreement by visiting the grave of Rabbi Joel Teitelbaum, the former grand rabbi, a place he and his allies had for years been barred from visiting.

"No stones were thrown at me and there was no spitting or yelling at me, no insults, just respect," Waldman told me afterward.

I also spoke to Abraham Wieder, the village's deputy mayor and a president of Kiryas Joel's dominant congregation, Yetev Lev (Strong of Heart), and he too was pleased that hatchets had been buried.

"I feel this is a victory for everyone because the primary purpose in life is that people should be able to live together," he said.

I asked him whether the prospect of having Rabbi Aaron Teitelbaum undergo a lawyer's interrogation motivated his decision and he acknowledged: "That would have been an embarrassment to the whole Jewish world."

But within a few years, another schism opened within Satmar, this time between Aaron Teitelbaum and his brother

Zalman. That fact allowed some observers to picture the conflict in biblical terms—as a Cain and Abel feud. But views of
the genesis of the feud depend on whom you talk to.

Moses died in 2006, having reigned virtually unchallenged
for five years after the 2001 death of his nemesis, his aunt
Faige Teitelbaum. According to accounts from the Zalman
camp, Moses, while he was still vigorous, had come to feel that
the Satmar movement had grown too large to be ruled by one
man, and sometime in the mid 1980s summoned Aaron, the
older brother, born in 1947 and a writer of scholarly essays
on Torah and Talmud, to his redbrick house at 550 Bedford
Avenue to tell him that he was dividing up the leadership of
the empire. He let Aaron choose where he wanted his seat—
Williamsburg or Kiryas Joel. Aaron chose Kiryas Joel. There-
after, Zalman, his third son, born in 1951, was named Moses'
deputy in Williamsburg, the base of the Satmar worldwide
empire. (The second son, Lipa, headed a small synagogue in
Williamsburg and administered the Satmar school system
there, and the fourth son, Shulum, led a small synagogue in
Borough Park.) But from his Kiryas Joel perch, Aaron, widely
regarded in the Hasidic world as the more learned, spiritual,
charismatic and personable brother, continued to act as if he
were the presumptive heir to the entire Satmar court.

Moses, however, became addled by Alzheimer's and, in
the years that passed until his death, Zalman's lieutenants,
handlers and institutional cadre became so entrenched in
Williamsburg that they regarded themselves as the rightful
successors. The Zalman faction, the Zaloynim, augmented by
the dissidents in Kiryas Joel, regarded Aaron as not an en-

tirely kosher Satmar leader: he had married the daughter of
the Vizhnitz Rebbe, who was considered too accommodating
with government leaders in Israel, a state that in Satmar eyes
has no validity because it was established before the arrival
of the Messiah. Meanwhile, the Aroynem, as Aaron's partisans are known in a transliteration from the Yiddish, let it be
known that the fight was less between the two brothers than
between Aaron and the secretary to his father, Moses Friedman, who did not want to relinquish power should the Rebbe
die. They shrugged off the story of Moses's talk to Aaron that
the sect had become too large for one rebbe to lead. If so, why
did he not designate which of the brothers would be in charge
of the Satmar colony in Britain or Israel or Brooklyn's Borough Park?

Whatever the interpretations of the feud's origins, when
Moses finally succumbed in 2006, the Zaloynim regime insisted it was the true heir to the Satmar throne. It claimed
control of the major properties like the white-brick Yetev
Lev D'Satmar synagogue at 152 Rodney Street, the United
Talmudical Academy yeshiva for boys and Bais Rochel yeshiva for girls, a kosher meat market and other institutions—
properties valued at the time at $372 million. As happened
in the Lubavitch feud, the Zaloynim too unearthed a competing last will and testament, one that did not favor Aaron
as the eldest son. Aaron's supporters labeled that will a fraud
and secured a rabbinical court ruling to bolster its case. The
Zaloynim, however, produced a transcript of a telephone call
in which Moses named Zalman as his successor and banished
the president of the synagogue congregation's board, Berl

Friedman, an Aaron acolyte. Berl Friedman and the other Aroynem denied that it was Moses's voice on the tape and blamed Moses Teitelbaum's secretary, Moses Friedman, for blocking Aaron's selection as overall grand rabbi.[*]

When backers of Aaron sued in New York State Supreme Court in Brooklyn, Zalman's handlers proved adept at turning the fight into religious quarrel, one in which the court eventually felt it could not intervene. The feud posed delicate challenges for outsiders dependent on the Satmar goodwill. After Moses died, Hillary Clinton, then United States senator from New York, made sure to pay a *shiva* call to each of the sons. And when Governor Andrew M. Cuomo in 2013 wanted to sell a square-block National Guard armory on the edge of Brooklyn's Williamsburg to the Satmar community, efforts were made to settle the dispute so he would not been seen as favoring one faction.

One building the Zaloynim could not stake claim to was the new grand synagogue going up on Ross Street, which the Aroynem contended had largely been paid for by seats bought by their loyalists. The city's Department of Buildings refused to step in the middle of the dispute and decide which brother's faction had title to the rising synagogue so it could grant a certificate of occupancy. As a result, that building has lain fallow, unfinished and boarded up for years.

Disputes have cropped up at every turn—over who owns which schools, synagogues, summer camps, real estate, even a matzo bakery. Indeed, the quarrel between the two factions

---

[*] Michael Powell, "Hats On, Gloves Off," *New York*, May 1, 2006.

has little to do with any standard political issue like taxes or abortion—the two groups both agree that Israel should not have established itself as a state until the coming of the Messiah, even if Aaron has been more flexible on dealing with political leaders in Israel.

"The fight within Satmar is over buildings, not ideology." Alex Rapaport told me when we discussed this issue.

When the Aroynem could not wrest control through appeals and legal stratagems, they began setting up a separate infrastructure in the low-rise, sometime ramshackle streets of Williamsburg. When I toured Williamsburg in the summer of 2012 with Rabbi Moishe Indig, a leader of the Aroynem faction, he showed me a new two-story stucco and cinder-block synagogue on Kent Avenue and Hooper Street that can hold 5,500 people on the High Holidays; it was built in two to three weeks after Moses' death so Aaron Teitelbaum could effectively claim the banner of his leadership by holding Rosh Hashanah services in Williamsburg. Indig, a developer, took charge of the round-the-clock construction, with work stopping only for the Sabbath. To avoid Tower of Babel pandemonium, he made sure the 180 plumbers, electricians, carpenters and other laborers did not get in each other's way (though critics say city construction regulations like the requirement for sidewalk sheds were openly flouted). By the time Aaron Teitelbaum celebrated the first Friday night service, the final touches had still not been applied; the wooden steps leading up to the arc had not been polished and cleaned of splinters, the floor was still concrete and the marble wall behind where Aaron was to stand was not fully tiled. But he conducted the service and stayed to deliver blessings to every male worshipper. The following week, a wooden floor was laid over the concrete.

"It would be very hard for Rabbi Aaron to dance for a couple of hours on concrete," Indig told my colleague Joseph Goldstein, then a reporter for the *New York Sun*.

The Zaloynim ridicule the building as "the Home Depot *shul*" but it is a sturdy structure that may outlast the internecine dispute (even if a seat for the year costs $2,000). It has its own men's *mikvah* where for $2 a day or $22 a month men can dip in warm water infused with rainwater for roughly three minutes before they study. The green-and-white tiled rectangular pool, about 10 feet by 12 feet, can hold 15 to 20 men at one time. (The facility also has 13 showers, a rebuke of sorts to those who malign Hasidim as unclean.)

Indig also showed me a yeshiva for 3,500 boys aged six through 13, another one not much smaller for girls, girls and boys high schools, a separate wedding hall and a separate meat market. The subsidized wedding hall, Rose Castle, allows Hasidic parents to stage a 125-person wedding for their daughters—catering, flowers, music and photography included—for $10,000, an important bargain since Hasidic parents often have five or six daughters whose weddings they must pay for. The Aroynem have also published a separate weekly newspaper—*Der Blatt* (The Page)—to rival the Zaloynim's *Der Yid*; it has weekly state circulation of 27,000. They have set up a separate social service organization—the Jewish Community Council of Williamsburg—to compete with that of the long-standing Zaloynim-led United Jewish

Organizations. They have even created their own matzo factory, so eager are they to create facts on the ground that might validate them as the dominant Satmar faction.

Socially, the split has been felt in the standard matchmaking efforts by Hasidic families. Many families headed by a father loyal to Aaron will not allow their daughter or son to marry a spouse whose father is allied with the Zalman faction. And vice versa.

America's temporal politics seem to be a key Satmar battleground. (There are also dynastic quarrels in the Bobov and Vizhnitz sects, but Satmar is the Hasidic whale, and together these schisms have complicated once-simple calculations about which candidate a Hasidic sect would support as a single bloc.) The impact of the Satmar quarrel was shown in the 2012 Democratic primary for Congress in the 7th Congressional District, which embraces Williamsburg. Nydia Velázquez, the incumbent, was supported by the Satmar Aroynem while her opponent, City Councilman Erik Martin Dilan, was backed by the Zaloynim.

"It could have been Tweedledum and Tweedledee—the two sides would have opposed each other," Samuel Heilman, the sociology professor at the City University of New York who is writing a book about Hasidic succession, told me. "Each of them wants to say we speak for Satmar so they can look as if they were the deciding factor, an important bloc in the election. Then when that particular candidate needs to turn to the Satmar community, he or she will turn to that faction."*

---

* Author's interview with Samuel Heilman.

Two days after Representative Velázquez's triumph in the June 26 primary, the Aroynem issued a news release claiming that their "political muscle" marshaled 4,000 of Velázquez's 16,000 votes and spelled the difference in her victory over Dilan. The Aroynem also claimed they were fast rivaling the numbers of the Zaloynim in their base of Williamsburg.

"Williamsburg is no longer under the complete control of the Zaloynim," Rabbi Indig, a top strategist of the Aroynem, declared in a statement issued after the primary by the influential public relations firm George Arzt Communications. "The Aroynem have just as much power and influence."

The claim—trumpeted in a banner headline in the Aroynem newspaper, *Der Blatt*, that said "Mazel Tov Williamsburg"—was quickly disputed as an exaggeration by partisans for Zalman Teitelbaum, chief among them Rabbi David Niederman. Rabbi Niederman let it be known that even though his candidate, Dilan, lost, the Zaloynim, with allies from other Hasidic sects in Williamsburg, proved their dominance by turning out more than 70 percent of the Hasidic vote for Dilan. It was the votes of non-Hasidim that prevented Dilan's election.

Since 1989, Niederman has been top executive of the venerable United Jewish Organizations of Williamsburg, the neighborhood's leading social service organization. UJO is the place to go in Williamsburg for food stamps, public housing spots, Section 8 housing vouchers, Social Security miscalculations, Medicaid, home care for the frail. (The Aroynem have their own social services agency, United Jewish Community Advocacy Relations and Enrichment, or UJ Care, but

I'm told it is not yet as robust about bestowing benefits for its followers as Niederman's group.) Niederman has a vast Rolodex of political and governmental contacts. There are photographs of him with Democratic and Republican governors and mayors, who make pilgrimages to Williamsburg to court his influence at election time. In the Velázquez primary, his intimates say, he chose to support her opponent, Dilan, because he felt, in the patchwork of ethnicities that make up Williamsburg, Velázquez had been favoring Hispanic families over Hasidim in allocation of public housing slots. The housing fight has been roiling Williamsburg since the 1960s. The Aroynem agree with the Zaloynim that whenever apartments become available in Williamsburg's housing projects they are given to Hispanic families, but they blame Dilan, not Velázquez.

Rapaport believes that the grand rabbis do not really immerse themselves in such petty politics, but leave it up to their handlers and sect administrators. "The rabbis don't see it as a priority," he said. "It's more secular. It's not religious. Assign the *machers*. Why do you need rabbis."

Nevertheless, politics plays an important role in enabling Hasidim to practice their particular faith, with zoning and buildings codes permitting synagogues to exist in certain spots and housing allotments allowing large Hasidic families to have apartments from which they can fulfill their sacred obligations. So rebbes do get involved—if only indirectly through their lieutenants.

Some political professionals contend that the dynastic succession squabbles have weakened the effectiveness of the Hasidim. Imagine, they say, if the warring Satmar factions had joined together on behalf of, say, Dilan. Dilan would have won.

Heilman, the expert in Hasidic succession, told me that one reason so many dynastic fights emerged in the past decade is that the grand rabbis are living longer, sometimes too long to have the vigor to conclusively determine whom their successors will be or so long that their increasingly entrenched institutional court refuses to cede power. In Hasidic Europe before World War II, a contender to the throne unhappy with a chosen successor could set up his seat in a neighboring village, Heilman said. But since the war, with the consolidation of Hasidim into relatively few sects, each sect's brand name has been enshrined so that successors want to become, say, the Satmar Rebbe, not the Kiryas Joel Rebbe.

Whatever the basis of the dynastic quarrel, pragmatism often trumps ideology and sometimes produces strange bedfellows. When the Aroynem wanted a *mikveh* for their followers in Williamsburg, they needed zoning permits and, according to community leaders, sought out the political muscle of both Niederman and two councilmen close to Vito J. Lopez (then Brooklyn's powerful Democratic boss), Dilan and Stephen Levin. With Rabbi Niederman's prodding, the two councilmen provided the needed help.

But such temporary cease-fires are not typical. In September 2012, the two Satmar sides were at it again—this time in a usually obscure race for Democratic district leader in the 50th State Assembly District, covering Williamsburg and neighboring Greenpoint. In this dispute loyalty to Lopez was at issue. (Lopez was a longtime assemblyman and Democratic leader but lost both positions after a sexual harassment scandal earlier in 2012.) The incumbent district leader, Lincoln Restler, who was all of 28, had come to power two years before by seizing the mantle of reform and defeating the Lopez candidate, an embarrassing setback. But in 2012 the old pol proved he had life in him yet when his newest candidate for district leader, Chris Olechowski, a leader of Greenpoint's Polish community, defeated Restler by 19 votes.

Key to the defeat were the Satmar Hasidim, with the Zaloynim championing Lopez's candidate and the Aroynem bitterly opposed. Restler's strategy was to round up as many of the newcomer urban professionals and artists, as well as some converts from the older Polish and other ethnic communities, to offset Lopez's strength with Williamsburg's Zaloynim. The Satmar on both sides streamed to their polling places in numbers that made it seem as if the election would determine the nation's president rather than the low-profile position of the district leader of a few Brooklyn neighborhoods. More than 11,000 people voted, the highest turnouts for any Assembly district in New York City. When I arrived I saw jostling crowds in front of a school polling place like I had never seen before in any election, though this time the crowds were entirely made up of black-hatted, black-suited men. The two sides even set up canopied electioneering booths outside the school manned by former Satmar members—some beardless, others with nose rings—who handed out campaign literature. Many of the Hasidim who voted for Olechowski (pronounced o-le-HOF-ski) struggled to pronounce his name and attributed actions to him—for example, saving four upstate Hasidic summer camps and distributing Section 8 apartments to Hasidim—that had more to do with Lopez than Olechowski. Indeed several Zaloynim I interviewed said they had been urged to vote for Olechowski by their rabbis or yeshiva officials. Eliezer Fried, a 21-year-old yeshiva student, told me in no uncertain terms that he had voted for Olechowski because "I like Vito Lopez—he's good for the community—he saved the summer camps."

When all the ballots were officially counted, Restler, who had earlier charged voter fraud and other irregularities, conceded and pointed out that more than 90 percent of Olechowski's votes were cast in Hasidic neighborhoods. He lost because in those neighborhoods the Aroynem simply were not able to match the numbers turned out by the Zaloynim.

It is hard to see anything uplifting in such seedy quarrels among supposedly pious people, but Rapaport does. He actually sees a hopeful aspect in the dynastic wars, a sense of how much Hasidim care about what happens to and who leads their congregations and institutions.

"Around New York there are so many synagogues collecting dust," he said. "Here you have synagogues that thousands of people are fighting over. People care who is the rabbi and who takes charge of our building. I see that as a promising thing."

20

THE LAW IN THESE HERE PARTS

He has a lush reddish beard and foot-long earlocks flowing from a half-bald head. He does not work from Friday at sundown to Saturday at sundown, or even drive a car in that period. You will never see him filling up on donuts and coffee at the local greasy spoon, the way other cops might. He is Deputy Shlomo, the Hasidic sheriff's deputy of Rockland County, New York, and the tale of how he became the nation's first Hasidic police officer is instructive of how Hasidim are wading into the mainstream out of necessity—whether it's good for them or for the mainstream—and raising subtle issues of how society should accommodate religious minorities.

Shlomo Koenig is a Hasid from the Vizhnitz sect, a particularly conservative Hungarian group whose members in America can mostly be found in Brooklyn's Williamsburg and in Kaser, the independent Hasidic village in Rockland County that was carved out of the town of Ramapo. The village has almost 5,000 inhabitants, every one a Vizhnitz

Hasid, and they live in an area of just one-fifth of a square mile, where the central institution is a plainspoken synagogue honeycombed with rooms for prayer and boys' and girls' yeshivas. Koenig for a time was Kaser's deputy mayor.

A squabble over zoning, though, was not the only issue that disturbed the peace in the Rockland County town of Ramapo and its unincorporated hamlet of Monsey. In the early 1950s, Monsey was a one-stoplight town with a single yeshiva and several bungalow colonies popular with Orthodox Jews. By 2002, Monsey had 200 synagogues and 50 yeshivas and had become an all-purpose place name for the Hasidic and Orthodox population of the area. The growth has stirred up awkward encounters with the gentile and secular Jewish populations.

A female police officer—whether town or sheriff's deputy—would write out a traffic ticket for a Hasidic man and he would refuse to take it from her hand, asking that she leave it on the hood of the car. Their faith, after all, does not allow them to casually touch a woman who is not a relative. Some Hasidim would simply walk away because they have internalized to a radical extent Hasidic scruples about engaging in conversation with unfamiliar women. On the other hand, Hasidim walking to synagogue on Sabbath—a day they cannot drive—often clog narrow country lanes and inadvertently block traffic, enraging secular drivers. When a mugging takes place, a Yiddish-speaking Hasid might not be able to describe what the assailant looked like; he might not know the word for jeans, hoodie or do-rag—the head scarf popular with rappers and motorcyclists.

"There are very big cultural misunderstandings," Koenig told me as we spoke in his Rockland County living room. "When you argue or fight with someone you have to understand what you're fighting about. I don't want to take a woman's hand, it's not because I disrespect her. So when you know a personal custom, you don't have problems."

Such misunderstandings were particularly common in dealings with the Hasidic community because almost no Hasids worked as firefighters, police officers, teachers or village clerks and had contacts that might explain some of the mystical culture of government bureaucracy and local politics.

Luckily, the county's sheriff, James Kralik, was enlightened enough to go beyond anger or even contempt to try to find a solution. He was intent on finding a Hasid to join the force.

"The police system is not closed to white guys with crew cuts," he told a local newspaper.

He had gotten to know Koenig and he made him an astonishing offer. His department has had a number of run-ins with Hasidim, he said, and in a county of 300,000 people, where Hasidim make up 20 percent of the population (and Jews one-third), it might be worthwhile to have a Hasid join the force.

"What about me?" Koenig replied.

Why was he talking to Koenig in the first place? Koenig is an unusual specimen in the black-hat world. He did not grow up in a Hasidic or *Yeshivish* household. He studied at yeshiva, but his father was a straightforward Orthodox man. However, he sent Shlomo to a Vizhnitz yeshiva and that led him into the Vizhnitz sect. Unlike other Hasidim, he speaks a well-turned and vernacular English and his patter is peppered with charming slang. So in the years before Kralik made his offer, Koenig had become the de facto go-between of the Vizhnitz Hasidim to the secular world of Rockland County.

From Koenig's point of view, many of the tensions between Hasidim and the wider society can be relieved by familiarity and education. Hasidim, he argues, have very little experience with public service other than as clients, victims or beneficiaries. They are seldom the official actors.

"Anywhere from seven to twelve percent of any population is made up of public servants—teachers, police," he said. "It's automatic grass roots, where in general your public servants will be a carbon copy of what your community is. But less than one percent of our community is actually in public service. So you have a situation where the people representing you are not part of your community. If someone makes a decision, you don't understand it. And in our community we don't watch TV and don't know how the police operate."

The suspiciousness that law enforcement provokes in Hasidim, who have never quite gotten over the terror their ancestors experienced in the Nazi era, combined with their ignorance of police methods makes for a volatile combination in crimefighting. Koenig offers the example of what might happen when a Hasid reports a crime. A Hasidic man dials up 9-1-1 and tells the dispatcher there's a suspicious person walking on the block. What makes him suspicious? the dispatcher asks. He doesn't look like he belongs in the neighborhood. Why not? the dispatcher replies. Koenig thinks many

Hasidim will get offended by this kind of dialogue. "If some-one who is not Hasidic garb is walking in the neighborhood at eleven p.m., it's pretty obvious he doesn't belong here, doesn't live here. Everybody's Hasidic. But the Hasidic guy is think-ing, 'He doesn't trust me or respect me because I'm Hasidic.' But the police officer wants to know why do you believe this person is suspicious. If you say it's three a.m. and only Hasidic guys are walking in the neighborhood at this time, you then give the officer probable cause."

His being a police officer is a reflection of how the modern world has had to adapt to the Hasidim in its midst and how the Hasidim have had to become more engaged in the wider society in order to sustain their lifestyles. When he was asked to join the sheriff's department, Koenig was a partner in a business that made plastic bags. But he soon found himself at the nearby New York State Police Academy attending 600 hours of classes in such non-Talmudic matters as firing guns, subduing suspects and other police skills.

"It was a whole new world to me," he told me. "I had to learn a lot of things. It was opening my eyes to a different world."

He of course skipped Saturday classes but he brushed up with notes from fellow students. He even won a marksman-ship award. He graduated with a tan uniform, shiny silver-star badge and a Smokey the Bear trooper's hat that takes the place of his black beaver-fur homburg when he is in uniform. Sheriff Kralik gave him a dispensation from the department's prohibition against beards.

Today, he may look like a character out of a Mel Brooks

comedy (*Blazing Saddles*)—the gun-toting deputy of a Dead-wood Gulch–like *shtetl* in the plains of Ukraine, perhaps. But he is a genuine deputy sheriff.

"I have generally been accepted," he told me. "Most people in the law enforcement industry look at your capability, your credentials, your training and who you are."

Koenig soon found himself working full-time as a police officer and greatly trimming back his role at the plastic-bag factory to that of investor. Still, when he pulled out his law-man's badge, the response was as often incredulity as it was fear. Much of his work was in the Hasidic community. In one case he was involved in even before he was officially sworn in, he helped the police track down and capture a Hasidic man accused of beating his estranged wife nearly to death. The case offered insights into some of the distinctive aspects of the Hasidic community. Family violence requiring police intervention is rare. Nevertheless, when a divorce is on the horizon, it exerts a particularly agonizing tension because of the singular Orthodox rules for divorce.

Under Jewish religious law, the husband must grant his wife a *get*, a Hebrew document of divorce obtained from a *bet din*, for the divorce to be accepted in the community. A woman who obtains a civil divorce without a *get* may be ostracized by her community, and a second husband married civilly without a *get* would suffer the same fate. Children of a second marriage will be considered illegitimate. (For years there have been rumors of rabbis who charge thousands of dollars and use physical force to prod a reluctant husband to grant a *get*. The scuttlebutt seemed to acquire some reality in October

2013 when federal prosecutors in New Jersey charged two rabbis, Mendel Epstein of Brooklyn and Martin Womack of Monsey, with arranging abductions of reluctant husbands for a $50,000 fee. The husbands—there were two dozen such cases, according to a criminal complaint—were tied up and shocked with Tasers and stun guns until they agreed to give their wives a *get*. "Basically, the reaction of the police is, if the guy does not have a mark on him then, is there some Jewish crazy affair here, they don't want to get involved," Rabbi Epstein was heard explaining to a female undercover FBI agent, according to the criminal complaint.)*

So when Blima Zitrenbaum, a mother of seven, asked her husband, Joseph, for a divorce and he refused to give it, the strains reverberated through Monsey and to Hasidic enclaves beyond. Joseph, a onetime furniture salesman, was not your ordinary Hasid; he was a secret cocaine user. But his refusal to grant a *get* still was paramount.

On February 20, 1996, a *Shabbos*, Mrs. Zitrenbaum, then 33, awoke in her Monsey home to find her husband standing over her with what appeared to be either a hammer or a hatchet, imploring her to abandon her quest for divorce. Blima refused again, so Joseph's hand came down on her head, again and again. He left her unconscious in what would turn out to be a four-day coma. She was discovered bleeding by her son. Koenig was called in on the investigation. By questioning Hasidim with whom Zitrenbaum hung around, he learned that

---

* Joseph Goldstein and Michael Schwirtz, "U.S. Accuses Two Rabbis of Kidnapping Husbands for a Fee," *New York Times*, October 11, 2013, p. A18.

Joseph was sometimes seen injecting himself with cocaine in the synagogue and that he terrified his fellow worshippers with his outbursts. Koenig also learned that Zitrenbaum often made his way to the Lower East Side of Manhattan to buy drugs.

Koenig alerted the Shomrim, a volunteer patrol of Ortho-dox Jews that was founded around 1980 and named after the Hebrew word for guardians. They do not carry guns or wear uniforms but respond when help is needed for anything from burglaries to lost children. Scores of its members distributed fliers with Zitrenbaum's photograph in the Jewish neighbor-hoods of Williamsburg and Borough Park, in Brooklyn, and on the Lower East Side. They figured that as an unemployed man he would need to *schnor*—beg—for food and money among the area's merchants. When they were tipped that Zitrenbaum was seen without a beard, they printed new fliers that showed him beardless.

As it turned out, Zitrenbaum, wearing traditional black garb but clean-shaven except for a mustache, was spotted not by a Shomrim member but by Michael Fleischer, the owner of a kosher takeout food establishment on Essex Street, a main Lower East Side commercial street. He is someone who also lives in Monsey and knew that Zitrenbaum was wanted. He first spotted Zitrenbaum walking through the neighborhood on the Tuesday after the attack, followed him for six blocks but lost his trail. Then two days later he spied Zitrenbaum eating a bagel with a cup of coffee at Motty's Bagels, a store near his own. This time Fleischer yelled to a neighboring mer-chant, a Torah scribe, to call the Shomrim while he flagged down a police office in a car on the other side of Essex Street.

The officer strode into the bagel shop and arrested a pale and shaken Zitrenbaum. David Wieder, a Shomrim volunteer, told me he was already in the store when the police entered and was blocking the doorway in case Zitrenbaum tried to get away. Other Shomrim streamed toward the store, alerted through two-way radios by their dispatcher in Williamsburg. Zitrenbaum was eventually convicted of attempted murder.*

The case also highlighted the impressive cohesiveness of Hasidim when someone in their community is imperiled or acts beyond the pale. That fierceness, resembling the posses pictured in films about the Old West, was exhibited, as we saw, in the disappearance in 2011 of eight-year-old Leiby Kletzky in Borough Park, even though he was soon found murdered by a mentally troubled Orthodox young man.

Koenig's police career, meanwhile, took some unusual twists for a Hasid. By 1999, Koenig was taken off what he calls "on the road police work" and assigned to a New York State electronic crime task force, looking for crimes, like credit card theft and child pornography, that involve computers or the Internet. He was also appointed to the FBI and Secret Service task forces on computer crimes.

"I was a computer geek when I was a kid," he told me. "I was into ham radio. I was into electronics. When I got into law enforcement I saw it as a need."

He went after hackers like those who harassed widows of New York Police Department officers killed on September 11,

---

* Joseph Berger, "Hasidic Volunteers Help Fund Suspect in a Beating," *New York Times*, February 16, 1996.

2001, in the destruction of the World Trade Center. Koenig traced the hackers through his computer work and they turned out to be three teenagers. He tracked down hackers who broke in electronically into the Federal Reserve Bank. His work has taken him to 40 states and several trials. With his sidelocks and yarmulke, he has become a curious but increasingly familiar presence at highly publicized trials like the bribery prosecution in 2012 of Sandy Annabi, a Yonkers city councilwoman, and Zehy Jereis, the city's Republican Party leader. Annabi was accused of changing her no vote on whether to allow two controversial construction projects totaling more than $1 billion after Jereis showered her with $174,000 in gifts. Jereis claimed he gave her the gifts out of romantic passion. But Koenig testified that the love notes he claims to have sent in 2005 and 2006 could not be found on Jereis' computer. Love notes from Jereis were found on Annabi's computer, but Koenig said, venturing into the kind of soap opera rare for a community of arranged marriages, there was evidence that 6,000 files had been deleted on her computer over two days after she became the subject of prosecution in February 2007, and that dates in her email folder—usually listed chronologically—were out of order, suggesting she had tried to alter the record to help her defense.

"That showed me that something about this folder is not the way it's supposed to be," Koenig testified.

Annabi and Jereis were both convicted and sentenced respectively to six and four years in prison.

Koenig said he relishes the technological challenge of solving such investigatory riddles and defeating hackers who wage cyberwarfare.

"The amount of damage you can do to someone on the Internet is enormous," he told me. "If you own a business and someone burns down the business you can be back in business tomorrow. But if a computer hacker steals his customer base he's out of business."

Koenig still prays three times a day, studies Talmud daily and clings to all the traditions of his Vizhnitz group. But he defies other Hasidic stereotypes by operating a ham radio and playing golf with business prospects for his manufacturing business. Golf?

"How do you write orders these days without playing a game of golf?" he said. "Do you have to be good at it? No. But do you have to play a little to write up an order? Yes."

"The reality is the world has changed and the community has to change," he said. "The notion of being able to make a living in this small community is not the way it used to be. There's also a bigger community so you have to have relationships with the outside world. But that doesn't mean I have to change. I can interact with the outside world and still not become like the outside the world."

At his daughter's wedding, he invited 15 federal agents who were not Jewish. Two of the agents were women and the men brought their wives, and all of them understood that the men and women would be eating in separate rooms and dancing separately.

"Being friendly with someone means respecting what they

do," he said. "I let them live their lives and they let me live my life."

But there is still a strong argument that Hasidim need to stay apart, and Koenig articulates that philosophy as well as anyone I spoke to.

"Sticking to themselves is not rude," he said. "That's how they differentiate. We don't stick to ourselves because we are better than the whole world. We are different. We don't eat the same foods. We don't go to the same schools. We don't play the same games. But we are also human and we do the same business and we do it together. Our private lives are different. Where we are the same we can do things with you, but where we are different we go different ways. Most people have to appreciate that and accept that. We can lead our separate lifestyles. And we can do the things we do together. But if you believe that we have to be like you to be able to interact with you then you have a problem."

21

THE BORSCHT BELT REDUX

For most of its settled life, the Catskill Mountains have been Currier & Ives country, Rip Van Winkle country, an archetypal American setting of sleepy towns, small farms, rushing streams and plainspoken folks whose days have an indolent, laid-back rhythm. This patch of the planet has not been—even during the Borscht Belt days of the stand-up Jewish comedians—a spot where one would find many Hasidim. Yet Hasidim today stride across a good deal of the landscape. They have set themselves up in ramshackle bungalow colonies that were forsaken in the 1970s and 1980s by the descendants of blue-collar and often not very observant Bronx and Brooklyn Jews. The parents had summered in them for almost a century until their more affluent descendants discovered air-conditioning, the Hamptons and cheap flights to the south of France. The Hasidim have now taken over those bungalows and even some of the large hotels—there were once 300 in the Catskills, though only a handful remain—and in recent years bought stand-alone summer houses for their large families.

When I exited off the New York State Thruway and drove westward along Routes 52 and 42 to Monticello, the seat of Sullivan County, I quickly started noticing the Hasidic presence. There in the lush landscape of fields and forests broken up by Victorian and clapboard villages, I saw a sign for Camp Bnos Belz, the girls' camp of the Belz Hasidim, followed by a sign for "Camp Emunah, The Rebbe's Camp, the Rebbe's Children," a girls' camp of the Lubavitch Hasidim. Soon I spotted a Hasidic hitchhiker in the uniform of black hat and frock coat in one hand gripping his *tallis* bag, covered in plastic as protection for rain and timidly holding out a thumb with the other. He was the first of dozens of hitchhiking Hasidim I was to notice. By the time I reached the hamlet of Woodbourne, Hasidim were everywhere. Next to an abandoned movie theater was a two-story building that had been turned into a synagogue—Congregation B'nai Israel of Woodbourne—with Hasidic men milling outside, prayer shawls around their broad backs and *tefillin* perched atop their foreheads. Some were gabbing animatedly while others continued to murmur what a large sign told passersby was "*Shachris*," the collection of morning prayers that Orthodox Jews utter every day.

In Fallsburg, the main street was lined with shops like Sprinkles Kosher Pizza & Ice Cream and Heimishe Bakery. In South Fallsburg, the Rivoli Theater was showing the Batman sequel *The Dark Knight*, but a sign in Yiddish hanging from the marquee said that that evening at 10 p.m. a man named Yosse Rokover would speak about the *get*—the Jewish divorce. Between those villages, among the ubiquitous yellow signs warning drivers of crossing deer, a woman in a black turban, long-sleeved blouse and ankle-length skirt—incongruous for a rather warm day—was scurrying along the side of the highway chatting on a cell phone while not too far behind her there were four teenage girls in long skirts and thick-seamed tan stockings. Yet another sign told me that a right turn would lead to Yeshiva Viznitz, which took over the old Gibber Hotel in Kiamesha Lake and fashioned it into a year-round school for boys from the Vizhnitz sect.

In short the Hasidim have turned the summertime Catskills into *shtetlech* reminiscent of the tumbledown villages of Eastern Europe from where emerged Yitta Schwartz, the Satmar woman who left behind 2,000 descendants. In a way they have restored *shtetl* life itself, at least during the summer. The Catskills in the 1940s, 1950s and 1960s were a place where one could hear Sid Caesar, Danny Kaye, Milton Berle, Jerry Lewis and a manic *tummler* (combination hotel social director and entertainer) like Grossinger's venerable Lou Goldstein tell groan-worthy jokes like this one: "Last year a lady stands right there and I say to her, 'What do you think of sex?' She says, 'Sex? It's a fine department store.'" But many of those hotels and their streamlined Miami Beach–style nightclubs have been torn down; when they imploded Grossinger's Playhouse in the late 1980s to make way for what was to be but never quite became a new upscale resort, Goldstein described his mixed emotions as "like watching your mother-in-law drive over a cliff in your new Cadillac."[*]

---

[*] Stefan Kanfer, *A Summer World: The Attempt to Build a Jewish Eden in the Catskills, from the Days of the Ghetto to the Rise and Decline of the Borscht Belt* (New York: Farrar, Straus & Giroux, 1989), p. 5.

Other faded dowagers have become New Age centers for yoga and meditation run by swamis and gurus (and taken off the tax rolls).

But among the remnants of the Catskills heyday the Hasidim have transplanted their singular institutions and unconventional lifestyle. Entire Hasidic communities shift for the summer from the jostling, clamorous streets of Brooklyn to the farm country a three-hour drive to the northwest.

The members of the Satmar sect alone inhabit several bungalow colonies, one of which has 300 families who dwell in an archipelago of snug cottages that surround a sprawling synagogue and study hall. The sect also operates six boys' camps in the area and one girls' camp. And everything is done in Hasidic fashion. For the largest of its boys' camps, the Satmar bought up Kutsher's Sports Academy, a satellite of a once grand but now fraying resort hotel that has been owned, though no longer operated, by the same family for more than a century. The Satmar Hasidim turned the sports academy into a summer playground for 2,500 boys. But the boys spend most of their day—from 10 a.m. to 4 p.m.—not canoeing or playing baseball or learning to pitch tents like most summer campers, but studying Torah and Talmud as they would in Williamsburg. The academy's dozen basketball courts stand moldering in the sun, overgrown with weeds, their hoops rusting, their pavement cracking. Yoel Landau, the camp's director, explained to me that Rabbi Joel Teitelbaum, the grand rabbi who founded Satmar in the United States, told his Hasidim that once children play ball they will continue to play and think about playing ball well into adulthood rather than focus on the study of Jewish texts. His word was law.

"The grand rabbi didn't want us to play ball," Landau said. "If you grow up with the ball, you never stop playing."

Rabbi Moishe Indig, a leader of the Aroynem faction of the Satmar, told me that ball "is not a Yiddishe game," though he joked: "If we played ball, we'd be a little skinnier—but that's what it is."

I was drawn to this summertime world because as a teenager my parents took my brother, sister and me to Catskills bungalow colonies with names like Broadlawn Acres and Jay's Lakeside Bungalows. There among other rough-cut tenement Jews we found relief from steambath apartments and sticky asphalt in the pine-scented air and chilling lakes. Friends— like my siblings and me, children of refugees who came to America after the losses of the Holocaust—and I spent the summer shagging fly balls or dashing around the bases of the disheveled ball fields, staging freestyle and backstroke races in the pool, catching fat bass among the weeds and lily pads from a rowboat and putting on shows like *South Pacific* in the day camp for the smaller children. At nights in the colony's "casino," cigar-puffing men kibitzed over gin rummy or nickel-and-dime poker, women gossiped over clacking mahjongg tiles and the teenagers would spin 45 rpm records like "Donna" and "Mr. Blue" on an old phonograph and clutch each other in slow tight dances, our first grapplings with the bodily wonders of the opposite sex. Sometimes the casino would feature a second-rate comedian, spritzing away bawdily in Yiddish-inflected English, or a mediocre juggler or magician. But it was a luminous interlude from the city's grinding dailiness of school and work.

Today's Hasidic world of the bungalow colonies and reborn hotels is very different from the world I knew. The Hasidic summertime world strays far less from its winter version than ours did. "The life here goes on just like in Williamsburg," Indig told me. "The only difference is that instead of an apartment they live in a bungalow." Yet I found that the Hasidim too appreciate the cut-grass fragrance of the air, the mercy of a shade tree and a bracing swim, the lazier pace of days unencumbered by schedules and commutes, and the consolation of tree-sheltered lawns and of neighbors like those in Brooklyn.

The Catskills proved particularly congenial for Hasidic vacationing because, as a result of its postwar heyday as a getaway for more generic Jews, it had all the infrastructure that Hasidic life demands—places to pray three times a day with a *minyan*, study halls, *mikvehs* and shops with kosher food. It was Rabbi Teitelbaum who encouraged the summertime migration to the Catskills. The Rebbe himself, accompanied by disciples, would take vacations in Sharon Springs, New York, thirty miles east of Cooperstown, a town that saw an ephemeral burst of Hasidic visitors drawn by the therapeutic spas and treatments paid for by the German government as a form of Holocaust reparations.

"He understood that people living in a little apartment with twelve children in the summer is like jail," said Indig, a 45-year-old father of five. "They needed a little air, a bungalow colony with a couple of acres and a big field. You can't let small children run around in the city. Here they have lots of room. The air is cleaner. And for religious reasons. He didn't want the men to see naked women in the city."

What happens is that the men, who seldom take what other Americans call vacations of a week or two, toil all week in the city and drive up either singly or in groups on Thursday nights or Friday mornings, making sure they leave time on Friday to help their wives, burdened with the needs of so many children, get ready for the Sabbath. On Friday mornings, after prayers, stores like Green Fresh Kosher Supermarket in Monticello are filled with men wheeling shopping carts around the aisles, picking out leafy vegetables that have been inspected as insect-free, impulsively deciding to treat their children with cookies and their wives with flowers. There are, to be sure, middle-aged and elderly women threading through the aisles and young mothers with babies perched in the shopping carts. But the Friday ambience is as male as a hockey game. The men can also be spotted queuing up at the local bakery, snapping up four and five loaves of *challah*, three and four pounds of rugelach and two or three chocolate babkas.

The morning prayers are men's time, too. At the largest Satmar colony in Monticello, the men precede the prayers with a dip in the *mikveh* at a more leisurely pace than normal—or at least it seemed that way from the two naked men, broad smiles amid their beards, whom I spotted languishing in the warm water. Then they make their way over to a low-slung but sprawling building that combines a study hall and synagogue with a half dozen *minyan* rooms. *Minyans* start at different times to accommodate the different schedules. In the study hall, some men spend hours bent over a volume of Talmud, but other just schmooze and gossip. Four I saw sat around a large box of marble cake that had been sliced into pieces, which the men picked on and munched as they chatted. Some of the *tefillin* wearers had drifted outside to gossip with friends they had not seen all week, catch up on business deals or do what the outside world describes as networking. One man with *tefillin* was busy chatting on a cell phone. Prayer is a routine part of daily living, no different from commuting or shopping, and slipping into other activities while costumed for prayer—something that might not be seen in a high Episcopal or even Reform Jewish service—is not astonishing.

After praying and shopping, a man may, if it's hot, go for a swim in the colony's pool. While not athletically inclined, Hasidic men and women do swim. There is even a passage of Talmud (*Kiddushin* 29a) instructing parents to teach their children to swim for their own safety, one of the three types of knowledge parents are obligated to pass on to their children (the other two are Torah and earning a livelihood). Hasidim take this passage literally. But Hasidim swim in peculiarly Hasidic fashion. The men swim only during afternoon hours reserved for men, with women swimming during the morning hours reserved for them. This separates the sexes, but for an extra precaution the colony pool is walled off by high plywood fencing so partially clad swimmers cannot be seen by the opposite sex. Modesty is strictly observed; there is no mixed bathing, not even for husbands and wives. Moishe Indig told me that the Satmar were renovating a bungalow colony they had just taken over and will build two separate pools, one for men, one for women, so there would no longer be a need for reserved hours.

The remainder of the weekend is structured around the Sabbath. On Friday afternoon at a secular bungalow colony of the past, the men might be playing pinochle around a card table or hit fungo balls to get ready for a Sunday morning softball game. But at the Hasidic colonies they head for the *mikveh* once again for their pre-*Shabbos* immersion. The wives light the candles and the men don their silken *bekishes* and fur *shtreimels* and head to synagogue for an hour or so of prayers. They return home to a kitchen fragrant with the aromas of chicken soup, gefilte fish and roast chicken, which they soon serve up followed by a medley of *Shabbos* songs. If the rebbe is in the vicinity, there is usually a *tish* that goes well past midnight and once again fosters a spirited camaraderie among the men. The next day, after morning prayers at the synagogue, is spent quietly, as it is in Brooklyn. The difference is the crisp mountain air and the greenery underfoot. It is, the Hasidim might say, a *mechaya*—a deep pleasure—an interlude that makes the expense and the long drives worth it.

On Saturday night, after *havdalah*, the blessing over a braided candle and spice box that ends the Sabbath, some Hasidim might take in a show at the Raleigh Hotel, one of the handful of remaining hotels and one that long ago gave up its Las Vegas–style nightclub act. Instead of Las Vegas, there is a *kumzitz* ("come sit") featuring Hasidic singers like Shloime

Daskal and Shragy Gestetner. There are no female singers; women are not permitted to sing for men because their voices are regarded as too arousing. But the entertainment is limited. In Hasidic colonies, the peculiarly named "casinos" (they never had any legalized gambling) that once harbored Saturday night comedians and magicians have been converted to small synagogues or grocery stores.

On Sunday, the men, eschewing the frock coats and wearing black vests over their white shirts as a concession to summertime heat, idle on the lawn with other men, watch their children caper across the lawn and feed them fruit or yogurt or ice cream. The wives sit apart chatting with their female friends. But by afternoon, the men, alone or in car pools, head home to Brooklyn.

The rest of the week the Catskills is largely a women's world. Since most Hasidic families, if they have a car, have only one driven by the husband, a Hasidic woman is stuck in the colony. Mayer Tzvi Schreiber, the owner of the 50-family Royal Bungalow Colony in Monticello, told me with tongue in cheek: "I'm the only man on the premises. That's what I like about it. I like when they complain. At least I have something to talk to them about."

Just as he said this his cell phone rang and it was one of his bungalow tenants letting him know a lightbulb was out. "Bring me the old lightbulb and I'll replace it," he told her.

A woman must run all her errands and doctor's visits by foot or by taxi, though many merchants have discovered they can do a land-office business by visiting a Hasidic colony with their wares. Of course this is an old, pre-Hasidic tradition, well portrayed in the movie *A Walk on the Moon*, which concerned a love affair between a wife stranded during the week in a bungalow colony and "the blouse man" who sold his clothing on the premises and took the wife to the Woodstock festival.

Families typically pay $3,000 to $4,000 for a nine-week season, but the bungalows are small and mothers with large families can have a hard time managing the crowding. The bungalows have one or two bedrooms, though a single room can hold six children—two bunk beds and a high-riser. That means other children must squeeze into the kitchen or into the parents' bedroom, or else the parents sleep, as Schreiber laughing told me, "next to the stove."

The women seem to revel in simply watching their children run across a grassy field or eat an ice cream under a tree. It's a sharp contrast to the stifling asphalt and gasoline-flavored air of Williamsburg or Borough Park in August. Sometimes they can even snatch a few minutes for time alone by dropping their children off with a neighbor. There are more than a few neighboring women happy to oblige because they will be reciprocated. At Pardess Bungalows, Chany Friedman, a 28-year-old mother of three young children who is in her third year at the colony, told me the best part of the day is the morning swim for "the ladies" in the heated pool. But there are other things to do as well, she said.

"Some ladies walk on the road every day to see the beauty of the scenery," she told me, standing outside her bungalow in a pink sweater, long white skirt and thick white stockings. "It's nice to see the trees and mountains. It's a half-hour walk to Walmart and they shop there. Mostly they sit around in a circle and talk. The main thing in the country is to see the kids enjoying themselves. It's very, very nice to me. The kids enjoy themselves running around on the grass. We have some chickens and the kids chase them and we drink and eat on the tables outside."

I was surprised how easily she spoke with me, the two of us standing at the foot of the short bungalow staircase. Her husband, Joel, who works in the city as a construction manager, was not there. So I could only imagine that she'd gotten a nod of permission to talk to me from one of the Hasidic *machers*, or movers-and-shakers. She even invited me inside to show off her new kitchen, and though it was snug, I could see it was in better condition than the ones I re-membered from my childhood, with sleeker appliances and fresher paint and air-conditioning. She offered me a yogurt and a peach, concerned that I might be wilting in the heat. As she grew more comfortable, her language became more lyrical.

"I enjoy myself every day," she said. "The fresh air is not polluted. When they cut the grass it makes it smell delicious. The fresh air, nothing beats it."

Simple pleasures, but Hasidim like her have never stayed in first-class Newport inns or Hampton mansions and have never seen television shows or movies about such hotels and so think that Pardess may be the acme of summer leisure.

I visited the Satmar boys' camp, a spread of 40 bunks, each with roughly 14 two tiered bunk beds, and dormitory for the older boys, all arrayed around a patchy lawn. Across the road there was a large pool surrounded by a 10-foot-tall green plywood fence and a corral that has a variety of farm animals like lambs, horses and cows. I accidentally wandered behind the pool fence and there were a half dozen women bathing in old-fashioned flesh-concealing bathing suits. They were the wives of the male teachers at the camp, who live there the whole summer and so bring their families. They were taking advantage of a break between the boys' swimming periods and were visibly upset when they spied me.

If there was no basketball or baseball, I asked Landau, the camp director, what activities, beyond swimming, do the boys do when they finish their studies at 4 p.m.? One afternoon, he told me, the boys gathered around a sheep and watched it being shorn of its wool coat as a rabbi explained that the wool is used for the *tzitzit* all the boys wear. Another time the boys took a bus trip to the cemetery in Kiryas Joel—about an hour away—where their rebbe, Joel Teitelbaum, is buried. It was his *yahrzeit*, the anniversary of his death, and they were performing a *mitzvah* that honored the sect's George Washington. A third time the boys were treated to a series of dioramas of scenes from the Old Testament. But not all the activities are religious, Landau told me. One afternoon the boys were entertained by a juggler.

Still, the ethos of spending one's days in serious pursuit of Torah study is set even in the bunks. Near the door, each cabin has a small library of colorfully covered Talmud volumes for the boys to read in their leisure time.

In taking a tour I was struck by the lack of organizational hierarchy, which I realized is characteristically Hasidic, indicative of a faith that is more tribal than individual. I asked Landau what was his title and he struggled to come up with "director," a title probably imposed by the needs of following state and local camp regulations.

"By Hasidim, it's not going by position," Landau said. "Everybody's helping."

Indeed, the Hasidim laugh at formalities forced on them by the secular world. Jacob Washal, a camp Hasidic supervisor who was driving me around in a golf cart for the camp tour, said of another Hasidic camp official: "He's the president of the laundry. I'm the president of this golf cart."

Pardess Bungalows has its own camp, but it is exclusively for a dozen mentally and physically disabled children. While talking to Mrs. Friedman, I noticed a young Hasid teenager, in full regalia of black hat and black frock coat, shuffling around the lawn while feeling the ground ahead of him with a long, pencil-thin cane. His name was Shimon, he was 17 and he had been born blind. But the Hasidim have worked on his remaining talents. His paraprofessional, or "shadow," David Schwartz, told me that he plays piano skillfully and delights in reading each week's Torah in Braille, and continues to do so all summer long.

"He loves the melody of the *leyning*," he said, referring to the Sabbath chanting of the week's Torah portion to a melody prescribed by cantillation symbols above the Hebrew letters.

But since the locale is Hasidic, working with Shimon is more than just a kind human impulse. It's part of the commandments involved in *binyan olam*—the building of a world, Schwartz told me.

"We build a world for a blind boy or man," Schwartz said. "We build them a world so they can survive."

The Hasidim have built their own world in the Catskills as well, a colorful, counterintuitive world that not only delights them, but helps them survive as Hasidim.

EPILOGUE

Rabbi Hertz Frankel is not a Hasid, but he has spent more than 50 years as the secular studies principal of a Satmar girls' elementary school and has watched the breathtaking growth of the movement, growth that has created a bittersweet crisis of classroom space.

In the spring of 2013, when he was 80 and still working as an administrator, I met with him at Bais Rochel d'Satmar, a girls' yeshiva that was housed in a century-old former public high school that was already packed to the brim with 2,400 girls. Frankel and his Hebrew counterpart, a Satmar Hasid, Benzion Feuerwerger, explained a dilemma that was architectural and mathematical as well as Talmudic. That June the school was graduating eight eighth-grade classes, but in September they would be taking in 16 first-grade classes.

They would need to create eight new classrooms and the school they were in was simply out of room. They might have to rent rooms somewhere in the neighborhood or hope that New York's Governor Andrew M. Cuomo could provide space for them in a National Guard armory that the state would soon be selling.

It was a painful but bittersweet crisis because the flip side of the dilemma was what it said about the robust growth of the Hasidic world, now becoming a major share of the city's Jewish population and poised to overtake the non-Orthodox Jewish populace within a decade or two. Like them or not, think them antediluvian or charming, they have become a force to be reckoned with. Rabbi Frankel, though his roots are in the *Yeshivish* world, could not help but boast and gloat.

The Satmar, he told me, have 30,000 students in Brooklyn's Williamsburg and Borough Park and in the upstate villages of Monsey and Kiryas Joel. That means their ranks comprise one-third of all the yeshiva students in the United States, he told me. By contrast, he said, look what is happening to the secular world, which scorned Hasidim for generations and now takes pleasure in a periodic sexual or financial scandal that gets the attention it does only because it involves hypocritical Hasidim.

That secular world is shrinking, including its devoted Yiddish world, he pointed out. In the 1950s there were dozens of neighborhood "Sholem Aleichem" schools and other schools with different names that taught Yiddish language and culture but little religion. They attempted to pass on Yiddish to secular children. Almost all of them have closed, Frankel said, quite accurately, and only a small fraction of secular Jews still speak Yiddish. The Yiddish newspaper the *Forward*, which once had 100,000 readers daily, is now a weekly with fewer than 5,000 readers and must rely on its lively and often news-breaking English-language edition to survive. In the 1950s many thinkers predicted that the Orthodox world would wither as more Jews assimilated into the secular American mainstream, but just the opposite has happened, Rabbi Frankel said.

"You're dying," he said. "We're living. The secular community is dead, dead, dead. There's no Yiddish press, no Yiddish theater [not quite accurate since there is one still-vibrant group, the National Yiddish Theater-Folksbiene]. Dead, dead, dead. There were hundreds of Sholem Aleichem schools, Peretz schools. Where are they? How many Yiddish books are being published? The secular people dominated everything and now they've lost. Hasidim are pushing everyone else to be more religious, more Jewish."*

His triumphalist comments were bolstered in October 2013 by a Pew Research Center survey of Jews across America, the first like it in a decade. It found that the intermarriage rate among all Jews had climbed to 58 percent and was a stunning 71 percent for non-Orthodox Jews—a sea change since the 1970s, when the overall rate was 17 percent. While the Orthodox made up only 10 percent of all American Jews, they were growing at a breathtaking clip; 27 percent of Jewish-American children younger than 18 lived in Orthodox households while only 11 percent of the age group between 18 and 29 were Orthodox. And only a third of the Orthodox were modern Orthodox.

I was here to speak with Rabbi Frankel because the *Times*

---

* Author's interview with Hertz Frankel.

had sent me on a story about a 3.2-acre National Guard armory in Williamsburg that was being put up for sale and that the Hasidim were interested in acquiring. It was telling that the administration of Governor Cuomo was eager to make sure the property wound up accommodating Hasidic needs for space for schools, wedding halls or housing. Locking the armory up for that group would secure thousands of reliable votes at a time when Hasidim were often drifting to the Republicans. That's how politicians made their hard-nosed calculations when it came to Hasidim, a recognition of their expanding power.

I noticed that among the books in Frankel's office there were several copies of *Little House on the Prairie*, the classic if sentimental novel by Laura Ingalls Wilder, based on her childhood on farms in the Midwest in the late 19th century. The yeshiva girls were reading the book in literature class. It is a very time-honored, quintessentially American book without enigmatic or disturbing themes about sex or cultural mixing that might stir up Hasidic concerns. When I asked him about the Americanness of the book, he did not respond directly to my inquiry, but said something worth noting.

"We love America," he said, "but culturally we want to maintain our tradition. We don't want to become a melting pot. There has been a spiritual Holocaust in America."

I was not surprised by the stridency of that last remark because I have often heard such observations from people who believe that assimilation and intermarriage may yet shrink the Jewish community more than Hitler did. I could have argued that assimilation has meant that Jews have become the presidents of Yale, Harvard and Princeton, schools where they were once excluded, that Jews like Henry Kissinger have become secretaries of state and, like Joseph Lieberman, Democratic vice presidential candidates, that they have contributed mightily to medicine, the arts and law and risen to top positions in those realms, that there is almost nowhere in the United States they cannot live, work and thrive. And their doing so well has made it possible for an outlier group like the Hasidim to thrive as well. I did not argue, because there was no point to doing so. To Frankel and others who share his viewpoint, the important thing is that the losses of assimilation were not happening among the Hasidim and other ultra-Orthodox Jews.

"We are the future of the Jewish people in America," he said, fairly pounding his chest in victory.

And as a fairly assimilated Jew who nevertheless attends synagogue and observes many biblical traditions, I still found it hard to counter his argument that Hasidim will become a more forceful part of the Jewish landscape. The numbers are irrefutable. Hasidim can no longer be dismissed as an odd curiosity. They are now a major and increasingly muscular player in the largest city in the United States and are important in other cities as well. They may save the municipal, state and federal governments tens of millions of dollars by not sending their children to public schools or they may cost those governments tens of millions of dollars by capitalizing on special education programs, food stamps, housing vouchers and other programs. They may do so corruptly or on the up-and up. But public officials will have to understand them and figure out— wisely and fairly—how to address their growing needs.

I have friends who may not like them, think them an archaic throwback, an anachronism, hypocrites who are cold to those who do not agree with them. But the Hasidim are mushrooming in numbers and becoming a more undeniable part of the Jewish landscape, and Americans, both Jewish and gentile, will have to learn to deal with them. Understanding who they are and why may be a sensible way to start.

GLOSSARY

Definitions for many of the Yiddish or Hebrew words that appear in the text:

Amah: a biblical measurement, about two feet.

Amud: The pulpit for the cantor or prayer leader.

Baalei Teshuva: Returnees to Orthodoxy, usually said of people who grow up in secular homes and adopt an Orthodox worldview or those who grew up Orthodox, tried a more secular life and returned to the fold.

Bashert: Predestined. Often said of an unanticipated but fortunate event or of a romantic match.

Beged: Item of clothing.

Beis Din: A rabbinical court.

Beis Medrash: A study hall for delving into Talmud.

Bentshn: Saying the blessings after a meal, a Jewish grace.

Bikur Cholim: Aid and comfort to the sick, often through a simple visit.

Bris: The circumcision of a male child eight days after his birth, often accompanied by a small feast.

Chametz: Any leavened grains or grain products that are forbidden during Passover. Five grains—wheat, barley, oats, spelt and rye—are specifically prohibited in Jewish law if they are leavened by water. Although matzo is made of grain, it is kosher when flour is combined with water for less than 18 minutes so no leavening can occur before the dough is placed in the oven.

Chavrusa: A study partner, usually someone of equivalent ability, in a system of exegesis practiced in yeshivas and *kollels*.

Chesed: A virtuous or righteous act, kindness.

Cholent: A savory stew usually made of meat, potatoes and beans that is put into the oven before Sabbath and so can be eaten during Sabbath without violating the prohibition against lighting a fire.

Cholov Yisroel: Milk favored by ultra-Orthodox Jews because it has been produced under the supervision of an Orthodox Jew and thus is indisputably kosher. However, even many modern Orthodox Jews find most store-bought milk perfectly fine.

Chumash: The Five Books of Moses, sometimes a synonym for Torah.

Chupah: The four-poled wedding canopy, often a synonym for a wedding or marriage.

Daf Yomi: The study of the Talmud by large numbers of Jews who every day dissect the same page—a *daf* is actually two pages that are part of a folio—until the entire Talmud of

5,422 pages is completed. The effort takes seven and a half
years and then the cycle begins again.

Daven: To pray, often with animated rocking and swaying.

Devekut: A cleaving to God, a philosophical concept to under-
score the fervor of Hasidim.

Eruv: A symbolic boundary, often of wires, set up within a
neighborhood or municipality to permit certain kinds of
carrying and other tasks on the Sabbath by extending the
domain of one's home. Orthodox Jews can thus carry house
keys and push strollers.

Eshes Chayil: Literally a woman of valor who holds steadfast in
her trust in God. Also the name of a Sabbath eve prayer
honoring the Jewish woman.

Frumakh: Hasidic slang, often used in jest, to describe someone
who is punctilious in fulfilling a commandment to an ab-
surd or even annoying degree.

Gebrochts: Broken matzo or matzo meal that might contain unbaked flour that when exposed to water would rise. Many
Hasidim and other especially rigorous Jews will not, for example, consume matzo ball soup and will use potato starch
instead of matzo meal for cooking.

Gemara: The second and greatest portion of the Talmud, con-
sisting of commentary on and analysis of the recorded rabbinic debates over Jewish law contained in the first part,
the *Mishnah*.

Get: A Jewish divorce, a document that a man must grant to his
estranged wife lest she be regarded as an *agunah*, a chained
woman who can never remarry.

Halacha: Jewish law.

Haredi: Ultra-Orthodox, a term that refers to both Hasidim and the non-Hasidic black-hat wearers who are as rigorous in their faith but may not adhere to a particular *rebbe*.

Havdalah: A ritual to mark the end of the Sabbath that features blessings over a braided candle, a box of spices and a goblet of wine.

HaShem: A more casual name for God, since other names can only be uttered in prayer. The term literally means "The Name."

Hazzan: Cantor.

Hoyzn-zokn: The custom among a few Hasidic sects like Ger of wearing the ends of pants—*hoyzn*—tucked inside socks—*zokn*.

Kallah: The bride.

Kapote: The long, often three-quarters-length frock coat worn by many Hasidic men, usually in one of many tones of black or charcoal gray.

Kiddush: Blessings over the wine for Sabbath and holidays. Also the refreshments after a synagogue service since those accompany a blessing over the wine.

Kollel: A school of advanced study of the Talmud and rabbinic commentaries, usually populated by married men who receive stipends to support their families.

Kolpik: Ukrainian version of the *shtreimel*.

Kugel: A baked pudding or casserole usually of potatoes or noodles.

Kvitl: A petition for help usually given to a *rebbe* believed to have miraculous powers.

Leyning: Chanting of the Torah to musical notations prescribed in the cantillation symbols above or below almost every word.

Lulav: A date palm frond, bound together with willow and myrtle branches, that is waved ritually in various directions during Succoth prayers in accordance with a biblical commandment to express joy during the holiday.

Makher: A mover and shaker, a big shot, a leader.

Mazel: Fortune or luck as in *mazel tov*, good luck.

Mashgiach: A supervisor of foods, restaurants or food factories who makes sure the food adheres to the Jewish laws of keeping kosher, known as *kashrut*.

Mechaya: A deep pleasure.

Mechitza: The curtain or other barrier separating the men and women during prayer among the Orthodox. Conservative, Reform and Reconstructionist men and women sit together.

Melamed: A teacher, usually of children in a *cheder*, the lower school for young boys.

Melaveh malkah: Literally "escorting of the queen," used to refer to the meal held just after *Shabbos* is over, often just a small token of food or drink to honor *Shabbos*'s conclusion.

Mesirah: Informing on a fellow Jew to secular authorities, generally considered a reprehensible deed.

Mesivta: A yeshiva for boys of high school age that emphasizes Talmud study.

Mezuzah: A small parchment inscribed with a biblical verse that is enclosed in a decorative container and attached to the doorpost of a home in accordance with a biblical commandment.

Minyan: A quorum of ten—adult men among the Orthodox— required for certain prayers, particularly the *Kaddish* prayer of mourning,

Mikveh: A small tiled bath or pool used for ritual immersion to regain purity. Used by women after their menstrual period, by men before study and by both sexes when undergoing conversion.

Misnagdim: Originally the opponents of Hasidism. The term sometimes overlaps with the *Yeshivish* or Litvak groups whose exacting Orthodoxy differs in some ways from that of Hasidim.

Mitzvot: Good deeds or commandments, usually ones pre- scribed in the Torah.

Moel: A person who performs a circumcision.

Neshama: Soul or spirit. Casually used for a sympathetic heart.

Motzaei Shabbos: Literally the departure of *Shabbos,* the time when it is over and normal activities can resume, technically after three stars have appeared in the sky.

Niddah: A woman during menstruation, or, colloquially, men- struation itself. The Torah prohibits sexual intercourse with a woman in *niddah.*

Niggunim: Melodies, often wordless, usually sung for religious purposes.

Parnosseh: Subsistence earnings, usually through a livelihood.

Peyes or *peyos:* Sidelocks, often elaborate and long spirals of hair dangling below the ears, that are favored by *Haredim* because of the biblical prohibition against rounding the "corners" of one's head.

Pidyon: Donation for the upkeep of a *rebbe*'s court.

Pidyon Haben: In accordance with a biblical injunction, the redemption of a firstborn son from priestly duties by the payment of five shekels to a *Kohen*, a descendant of Jewish priests.

Punim: Face.

Rebbe: A grand rabbi, the venerated leader of a Hasidic movement or sect.

Rebbitzin: The rabbi's wife.

Rekel: An elongated frock coat worn by Hasidic men as an everyday outfit.

Ruach: Spirit or energy.

Schnor: Literally beg, but also to manipulate circumstances to obtain something small for free. The root of *schnorrer*, a manipulative freeloader.

Seudah: A festive or celebratory meal, often accompanying a *mitzvah* (commandment).

Shabbos: The Sabbath, which runs from sundown Friday until approximately one hour after sundown on Saturday.

Shatnez: A biblically forbidden mixture of linen and wool in clothing.

Sheimos: Worn religious books containing the name of God that must be ritually buried. Collection of such books typically occurs before Passover.

Shiduch: An arranged match, usually orchestrated by parents or a professional matchmaker or *shadchan*.

Shiur: A lecture in Talmud, usually by a rabbinic scholar.

Shiva: The seven-day period of mourning after a death, with the day of the funeral customarily counted as the first day. One sits *shiva* for parents, siblings, children and spouses.

Shmurah: Matzo that has been watched over by rabbis from the time its grain is milled.

Shofar: The ram's horn blown on Rosh Hashanah.

Shpatzir: A pleasurable stroll that for some Jews has become a Sabbath or holiday ritual and a way of running into other Jews.

Shtetl: A small, often impoverished Jewish village of the kind that was found in rural areas of Eastern Europe until such places were decimated by the Holocaust.

Shtibl: A small, room-sized synagogue.

Shtreimel: A round fur hat worn by married Hasidic men on *Shabbos* and Jewish holidays or on festive occasions like a wedding.

Shul: Synagogue.

Shulchan Aruch: The Code of Jewish Law.

Simcha: Joyous occasion like a wedding.

Spodik: Polish version of a round fur hat, usually higher than the *shtreimel*.

Succah: A hut roofed with branches or reeds in which observant Jews spend considerable time during the eight days of the Succoth holiday to remind them of the flimsy dwellings used by the ancient Hebrews as they wandered across the desert.

Sugya: The argumentation, debate and analysis that follows a rabbinical statement or legal position, thus the essential literary style of the Talmud.

Tahorah: Ritually clean, or the cleansing of a body before burial to makes sure it is ritually clean.

Talesim: Prayer shawls, plural of *tallis*.

Tashmish Hamitah: Sexual relations.

Tefillin: Phylacteries, or a set of leather boxes containing verses from the Torah and their attendant leather straps. Worn, usually by males, during weekday prayers.

Tisch (tish): Literally a table, but in the Hasidic world a reference to the table of the *rebbe*, or grand rabbi, around which Hasidim gather on *Shabbos* to listen to the *rebbe*'s wisdom, sing songs and partake of his *shirayim*, literally leftovers, but often just small servings of the food he is eating.

Torah lishmo: Study of Torah for its own sake, for the sheer performance of a Godly mitzvah, not for a reward in this world.

Tzadik: A righteous man or spiritual leader. Often used for the most venerated grand rabbis.

Tsimmes or *tzimmes*: A sweet stew made of carrots; its name has become a colloquialism for a big fuss or exaggerated crisis.

Tzedakah: Charity.

Tzitzit: The fringes on the four corners of a *tallis*, but also the term for the daily poncho-like fringed undergarment worn daily by observant Jewish men and by many Hasidim over their shirts.

Tznius: Modesty, as shown in the concealing clothes a Hasid will wear.

Upsherinish or *upsherin*: The ceremonial first haircut for a boy, usually when he reaches three years old. Like the *bris* it too is accompanied by a feast.

Yahrzeit: Literally a year's time, but used for the anniversary of a death in the Hebrew calendar when *Kaddish* is recited for close relatives.

Yeshiva Gedola: A post–high school yeshiva.

Yeshivish: A term describing ultra-Orthodox but non-Hasidic Jews who emphasize exacting study of Torah more than spiritual fervor and do not venerate a particular *rebbe*. Synonyms are "black-hat" or *Litvak*, referring to the groups' roots among the Lithuanian yeshivas.

Yichus: Pedigree, usually a prestigious one.

Zmiros: Special Sabbath or holiday songs.

ACKNOWLEDGMENTS

Many Americans, even Jewish Americans, regard the Hasidic world as impenetrable, but I found that genuine curiosity, common courtesy and a spritz of Yiddish pried open that world and made it less enigmatic. But I would not have been able to craft more than a glancing look at the community without the help and generous gift of time that many Hasidim gave me. Perhaps they realize that for their own well-being, bridges need to be established to the secular world that would render their tribe less inscrutable. Foremost I'd like to thank Alex Rapaport, the head of a nonsectarian soup kitchen organization called Masbia, for giving me several extended tours through the Hasidic world in its granular, offbeat charm and informing me about cryptic Hasidic customs and folkways. His observations were always leavened with humor and deep enjoyment and pride. Several Hasidim submitted to lengthy interviews about their lives even as they had doubts about what the value of such exercises were for their communities: Nechuma Mayer, who told me the story of her remarkable mother, a matriarch of 2,000 descendants; Shlomo Koenig, the deputy sheriff of Rockland County; and Mendel Werdyger, the passionate self-taught student of cantorial recorded music. Rebellious or former Hasidim like Shulem Deen and the Hasid who has blogged under the pseudonym Shtreimel were quite open about their lives and feelings. Rabbi Hertz Frankel, who is not Hasidic but works in a Hasidic yeshiva, shared his views on the heady growth of the Hasidic world. Rabbi David Niederman and Rabbi Moshe Indig explicated the politics and organizational life; Rabbi Mayer Schiller helped me plumb Hasidic philosophy and its Skverer manifestations. Others who were especially helpful, either Hasidim or people who have worked closely with the communities, include Rabbi Yehuda Krinsky, Assemblyman Dov Hikind, Ruchama Clapman, Menashe Mayer, Yeedle Melber, Levi Meisner, Irwin Botwinick, Yitzchok Fleischer, Yosef Rapaport, Barbara Shine, Isaac Abraham, Amram Weinstock, Jacob Roth, Nuchem Sanders, Raphael Waller-stein, Motti Seligson, Akiva Kizelnik, Joseph Waldman, Stephen Bernardo, Abraham Wieder, Solomon Rottenberg, Mendel Hoffman, Chany Friedman and Yoel Landau.

Academic or organizational experts I consulted and were generous with their time and thoughts included Samuel Heil-man, who has always been especially helpful in elucidating a world he has written eloquently about, William Helm-reich, Menachem Genack, Daniel Retter, Allan Nadler, Lani Santo, Rabbi Moshe Tendler, Rabbi David Zweibel, Benja-min Blech, Alan Silverman and Bernard Beer. For their very different but probing books on Hasidim I also want to thank

Jerome Mintz and Elie Wiesel. Others who were helpful in fleshing out various stories were Anita Altman, Paul Adler, Herbert Reisman, Sima Rabinovicz, Abe Weiss and Michael Sussman.

I am indebted to the *Forward* and *Jewish Week* and the blog Failed Messiah for their incisive reporting on the sex abuse and other scandals in the ultra-Orthodox community that saved me time, phone calls and research; their publishers and editors, Samuel Norich, Jane Eisner and Gary Rosenblatt; and too many of their writers to mention. At the *New York Times* my colleagues Sharon Otterman, Ray Rivera, Michael Powell, Ben Weiser, Christine Haughney and Joseph Goldstein shed light on some of these same issues with potent depth and insight.

I want to especially thank the *New York Times* for allowing me, on so many occasions, to follow my enthusiasm and curiosity in ways that I felt would illuminate the world for the newspaper's readers, enabling me to do the reporting that was essential for this book as well as the articles it produced. Editors or former editors I'd like to single out include Wendell Jamieson, Jan Benzel, Arthur G. Sulzberger, Carolyn Ryan, Jon Landman, Jill Abramson, Joyce Purnick, Michael Oreskes, Anne Cronin, Joe Sexton, Susan Edgerley, Diego Ribadeneira, Jack Kadden, Bill McDonald and John Darnton.

I feel grateful to Claire Wachtel at HarperCollins for having the foresight to know that a book chronicling the Hasidic world and its foibles is important at a time when Hasidim are a mushrooming sector of the American Jewish community and an increasingly muscular political and sociological subculture on the wider American scene. Her associate, Hannah Wood, has always been diligent in seeing that the book moves toward publication. Jane Dystel, my agent, has always promoted my books with vigor, affection and care. Carolyn Hessel of the Jewish Book Council has been in my corner for years now.

My daughter, Annie Berger, who recently became an associate editor at HarperCollins of young adult and children's books, was hard-nosed and practical about the exigencies of publishing. My wife, Brenda, was there with patience and love to make it possible for me to work on another book even if I deprived her of companionship on more than a few Sundays. Finally, I will forever be grateful to my late parents for embodying in the most soulful fashion the lost European world, down to its foods, music, spirit and joy in Jewish life, that Hasidim stemmed from and still try to sustain.

ABOUT THE AUTHOR

J oseph Berger has been a reporter with *The New York Times* for 30 years, writing about religion, education, neighborhoods and issues in the Jewish world. In 2011, he won the Peter Kihss Award for a career's work given by the Society of Silurians, a leading association of journalists. He is the author of *Displaced Persons: Growing Up American After the Holocaust*, a memoir about his family's experience as refugees that was chosen as a notable book of 2001. He also chronicled the dramatic changes in American ethnic life in *The World in a City: Traveling the Globe Through the Neighborhoods of the New New York*, published in 2007.